4
8
2003

DREAMS OF FLIGHT

NUMBER FOUR
Centennial of Flight Series
Roger D. Launius, General Editor

DREAMS

OF

FLIGHT

General Aviation in the United States

By Janet R. Daly Bednarek

with Michael H. Bednarek

Texas A&M University Press   College Station

Library of Congress Cataloging-in-Publication Data

Bednarek, Janet R. Daly, 1959–
    Dreams of flight : general aviation in the United States / by Janet R.
    Daly Bednarek, with Michael H. Bednarek.—1st ed.
        p. cm.—(Centennial of flight series ; no. 4)
    From first seeds to early blossoms—The "Golden Age" : 1926–39—
    For the duration : 1939–45—Up from the ashes : 1945–80—Dreams once
    again deferred : post–1980.
    Includes bibliographical references and index.
    ISBN 1-58544-257-7 (cloth : alk. paper)
        1. Private flying—United States.   I. Bednarek, Michael H., 1956–
    II. Title.   III. Series.
    TL721.4.D35   2003
    387.7'0973—dc21   2002152893

To Edwin Wick

Clay McCutcheon

Nancy Drew

and the Flying Angels—

they all inspired us to fly.

Contents

List of Illustrations   ix

Preface   xi

CHAPTER

   1. From First Seeds to Early Blossoms   3

   2. The "Golden Age": 1926 -39   25

   3. For the Duration: 1939- 45   65

   4. Up from the Ashes: 1945–80   87

   5. Dreams Once Again Deferred: Post-1980   121

Notes   153

Sources for the History of General Aviation   169

Index   183

Illustrations

Wright brothers' 1910 winter flying school at Montgomery,

    Alabama 2

1930 Fairchild KR-21A powered by a Kinner K-5 engine 24

Piper L-4 (J3C-65) powered by a Continental A-65 engine 64

1955 Cessna 310 powered by a Continental O-470 engine 86

1965 Cessna 172 powered by a Continental O-300D engine 120

Vans RV-6 homebuilt powered by a Lycoming O-360 engine 152

Preface

What is general aviation? This question is perhaps most simply answered by explaining what general aviation is *not*. General aviation is not the scheduled commercial airlines and it is not military aviation. Pretty much all other aviation activities—including private and sport flying, aerial photography and surveying, crop dusting, business flying, medical evacuation, flight training, and the use of police and fire-fighting aircraft—fall under this broad heading. General aviation aircraft include everything from small, single-engine, fabric-covered planes to multimillion-dollar business jets—with helicopters, converted airliners, restored war birds, and homebuilt aircraft all falling within that range. General aviation, therefore, is defined not so much by the types of aircraft involved, but rather by the use to which those aircraft are put. Although what we now call general aviation—which before the 1950s was most often referred to as private or personal aviation—did not begin to blossom until the 1920s, its origins, like the origins of all aviation, began with the invention of the airplane and those who first dreamed about how this modern marvel might be used.

Almost from the moment Americans first realized that Orville and Wilbur Wright had indeed invented the airplane, certain beliefs and myths began to surround the use of this wondrous new machine. Joseph Corn called them "the winged gospel." Many Americans saw the advent of the airplane as the dawn of a new age: an air age that would bring with it profound social and cultural changes. Some proponents of the winged gospel promoted military use of the airplane, claiming that it would change the nature of warfare. Others envisioned a future in which aircraft would allow people and ideas to travel farther and faster, erasing the barriers of time and space and drawing the world closer together. Still others focused their hopes and dreams on what came to be known as general aviation. They believed that flying an airplane would become as commonplace as driving an automobile in the coming air age foretold in the winged gospel.[1]

The latter was one of the most stubborn myths of the winged gospel, one that profoundly shaped general aviation. Despite any evidence to the contrary, there was a persistent belief that a majority of people, if not everyone, would someday soon own and operate their own air vehicles. There would be, as some put it, "an airplane in every garage." Envisioning a time when a significant percentage of Americans would routinely fly, manufacturers of personal aircraft began to emerge in the early 1920s.[2]

Another part of the winged gospel that helped shape the course of general aviation history was the belief that participation in aviation could put one on a path toward greater equality in American society. In particular, women and African Americans came to see aviation as a way to assert their ability to fully participate in American society and culture.[3] The result was that for much of the twentieth century, general aviation was far more important to women and African Americans who wished to participate in flying, especially as pilots, than it was to white males. Both women and African Americans were effectively barred from serving as pilots in both the commercial airline industry and military aviation until World War II. Before that time, women (and only white women at that) were allowed only one role in commercial aviation: that of stewardess. During the war, African-American men broke the color barrier in the Army Air Forces. Although some women flew for the military during the war, they did so as civilians—and the government terminated the program that allowed them to fly before the war ended. Although African-American males continued to fly for the military after World War II and gradually made their way into commercial airline cockpits, women were not allowed to serve as either commercial or military pilots until the 1970s. General aviation thus served as the vehicle through which both blacks and women entered the world of aviation for much of the twentieth century. The civil and women's rights movements did much to help shape the history of general aviation as African Americans and women fought for and found expanded roles in aviation. Yet, while the roles open to them expanded during the second half of the twentieth century, women's participation in aviation has not grown to the degree that many had hoped it would. It is a circumstance a number of organizations are attempting to address.

In fact, the number of American pilots has declined in recent years. After peaking in the late 1970s, the number of pilots and student pilots has fallen. Although this is an issue for all forms of aviation, it has become a source of particular concern for a number of organizations involved with general aviation. Joseph Corn argues that America's romance with aviation ended in the 1950s, but the waning of its attraction did not become glaringly apparent until the late 1970s and early 1980s.[4] Any number of factors seem to have been involved. Regardless, efforts to significantly reverse the decline have yet to achieve marked success. Unless the number of Americans choosing to become pilots changes dramatically, not only will there be a shortage of trained pilots for all sectors of aviation, the still-persistent dreams of those who envision an airborne future for a large number of people will remain unrealized.

While the themes suggested by Corn in *The Winged Gospel* proved important throughout the history of general aviation, others have proven to be influential as well. One interesting theme is the differential impact of European competition. For much of the twentieth century, U.S. manufacturers dominated the general aviation market. Even the long-term slump that began in the 1980s had its roots in domestic rather than international factors. While global competition created some issues, light aircraft manufacturers were only slightly affected. Glider manufacturers, on the other hand, were gradually overwhelmed by European competition. Europeans captured an increasing share of the market after World War II and eventually drove U.S. manufacturers out of the field. Additionally, while domestic glider manufacturers decided not to adopt European manufacturing techniques as a means to compete, those techniques—which involved the use of composite materials—became important to the designers of homebuilt aircraft kits. In that arena, the adoption and modification of European techniques proved revolutionary.

The history of general aviation reflects any number of events, trends (both long and short term), and developments in the broader history of the United States. As already suggested, the civil and women's rights movements provided additional outlets for activity for groups previously confined to general aviation. The globalization of the American economy has also had a differential impact on general aviation. The Great Depression and the New Deal that arose in response to it resulted in a number of programs that influenced general aviation, including programs for pilot training, safe aircraft design, and airport development. In fact, the relationship between general aviation and the federal government has gone through a number of different phases. At times, strong advocates such as Eugene Vidal and Theodore Wright championed the interests of general aviation. At others, the relationship proved more embattled in nature as federal regulators sought to rein in what they saw as some of the sector's more freewheeling elements, and general aviation's advocates fought to retain what they viewed as essential freedoms.

World War II proved to be a boon to general aviation. However, the overexpansion that resulted contributed to a postwar slump and a major shakeout in the industry. The survivors in the light-aircraft sector subsequently enjoyed a period of sustained growth during the prosperous 1950s and 1960s. Meanwhile, the environmental movement that emerged in the early 1960s proved challenging to agricultural aviation. High fuel costs caused by the restructuring of the global oil market, rising insurance premiums due to litigation, and a lack of significant technological advancement all contributed to the rapid and sustained depression of the light-aircraft market in the last quarter of the twentieth century. Finally, the tragedies of September 11, 2001, had immediate and severe consequences for general aviation. While most of the restrictions imposed in the wake of the terrorist attacks have been lifted, the long-term consequences for general aviation have yet to be fully realized and understood.

In the late 1990s, Roger Launius, the National Air and Space Administration's chief historian, proposed a "Centennial of Flight" series of books. These books, each to be about two hundred pages long, would cover a number of topics in a style lacking scholarly apparatus and appealing to a general audience. Each would provide an overview of the topic, and, in the terminology of the profession, be a synthetic work based primarily on published sources. One of the proposed topics was a history of general aviation. As a historian and a general aviation pilot, I found the idea intriguing. Not only was the subject of some personal interest, it was also one with which I could do collaborative work with my husband, who is an aeronautical engineer and pilot. He would provide the technical expertise and sketch out the "Planes and Power Plants" sections of the various chapters. We began work in 1999 intent on having a finished manuscript by the fall of 2001 so the press could begin its review process.

The manuscript began and unfolded with the original aim of the Centennial of Flight Series in mind. It was not going to be a definitive work; it would be based almost exclusively on secondary sources representing the best available scholarship (as it turned out, some subjects demanded a small measure of primary source research as no secondary works existed); and it would offer a synthesis of the major topics in the history of general aviation. There would be no source citations. Instead, it would conclude with an essay pointing readers to available source material. It would not be written for a scholarly audience. Rather, it would be written to appeal to a general audience. In many ways, my model was Roger Bilstein's work—both his textbook on aviation history and his study of the aerospace industry. Bilstein is known as a skilled historian who excels at synthesizing difficult and complex topics.

In trying to provide an overview of general aviation's first century, a number of choices had to be made to keep within the series' page limit and time constraints. I therefore decided to focus on heavier than-air flight. Although balloons, dirigibles, and blimps are all part of the general aviation story, they have a history—indeed, something of a culture—that sets them apart. There are also a number of excellent books available on the subject of lighter-than-air flight.[5] Thus, people interested in that aspect of general aviation have other sources from which to choose. I also decided at the outset to focus on powered flight and so did not include coverage of gliders in the original manuscript.

Additionally, I had to make choices regarding who and what to include after deciding to focus on powered, heavier-than-air flight. I take full responsibility for those choices. For example, the manuscript included information on Don Luscombe, a general aviation pioneer who is not well known outside the general aviation community. Among other accomplishments, Luscombe designed and built one of the first all-metal light aircraft. Production of his planes ended in the early 1950s, but Luscombe enthusiasts have been attempting to bring certain models back into production for many years (see chapters 2, 4, and 5). At the other end of the spectrum, I did not include a section on Henry Ford, who famously (or infamously) was involved in general aviation. His company built an early airliner, and his airport near Detroit was the first in the United States to have a paved runway. Although his most successful ventures were in the category of commercial aviation, he did sponsor a short-lived attempt to build a small, affordable aircraft. Because he was Henry Ford, that effort received a great deal of media attention. However, the aircraft—the Ford Flivver—was never put into production. In fact, Ford abandoned the project after the pilot testing the aircraft was killed in a crash. Ford essentially left the aviation business after only a few years of activity. In a similar vein, the manuscript included sections on helicopters, but did not deal with the autogiro. The former has become an important component of general aviation, whereas the latter, despite its own fascinating history, had no long-term impact the industry. I attempted to remain as representative as possible when choosing what subjects to cover. That presented a particular challenge, especially in a work aimed at a general audience, as even some of the most obscure figures and aircraft have devoted champions. Those who are fascinated by the Funks (twin brothers from Ohio known both for their gliders and for the 365 aircraft they built, of which there are about two hundred today) or who lovingly restore Davis aircraft (about five still exist) may be disappointed. I did try to include those persons I felt were the most important representative figures. The "Planes and Power Plants" sections of each chapter were designed, in part, to touch on the history of the most representative aircraft and the engines that powered them.

Somewhere between the original conception for the Centennial of Flight Series and the initial submission of our manuscript, the nature of the series changed dramatically. Roger Launius, the series editor, half-jokingly told me that the change was largely of my own doing. In 1998, I completed a monograph on the history of municipal airports in the United States that examined the period between the end of World War I and the end of World War II (*America's Airports: Airfield Development, 1918–1947*). A standard scholarly work, it was grounded in primary sources, with source notes and a bibliography. As it neared publication, Roger Launius and Texas A&M University Press decided to make it the inaugural book in the Centennial of Flight Series. In the meantime, a number of other authors engaged in preparing works for the series began submitting project ideas and manuscripts that differed significantly from those originally envisioned. The series thus evolved from one emphasizing short, synthetic works to one encompassing both synthetic works and original monographs. Most importantly, each author was instructed to fully document all of the sources used.

Documenting a manuscript after the fact is a daunting challenge. The published sources, while sometimes difficult to dig up again, proved to be the easiest to retrieve. More challenging were sources located on the Worldwide Web. Fortunately, when I found such sources, I usually printed out a copy of the Web page. The conventions for using and citing Internet sources are still evolving. I have in my possession print copies of all information drawn from the Web. In the source citations I give the Internet "address" for the Web sites that hosted the information. These references provide sufficient detail for readers desiring to find and verify the material or to learn more about the subject to do so. I limited myself to Web sites hosted by known professional associations, government agencies, and established aviation organizations. Although Internet documents often see little of the kind of review accorded traditionally published documents, I have some confidence in the publishers of the Web sites I used. I anticipated, for example, that I could have the same level of confidence in statistics posted on the Internet by the Federal Aviation Administration as in those appearing in published form. Similarly, corporate and organizational histories appearing on the Web probably have the same level of reliability as traditionally published corporate and organizational histories. In other words, I tried to evaluate Internet sources in much the same way I would evaluate printed sources, particularly keeping in mind the source responsible for publishing the information on the Web.

In addition, the reviewers challenged me to revise the manuscript in a number of ways before publication. I responded to a number of their suggestions for additional topics. Most importantly, I added information on the history of gliders. In the United States, that history in many ways centers on Elmira, New York, home of the Soaring Society of America, and on the Schweizer Aircraft Corporation—the foremost producer of gliders in America. The published sources focus on Elmira and Schweizer Aircraft. Although others, including the above-mentioned Funk brothers, also played roles in the history of soaring, much of the tale could be told by focusing on that town and the still-existing company. I also expanded the coverage of ultralights and added a little on hang gliding. I had included discussions on the history of the homebuilt movement. In these my focus was on the Experimental Aircraft Association (EAA). I had made mention of both plan- and kit-built aircraft and the fact that the latter employed the use of composites in their construction. I had not mentioned many individual designers of homebuilt aircraft, however. One reviewer suggested that I include a section on Burt Rutan, probably the best known of the homebuilt aircraft designers, and his aircraft designs. So, now there is a section dealing with Rutan and his airplanes, including the Voyager.

Although it has been part of the world of aviation practically since the invention of the airplane, general aviation has often been thought of as "the other" form of aviation. Military and commercial aviation have attracted the most attention, both from scholars and from the public. The massive use of airpower and the evolution of commercial aviation into something of a form of mass transit have served to make the influence of those forms of aviation quite visible. General aviation's impact on Americans has been less obvious, but in many areas no less important. Business aircraft provided American corporations with previously undreamed of mobility and flexibility. Both people and parts could be moved quickly and efficiently. With the introduction of the business jet, that mobility and flexibility became global in scope. Agricultural aviation helped contribute to the dramatic increases in farm yields, not just in the United States, but also around the world. In fact, some might argue that the misuse of agricultural aviation helped contribute to the rise of the environmental movement. Helicopters used for rapid medical evacuation have saved countless lives. Air shows continue to be a popular form of entertainment, although their popularity does seem to increase with the number of military aircraft involved. Nevertheless, the annual EAA gathering at Oshkosh, Wisconsin, which focuses almost exclusively on general aviation, attracts upward of eight hundred thousand people. As this is being written, aerial tankers are being used to help battle massive forest fires in Colorado, Arizona, California, and the Pacific Northwest. Whether any aircraft will ever approach the automobile as a form of personal transportation remains to be seen. Both serious skeptics and hopeful optimists continue to debate this. As interesting as the history of general aviation has been during its first century, it will undoubtedly continue to prove of interest during its second century.

DREAMS OF FLIGHT

The Wright brothers' 1910 winter flying school in Montgomery, Alabama. Photo courtesy Special Collections and Archives, Wright State University.

CHAPTER 1

From First Seeds to Early Blossoms

The period before 1926 witnessed the beginnings of a number of activities that would become part of general aviation. First, pioneer aviators began to explore the limits of the new invention and potential uses for it beyond military and commercial applications. The first of these aviators were the birdmen and bird women of the exhibition era between 1910 and about 1915–16. After World War I, a second group of exhibition pilots emerged: the barnstormers. Second, as enthusiasm for flight grew, more and more individuals sought to take to the skies. Many early aviators were forced to learn to fly by trial and error. However, beginning around 1910, a number of flight schools opened up around the country. Third, at many of the early airfields hosting flying schools, individuals also offered fuel, maintenance, and other services. These were the first of what have since become known as fixed-base operations and those running them as fixed-base operators. Others looked for additional ways to earn a living in aviation. They were the pioneers of aerial surveying and photography, crop treatment, and corporate flying.

Shaping much of what happened by providing the opportunities for and setting the limits to aerial activity were the planes and their power plants. Through World War I, both aircraft and power plants were rare and expensive to purchase and maintain. The three most important aircraft types were those produced by the Wrights, Glenn Curtiss, and Louis Blériot. In addition, a number of individuals around the country produced aircraft based on those types and, to a certain extent, on their own designs. Some of these pioneers survived to emerge as important general aviation aircraft manufacturers. Others, in a demonstration of both the wide-open and highly risky nature of early aircraft manufacturing, soon moved on to other endeavors. Powering these first aircraft primarily were Wright engines (found mostly in Wright aircraft), Curtiss engines (found mostly in Curtiss aircraft) and imported French Anzani and Gnome/LeRhone engines. Again, a number of individuals also produced aircraft power plants of their own design.

Between the war and 1926, the most common aircraft types used in general aviation were the plentiful and inexpensive military-surplus trainers: the Curtiss JN-4D "Jenny" and the Standard J-1. Although a number of new general aviation aircraft were designed and built during the early 1920s, most fell victim to economics. As during the prewar period, all of these aircraft were of wood and fabric construction. However, by the end of this early period at least two companies, Travel Air and WACO, were beginning to build personal aircraft with steel-tube fuselages.

The period between 1903 and 1926 thus proved to be an important formative one. While general aviation did not fully emerge until the mid-1920s, the seeds for future general aviation activity were planted in the first quarter of the twentieth century and many of the first blooms began to come forth.

The Origins of General Aviation: The Birdman Era through World War I

By the time the Wright brothers began their quest to solve the problems behind the achievement of heavier-than-air flight, the idea of a flying machine was one that more and more people were beginning to take seriously. Other pioneer experimenters—such as Otto Lilienthal, Octave Chanute, and Samuel Langley—had lent respectability to the pursuit of heavier-than-air flight. Balloons and, more importantly, dirigibles had proved to the public the reality of lighter-than-air flight. Heavier-than-air flight thus seemed a more realistic next step. Even as the Wrights succeeded at Kitty Hawk, North Carolina, and worked to perfect their craft on the Huffman Prairie outside of Dayton, Ohio, those close to the development of aeronautics in the early twentieth century began to speculate on what uses might be made of heavier-than-air craft.

The Wrights themselves saw military and commercial applications (transporting freight, passengers, and the mail) as the most likely uses for their invention—uses that would assure them a return on their investment. However, the airplane was a frail and unproven technology in its infancy, and while the Wrights succeeded in gaining military sales both at home and abroad, they and other pioneer aviators also sought to profit from the sport or exhibition use of their aircraft, so they opened up some of the first flight training facilities.

The Wrights, Glenn Curtiss, and others formed exhibition teams to travel around the country and demonstrate their flying machines. Once the Wrights had successfully demonstrated their invention in Europe and at Fort Myer, Virginia, the American people craved their own look at this new wonder. Local aviation enthusiasts organized air meets all across the country, and both the Wrights and Curtiss were able to charge premium prices for the appearance of their airplanes and pilots. The Wright and Curtiss fliers competed not only against each other, often for prize money, but also against European pilots and their airplanes. Large and enthusiastic crowds were on hand to greet them everywhere.

These pioneer aviators discovered both the possibilities and the limits of profiting from aviation by using aircraft for entertainment. As first, simply the promise of seeing one of these miraculous flying machines was enough to draw thousands of people to aviation meets. Soon, however, the public began to demand more. In part out of a desire to continue to draw large crowds and in part out of their genuine enthusiasm for flight, pilots began to push their fragile craft to their limits. Dips and dives and eventually loops and rolls became standard fare. Pushing the limits, though, came with a high price tag: crashes were common and often resulted in fatalities. The high death rate itself began to dampen some of the public's enthusiasm for exhibition flying. Yet, no matter what stunts the pilots devised, the American public soon came to view flying as somewhat commonplace. Exhibition flying peaked in 1910 and 1911, and although air shows continued through 1913 and 1914, by 1915–16 the first era of exhibition flying was at an end.[1]

Lincoln Beachy emerged as one of the most famous and daring of these early exhibition pilots. Beachy, born in 1887, came to aviation from what became a somewhat familiar path. He started with bicycles, then moved to motorcycles and finally got interested in balloons. After learning the fundamentals of balloon flight, Beachy quickly moved into dirigibles. By 1906 he was on the exhibition circuit flying his own craft, nicknamed the "Rubber Cow." Beachy continued to pilot his dirigible on the circuit for a number of years. In 1910, however, he saw a French aviator flying a Farman airplane. Sensing that the future lay in heavier-than-air flight, Beachy sought lessons at the Curtiss Flying School. After a somewhat difficult start, Beachy completed the course and by the end of 1911 was the highest earning performer among the Curtiss birdmen.

Beachy specialized in highly risky and thrilling maneuvers. He became widely known for his dips, dives, loops, and spins. By 1913, however, Beachy began to sense that the business of exhibition flying was perhaps a bit too dangerous. During that year he "retired" no fewer than three times, once after accidentally killing a young woman spectator. Following his third retirement, Beachy returned to the exhibition circuit partnered with racecar driver Barney Oldfield. The two toured the country racing aircraft against automobile. Beachy also continued to pursue his stunt flying. In early 1915, while test flying a new acrobatic monoplane, Beachy crashed and died. He was not the first of the exhibition pilots to lose their lives. In fact, the number of deaths had grown so high that by the time Beachy died many had come to the conclusion that exhibition flying was simply too dangerous, too deadly. The large number of deaths on the circuit eventually contributed to the end of the early exhibition era.[2]

The men who flew for the exhibition companies were among the first formally trained pilots in the United States. Both the Wrights and Curtiss had basically taught themselves to fly. The process had been long and dangerous and they were all probably quite lucky to have survived it. They realized that for the airplane to be practical it not only had to fly, it also required someone at its controls who knew how to fly it. By 1910, both the Wrights and Curtiss were selling aircraft to the military and showing off their exhibition companies. In order to train the pilots the military needed to fly their new purchases as well as those for their own exhibition companies, the Wrights and Curtiss each opened flight training schools. Most of the early students were either pioneer military aviators or would-be birdmen like Lincoln Beachy. However, the schools soon began to attract others drawn to aviation, as well. Students included a number of wealthy individuals who needed to learn how to operate their newly purchased flying machines. The schools accepted both men and women as students, but excluded African Americans. Although a number of pioneer aviators continued to teach themselves to fly, and pilot licenses were not required until 1926, a number of flight schools began operating successfully around the country.[3]

While both military and commercial aviation for the most part would be closed to women throughout much of the twentieth century, they were able to find a niche, albeit a small one, in general aviation. As noted, the early exhibition era included not only intrepid birdmen like Lincoln Beachy, but also a number of bird women. Like their male counterparts, they delighted in flying and participated fully in pushing aviation technology to its limits. In doing this, though, they shared the fate of many of the birdmen. One of the most famous bird women of this era was Harriet Quimby, who in 1911 became the first American woman to earn a pilot license. The following year she gained international fame as the first woman to fly an aircraft across the English Channel. Shortly thereafter, however, she was killed in a fall from an aircraft she was piloting. Other pioneer women fliers, such as Katherine and Marjorie Stinson and Ruth Law, managed to live through the exhibition era while setting aviation records as they engaged in the same type of stunt piloting done by the men.[4]

Katherine and Marjorie Stinson, along with their brother Eddie, in addition to continuing their exhibition careers, opened an early flying school. Katherine had learned to fly at the Max Lillie Flying School in Chicago and Marjorie trained with the Wrights. Both women thus had licenses and a familiarity with more formal flight training. When war broke out in Europe in 1914, the Stinson family realized that there might be an opportunity to use the new airfield they had just opened near San Antonio, Texas, as a flight-training center. In addition to the fact that the U.S. military often employed civilian flight schools to train military aviators, in 1915 the Canadian government sought to find a way to train airmen for service in the British military. As a result, the first graduates of the Stinson School of Flying, all trained by Marjorie Stinson, were Canadian citizens. During 1915 and 1916 the school attracted not only more Canadian flight students, but also a number of young men interested in flying for the U.S. military. Although the Stinson family invested much in equipment and worked hard at maintenance, training operations were hard on the school's aircraft. Eventually, a combination of accidents, the fact that the U.S. military had opened its own training fields, and the wartime ban on civilian flying forced the school to close in 1917. Stinson Field remained, however, and eventually evolved into Stinson Municipal Airport, an important satellite airport in San Antonio. As owners and operators of an airport and flying school, the Stinson family became one of the first fixed-base operators in the country.[5]

During World War I, Katherine Stinson attempted to find a role for women in aviation that went beyond exhibition flying and flight training. In 1918, the U.S. Post Office began experimenting with using airplanes to move the mail. At first the planes and pilots were borrowed from the military, but the Post Office soon began to buy its own planes and hire its own pilots. Although the experiment began with a number of problems and missteps, the idea of an airmail service captured the public's attention. Following an exhibition tour of Canada, Katherine Stinson returned to the United States and presented herself to Post Office officials as a potential airmail pilot. Not willing to take no for an answer, Stinson eventually convinced the Post Office to give her the opportunity to fly the mail. On September 26, 1918, Stinson, along with an escort pilot and plane, flew the mail route between Washington, D.C., and New York City. The next day, she and her escort flew back to Washington. Her flight, although of some importance, failed to permanently break the gender barrier barring women from flying the mail. For reasons never fully explained, Katherine Stinson resigned immediately after her one and only airmail flight. Stinson's health may have been the deciding factor: within months of her resignation she began a six-year battle with tuberculosis. She never played an active role in aviation again, particularly after her marriage in 1928, and women's place in aviation remained in general aviation.[6]

The few companies involved in aircraft manufacture before World War I saw the military as their prime market. Nonetheless, the Wrights, Curtiss, and others also sold aircraft to individuals. Given the cost of their machines, the personal aircraft market was limited primarily to the wealthy, although many of the early exhibition pilots used their earnings to purchase their own planes. One of the most prominent of the early wealthy aviation enthusiasts was Harold McCormick of Chicago. Heir to the McCormick Reaper fortune, Harold McCormick belonged to the Chicago Aero Club and in 1911 not only helped plan a major air meet, but also allowed the Aero Club to develop the area's first airport, Cicero Field, on 180 acres of land he owned. McCormick even tried his hand at aircraft design. The strange looking craft flew, but not very well. Within two years McCormick's attention had shifted from land-based aircraft to water-based aircraft or hydroplanes. In 1913, he purchased a hydroplane from Glenn Curtiss. That first machine was destroyed in a crash, but McCormick quickly bought a second and hired a pilot so that he could use the plane to commute from his home to Grant Park, near his downtown Chicago office. His enthusiasm soon waned, however, and McCormick withdrew from aviation in 1915.[7]

McCormick's commitment to the Aero Club field was also limited. In 1913, only two years after permitting use of the site, McCormick sold the land upon which the Aero Club had developed Cicero Field. Although it closed in 1916, Cicero Field was a hotbed of aviation activity in the Chicago area during its short life. The field was so heavily used that the Aero Club hired a manager, Andrew Drew, and paid him $40 per week to serve as the region's first airport manager. Max Lillie operated his flying school on the field from 1911 until his death in 1913. The Aero Club used the field for testing pilots before issuing them a license. In addition to Katherine Stinson, pioneer aviators Glenn Martin, Norman Prince (who served in the Lafayette Escadrille), and Chauncy "Chance" Vought all learned to fly at Cicero Field.[8]

Although a number of individuals shared McCormick's enthusiasm for flight, few had the means for indulging it. Many of them wanted to join the ranks of the birdmen. For them, the best chance of getting airborne was to build their own airplane. The field was fairly wide open despite the Wright-Curtiss patent fight. The Wrights closely guarded their design and any use of it, whereas Glenn Curtiss freely allowed others to copy his early aircraft, making it possible for people with a desire to fly and a certain amount of mechanical aptitude to at least briefly set themselves up as aircraft manufacturers. For example, three brothers from Omaha, Nebraska, found their way into aviation and exhibition flying by building their own version of a Curtiss airplane.

Brothers Otto, Charles, and Gus Baysdorfer arrived in Omaha with their parents in 1887. Otto opened a bicycle shop in the early 1890s, but soon focused his efforts on another hot new technology, the automobile, completing the first one built in Nebraska in 1897. Another new technology caught the attention of the mechanically minded brothers three years later. In 1900, Charles witnessed a balloon flight at a local festival and two years later forged a friendship with noted balloonist John Waldorf Hall, who offered to train him. By 1903, Charles was out on the air show circuit, flying his balloon and parachuting from it. A year later, a severe bout of typhoid fever forced him to return to Omaha in order to recuperate. While he was home, he convinced his brothers to join him in aviation.

The brothers built and successfully flew their first flying machine in 1908, a dirigible named *The Comet*. By the following year, however, the nation was abuzz with news of the Wright brothers' and Glenn Curtiss's success with heavier-than-air-flying machines. Like many of those longing to get airborne, the brothers modeled their first aircraft after Glenn Curtiss's 1908 *June Bug*.[9] The brothers gained firsthand experience with Curtiss flying machines in July, 1910, when the Curtiss exhibition team came to Omaha. They had the opportunity to see a working airplane up close and were able to talk with the mechanics and pilots. By November, the brothers were ready to take their airplane out for its first flight. Charles, the only brother with any kind of flying experience, was at the controls.

The Baysdorfers conducted their flight tests in an open field near the small town of Waterloo, Nebraska. As news of their achievement spread, people began to travel out to watch. Once they felt they had perfected their new craft, Gus (as mechanic) and Charles (as pilot) joined the Moisant Exhibition Company and began traveling on the air show circuit. Gus soon tired of life on the road and returned home, but Charles continued to fly for several years. In 1916, while performing as a stunt pilot in an early movie, Charles crashed and destroyed his airplane. He decided it was time to retire from aviation and moved the Florida. Between 1910 and 1916, the Baysdorfers built perhaps four aircraft. Charles used one on the exhibition circuit and Katherine Stinson, according to local sources, bought another. However, just as the brothers had moved from bicycles to automobiles, from automobiles to dirigibles, and from dirigibles to airplanes, they soon moved from airplanes to other interests. Charles took up fishing in Florida and Otto and Gus ran the family machine shop in Omaha, where they continued to work on other new inventions.

The Baysdorfers built their aircraft primarily as a vehicle for participating in the lucrative world of exhibition flying. They represented the many individuals who sought fame and fortune in the aviation industry only to find that the opportunities involved a great deal of personal risk.[10] There were others, however, who began to think about building aircraft solely for what they believed would become a large market for personal aircraft. The wealthy could afford to buy airplanes from the same companies producing aircraft for the military, but a number of pioneer aircraft manufacturers began to dream of building planes that less affluent buyers could afford. Among them was Clyde Cessna, who got his start in aviation before World War I and, unlike the Baysdorfers, emerged from that conflict as one of the earliest manufacturers of general aviation aircraft.

Born on December 5, 1879, in Hawthorne, Iowa, Clyde Cessna moved
to Kansas with his family in 1881. By the time he reached his teenage
years, Cessna had earned a reputation for his considerable mechanical
abilities. His talent came in handy after he and his brother Roy bought
their first automobile, a one-cylinder, four-horsepower affair that proved
very inappropriate in Kansas' sandy soil. Cessna bought a second automobile, an eight-horsepower Reo, in 1907. As he gained more experience with automobiles, he developed a desire to learn more about them.
He soon made friends with an Overland car dealer and by 1910 was earning a living managing a dealership in Enid, Oklahoma. The following
year he traveled to Oklahoma City to attend an air show, where he witnessed the flight of a Blériot Type XI monoplane. Convinced that he
wanted to fly and that a monoplane was the best way to do it, he immediately sought to purchase his own airplane.

Cessna traveled to New York City and visited the Queen Aeroplane
Company, which built reproductions of the Blériot Type XI. After spend-
ing several weeks at the plant learning about aircraft construction and
going up for a few flights, Cessna arranged for the company to ship his
new $7,500 aircraft home to Enid. He planned to assemble the craft
himself and fly it at a local fair on March 5, 1911. He failed to make that
scheduled flight. Over the next two years, Cessna struggled with his new
airplane, which proved far more difficult to fly and maintain than he
had anticipated. Despite long struggles with the power plant and innu-
merable crashes, he learned much about airplane construction and flying. By 1913, he was ready to build the first aircraft of his own design.

Cessna's 1913 aircraft was clearly based on the one he purchased in
1911, but it proved to be a major improvement over the earlier machine.
Although Cessna had purchased his first aircraft with the idea of flying
it in exhibitions, his career as an exhibition pilot proved less successful
than he had hoped. He planned to fly in several exhibitions in 1913, but
by that time he had also convinced himself that there was a market for
personal aircraft. He and his brother Roy traveled to Wichita, Kansas, in
October, where they announced—somewhat prematurely as it turned
out—that they planned to start manufacturing aircraft and open a flying school.

Cessna built a second monoplane of his own design the following
year, and during the 1914–16 flying seasons continued to travel the air
show circuit. He did not, however, give up on the idea of starting an
aircraft factory and flying school. His chance to realize that part of his

ambition finally came in 1916. A group of Wichita businessmen, many of them members of that town's local Aero Club, invited Cessna to come to their city. When he arrived they offered him factory space and the use of seventy-three adjacent acres for a flying field. Cessna and his Cessna Aeroplane Exhibition Company accepted the offer and moved to Wichita, where he established his factory and flying school in early 1917. Although Cessna received a number of inquiries about his airplanes and about flight training, timing was against him: the United States entered World War I in April. While Cessna continued to earn some money flying at exhibitions, and a few civilians learned to fly at his new school, the war brought a temporary end to civilian aviation. Cessna returned to farming in 1918, but he did not give up on his dream of building an affordable aircraft. Nonetheless, he knew that its fulfillment would have to await the return of peace.[11]

General Aviation Takes Root, 1919–26

The end of World War I marked the beginning of a new period of aerial enthusiasm: the age of the barnstormer. Surplus military aircraft provided a large and inexpensive supply of aircraft for a new group of aviators eager to share the wonders of aviation with the American people. Even though surplus military aircraft in many ways flooded whatever market there was for general aviation planes, a number of pioneer manufacturers hoped to appeal to what they believed would be a growing demand for affordable personal aircraft. In addition, experiments sponsored by various branches of the federal government demonstrated that there were a number of practical uses for aircraft, including crop dusting and aerial surveying. Pioneer air taxis and charter services pointed the way toward corporate flying.

The world of these gypsy fliers—or barnstormers, as they came to be known—was different from that of the prewar birdmen. The country's earliest fliers had been able to command up to $1,000 per day simply for getting airborne. Moreover, even though air show crowds demanded ever-greater stunts between 1910 and 1916, the pay remained high as both planes and pilots remained rare. Neither was as precious a commodity by the early 1920s. Both planes and pilots were in greater supply thanks to wartime training programs. While a few prospered, many more struggled to earn a living while keeping their hard-to-maintain aircraft in flying condition as they competed for the public's attention. Beginning in 1918, a small number of elite pilots captured the nation's imagination while flying the airmail. These men, like the birdmen before them, emerged as popular heroes as their exploits matched or surpassed everything the barnstormers did. Yet, while both groups sought to promote aviation, their actions more often than not produced caution rather than excitement.[12]

Although the surplus military aircraft used by the barnstormers and airmail pilots provided greater safety and performance than the fragile, kitelike airplanes of the prewar period, accidents and fatalities remained all too common. As noted, the public demanded ever more spectacular stunts. The barnstormers, eager to engage the public, enthusiastically obliged. However, when their efforts ended in failure and death, the impression they left with the public was not an enthusiasm for flight, but a fear of aviation. Like the birdmen before them, the barnstormers received intense criticism. Their actions, some argued, were inhibiting rather than promoting aviation's growth. Simply put, the aviation industry would not grow as long as the American people were afraid to fly.

In addition to the competition they faced from airmail pilots for the hearts and minds of the American public, barnstormers faced competition from another quarter as well. In part due to efforts to focus the public's attention on the safety and reliability of aircraft, attention gradually shifted from the daring barnstormers and their hair-raising stunts to the somewhat better equipped and more narrowly focused air racers. Even before World War I, many in both the United States and Europe argued that air races—quests by pilots to go farther and faster—would promote aviation more responsibly than the colorful exhibition pilots. After the war, organized air races focused on distance and speed captured more and more of the public's attention. These air meets, held in both the United States and Europe, attracted the best pilots and the most advanced aircraft. The barnstormers in their increasingly obsolete Jennies and Standards could take aviation into the nation's remotest corners, but the air races emerged as the major aviation events.[13]

Although barnstorming did not bring the same degree of fame and fortune as that granted to the earlier birdmen and women, it nonetheless attracted former military pilots and a host of others seeking to take to the skies. Young Charles Lindbergh started his storied career in aviation as a barnstormer. Lindbergh longed to learn how to fly. To earn money for both flight training and his first aircraft, Lindbergh learned to parachute and wing walk. While traveling on the exhibition circuit, he received a few flying lessons. Once he had scraped together sufficient money, he bought his own airplane. Unfortunately, he lacked the funds to pay for additional flight training. After his first attempt at solo flight nearly ended in disaster, a fellow barnstormer took pity on him and provided him enough training to start his new career.[14]

Women also joined the barnstormers' ranks. Most of them, however, focused on racing and record setting rather than performing elaborate stunts. One who sought to match the spectacle of her male counterparts was Ruth Law. Law, one of the early bird women, earned her pilot license in 1912 and soon joined the air show circuit. During World War I she flew exhibitions in order to raise money for the Red Cross and to support Liberty Loan drives. When the war ended, Law realized that the vast number of male pilots trained by the military had turned aviation into a far more crowded field. She and her husband decided to take a different tack and took her show overseas to the Far East. Upon returning to the United States in 1920, Ruth Law's Flying Circus performed a number of breathtaking stunts—including a plane-to-car transfer. The work was dangerous, though. One morning in 1921, Ruth Law opened her newspaper and saw a story announcing her retirement. Despite the fact that her Flying Circus earned up to $9,000 per week, her husband had decided it was time to stop tempting fate. He told her that he had given the story of her retirement to the newspaper. Rather than argue, Law gave up her career in aviation.[15]

Bessie Coleman took up aviation about the same time Ruth Law retired. Coleman, an African American born in 1893 to a former slave, became fascinated with flight during the war, and in 1919 began a search for a flight instructor. After discovering that no one in the United States would teach her to fly, Coleman—encouraged by Robert S. Abbott, founder and editor of the *Chicago Defender,* a prominent African-American newspaper—went to Europe, where she earned her pilot license at the Federation Aeronautique Internationale in Paris on June 15, 1921.

She returned to the United States and began flying on the exhibition circuit. Her ultimate goal was to earn enough money to open a flight school where other African-American women could learn to fly. Coleman followed the air show circuit for the next five years. Along the way she not only impressed many with her flying ability, she also won a few small victories for equality. In Texas, for example, she succeeded in getting air show officials to allow African Americans to use the same entrance gate as whites. They were still segregated once they were inside, but just being allowed to use the same gate was a step forward. Coleman, however, did not live to accomplish her ultimate goal: establish a flying school. "Queen Bessie," as she became known, died when she fell from her plane while practicing to make a parachute jump for an air show in Orlando, Florida, on April 30, 1926. Although she did not realize her ambition of teaching other African-American women to fly, Coleman succeeded in blazing a path for African Americans in general aviation. Others, both male and female, would follow.[16]

Although surplus military aircraft dominated the general aviation market in the early 1920s, there were many who believed that there was a market for affordable, better-performing personal aircraft. Such airplanes could be sold to some of the more successful barnstormers as well as to other individuals hoping to buy their own aircraft. As early as 1919, Jacob Melvin "Jake" Moellendick, a Wichita, Kansas, businessman, saw the opportunities in postwar aviation. He and a small group of Wichita businessmen funded the Wichita Airplane Company. Initially, the company sought to earn money from the exhibition circuit, to provide flight training, and to operate an air taxi and joyride service. Moellendick, however, soon saw a need for an aircraft different from the available Standards and Jennys, an aircraft with a greater load and passenger capacity. Hoping to be the first to produce such an aircraft, Moellendick sent his firm's manager to Chicago to convince airplane designer Emil Matthew "Matty" Laird to come to Wichita. Moellendick eventually lured Laird, his brother Charles, and another young man, George "Buck" Weaver, to Wichita to join his fledgling company. Laird's new aircraft, the Swallow, made its first successful flight in April, 1920.

The company planned an initial production run of ten aircraft, but orders soon eclipsed the original production plan and the company had to hire additional employees to meet the demand. One of its first new hires was Lloyd Carlton Stearman, a former navy pilot with a strong desire to learn aircraft engineering. Another early employee was ex-barnstormer and salesman Walter Herschel Beech. Between 1920 and 1923, the company produced and sold forty-three aircraft. By that time, however, it had begun to experience some internal problems. Weaver left in 1921 for Ohio, where he used the experience he had gained in Wichita to start the Weaver Aircraft Company. Matty Laird left in 1923. With his departure, the company reorganized and began operating as the Swallow Airplane Manufacturing Company in January, 1924. By the end of the year, however, disagreements between Stearman, Beech, and Moellendick led the younger men to leave the company. Stearman had wanted Swallow to move from wood to steel-tube construction. Moellendick insisted on using wood. Stearman and Beech, wishing to form their own aircraft manufacturing company, turned to local aviation pioneer Clyde Cessna. He was intrigued by their ideas and in early 1925, Stearman, Beech, Cessna, and local banker Walter Innes Jr., formed the Travel Air Manufacturing Company.

Travel Air sold its first aircraft in the spring of 1925, and orders for additional planes soon taxed the company's resources. Yet despite its early success, disagreements arose. Travel Air produced biplanes, the design favored by Stearman and Beech, whereas Clyde Cessna wanted to produce a monoplane. Using his own resources, Cessna designed and tested a successful monoplane in June, 1926. That design evolved into Travel Air's first monoplane, the Type 5000. Even though Travel Air had adopted a monoplane design, Cessna was still anxious to build his own kind of airplane: an affordable personal aircraft. He left Travel Air in early 1927.

Wichita served as an important incubator for general aviation aircraft manufacturing during the first half of the 1920s. By 1926, the city had seen or would soon witness the creation three pioneer general aviation manufacturers: Swallow, Travel Air, and the Cessna Aircraft Company. While the personal or light aircraft industry would not enter its so-called golden age until after the enthusiasm generated by Charles Lindbergh's nonstop New York to Paris flight in 1927, a base clearly had been built by the mid-1920s.[17]

Similarly, the base for a number of new, practical uses of aircraft was also laid in the early 1920s. The early experiments were done not so much by private individuals, but by the military or under the sponsorship of various branches of the federal government. Among the activities explored were crop dusting, forest-fire patrols, and aerial surveying. Although each of these activities was initiated in the public sector, by the mid- to late-1920s private sector individuals had begun building on these early experiments.

In 1921, the state of Ohio faced something of an agricultural emergency. Catalpa sphinx and catalpa midge threatened widespread destruction. The state's Agricultural Section joined Army Air Service personnel at McCook Field in Dayton to devise a way to deliver chemicals by air to treat a grove of catalpa trees near Troy, Ohio. Within minutes, the pilot, flying a plane equipped with experimental "dusting" equipment, had completed what would have taken field hands hours using conventional methods. News of the successful effort spread quickly. Over the next few years, the Air Service continued to support other experiments involving aerial crop dusting. By the mid-1920s, private interests began to recognize the value of delivering chemicals by air, and a number of crop-dusting companies soon appeared on the scene. They included the Huff-Daland Airplane Company (which also saw an opportunity to sell its airplanes), the Southern Dusting Company, and the Quick Aeroplane Dusters. Most of the activity centered in the South, where the main target was the boll weevil.[18]

In addition to conducting crop-dusting experiments, the military and other branches of the federal government explored a number of other potentially practical uses for aircraft. The Department of Agriculture used aircraft to help it compile crop estimates. The Coast Guard used aircraft to help guide commercial fishermen to schools of fish, aircraft were used for forest-fire patrols, and the U.S. Coast and Geodetic Survey began using aircraft to conduct aerial photographic surveys to help it meet its mandate to provide updated charts of seaboard cities and the coastline of North America. While private interests did not become involved in many of these types of activities until after 1926, the government's efforts did serve to demonstrate a number of potential uses for aircraft.[19]

Planes and Power Plants

Although there has always been something of an overlap between general aviation aircraft and airplanes used for military and/or commercial purposes, this was particularly true between 1910 and 1926. Aircraft used for exhibition and personal flying were, in many cases, the same planes, or versions of the same planes, used for other purposes—particularly military purposes. Between 1910 and 1926, the planes themselves evolved from craft with open, kitelike structures to more robust vehicles, while the materials used—wood, fabric, and wire—remained constant. Not until the end of this period was there a move toward steel-tube construction in smaller aircraft. Throughout, the engine remained the most troublesome and expensive part of an airplane. Aircraft engines continued to be underpowered and unreliable. Moreover, with the exception of the World War I–surplus Curtiss OX-5 engine, they were expensive. Certain manufacturers began to design and build aircraft for the emerging general aviation market, but their high prices—driven in most cases by the cost of engines—kept the market for new aircraft small. The result was that surplus military aircraft dominated the market in the early 1920s.

Through 1916, the three primary aircraft types were those made by the Wrights, Curtiss, and Blériot. Wright aircraft built between 1910 and 1916 (by which time Orville, the surviving brother, had sold the company he and Wilbur founded) were open structured, two-place biplanes. The pilot and passenger sat upright on seats placed on the lower wing. The wing-warping system and elevator were manipulated by two hand-held control sticks. A bar moved by the pilot's feet controlled the rudder. While the earliest Wright planes were canards, with the elevator at the front of the aircraft, later models moved the elevator to the rear of the aircraft with the rudder. All were "pusher" aircraft, with chain-driven twin propellers mounted at the rear of the wings. The earliest models employed skids for landing gear; later models added wheels.

Wright engines powered all Wright aircraft. These engines, evolved from the one that powered the original Kitty Hawk Flyer, are best described as having been adequate. The original Wright aircraft engine, built by Charles E. Taylor to the brothers' design specifications, was a four-cylinder inline engine that operated while lying on its side. The engine provided sixteen horsepower when first started. Once in operation, it offered a steady twelve horsepower, which provided just enough power while running wide open to get the Kitty Hawk Flyer aloft. The post-1903 descendants of that first engine incorporated throttle controls and a normal carburetor. By the time the original Wright company ceased its initial manufacturing run, the engine line had evolved through a thirty-horsepower, four-cylinder engine and a sixty-horsepower, six-cylinder version.[20]

In many ways, early Curtiss aircraft structurally resembled the Wright models. Both were open-structured pusher biplanes in which the pilot and passenger sat exposed on the aircraft's lower wing. There were, however, important differences. The most important one was the control system. The Wright aircraft induced roll by warping or twisting the surface of the wings, whereas Curtiss aircraft induced roll by use of an aileron, a small control surface initially placed between the wings. The Curtiss aileron was a distinct improvement over the Wright's wing-warping method, especially when aircraft designers began building larger and faster aircraft. The wing-warping system quickly proved something of a technological dead end at that point.

When the Wrights developed their first aircraft they left the purchase or development of an adequate power plant to the last. In contrast, Glenn Curtiss's first exposure to flying came about because of his expertise with engines. In 1904, "Captain" Thomas Scott Baldwin approached Curtiss and asked him to develop an engine for his dirigible. The engine was a success and, bitten by the flying bug, Curtiss joined the Aerial Experiment Association headed by Alexander Graham Bell. Curtiss's earliest aircraft engine was a V-8 similar to the one on the motorcycle he used to set the land speed record in 1906. He then produced a four-cylinder engine (E-4) generating fifty horsepower and an eight-cylinder version (E-8) producing a hundred horsepower, both of which were air-cooled. Curtiss's later prewar engines were water-cooled V-8s that evolved into the famous (or infamous) OX-5, introduced in 1910. The OX-5 emerged as one of the most important engines during the early 1920s—not so much for its power or reliability, but because it was cheap and plentiful. The OX-5 powered one of the two main training aircraft used by the U.S. armed forces: the Curtiss JN-4D Jenny. As a result, the military ordered the engine into mass production. When the war ended, the by-then technically obsolete engine was available in large numbers.[21]

The third type of aircraft available in the United States was the Blériot Type XI monoplane. In addition to having a single wing rather than two, Blériots differed from Wright and Curtiss aircraft in other significant ways. Blériots were tractor-type aircraft rather than pushers, with the engine and propeller located in the aircraft's nose in front of the pilot, who sat inside a partially enclosed fuselage. The elevator and rudder were located at the tail end of the fuselage. Although the Blériot employed the Wright's wing-warping system, it used the now standard "stick" to control the plane's pitch and roll. The Wright control system used dual sticks for pitch (elevator) and roll (wing warping). The early Curtiss used a stick to control pitch (elevator) and a shoulder yoke to control roll (aileron).[22]

In addition to these three major types of aircraft, the pioneer bird-men employed a number of other airplanes. However, almost all of these were based on the Wright, Curtiss, or Blériot designs. These prewar aircraft, like those built by the Baysdorfers in Nebraska and Cessna in Kansas, were built in very small numbers—often for use by the builder, although Cessna did plan to manufacture planes for what he hoped would be a significant personal aircraft market.

As noted above, Wright aircraft used Wright engines and Curtiss aircraft used Curtiss engines even though other domestic engines, such as the Etheridge, Roberts, and Hall-Scott, were available. Their supply was limited, however, because, with only minor exceptions—the Hall-Scott was used on the Standard—they were not used by any of the major U.S. aircraft-manufacturing firms. In addition, expensive imported engines were available. The most common of these were the Gnome and LeRhone rotary engines, and the Anzani fan and then radial engines—all built in France.

Following World War I, whatever general aviation aircraft market there was found itself flooded with surplus trainers, particularly Curtiss JN-4D Jennies and Standard J-1s. The Jenny, with its OX-5 engine, proved to be especially popular because a basically new aircraft and engine could be purchased for under $500—considerably less than its competitors. The wartime trainers were quite different than the prewar designs, reflecting the technological strides made during the war. Both were tractor-type aircraft with fully enclosed fuselages. In terms of construction, however, they shared important similarities with their prewar predecessors: both were made of wood, fabric, and wire, and both were biplanes.

Engines remained the most difficult challenge. As noted, the ninety-horsepower Curtiss OX-5 was plentiful and cheap. Engines with more horsepower and greater reliability were available, but their cost was prohibitive for the general aviation market. If one could afford it, one could replace a plane's OX-5 with a Wright–Hispano Suiza (or Hisso) engine. Built under license by Wright Aeronautical, a descendent of the Wright brothers' original firm, the Hisso was far more reliable and twice as powerful as the OX-5. However, these benefits did not come cheaply. Imports, especially the Anzani, remained available, but they, too, were expensive.[23]

Many of the general aviation aircraft built during the early 1920s were designed to use the cheap, readily available OX-5 engine, and this engine choice drove design. The heavy OX-5 required an airplane with considerable lift. Therefore, a two- or three-place biplane was the most common design.

Despite the tight market and the limitations posed by engine cost, a number of innovative designs emerged shortly after the war. These included the Loughhead S-1, the Curtiss Oriole, the Bellanca CF, and the previously mentioned Cessna monoplane. The Loughhead S-1, designed by Jack Northop, employed molded plywood construction. The result was a cigar-shaped, monocoque ("single shell") fuselage. Northop and the Loughhead brothers (the brother who remained in the aviation business later changed the spelling of his last name to Lockheed) hoped their plane would be affordable and appeal to a large market. In the end, however, its high price discouraged sales. The Oriole was Glenn Curtiss's attempt to build a small aircraft for the personal aircraft market. Similar to the other small planes being produced at the time, it also fell victim to economics. Wings built for the plane, however, were purchased and used by Harold Pitcairn for his first production aircraft. The Bellanca CF, designed by Italian immigrant Giuseppe Bellanca, grew out of the partnership between the designer and a group of Omaha, Nebraska, investors eager to bring the aviation industry to their city. Although the manufacturing venture soon failed, the CF proved to be a highly successful, if expensive, design. The CF, one of the first successful enclosed cabin monoplanes built in the United States, fathered a series of remarkable planes, including the Wright-Bellanca 2 that Charles Levine and Clarence Chamberlin flew from New York to Berlin two weeks after Lindbergh reached Paris. Thus, despite the innovative nature of each of these aircraft's design, their price tags—ranging from $3,000 to $5,000—kept the number produced and sold low.[24]

By the mid-1920s, a few U.S. general aviation manufacturers began to employ steel-tube fuselage designs following Anthony Fokker pioneering the use of metal in aircraft construction in Europe. A campaign of sorts emerged during the period promoting the use of metal. Although many proponents claimed that all-metal aircraft would be safer (or at least be perceived as safer) in a fire than one constructed of wood, fabric, and wire, their argument was not entirely grounded in technical considerations. In many ways, aircraft were viewed as modern machines, and metal as a modern material. Wood, on the other hand, was associated with old-fashioned, craft-style construction. Metal proponents apparently came to believe that modern aircraft should be constructed of a modern material, even though the use of metal increased both material and labor costs.[25] As noted, Cessna, Stearman, and Beech founded Travel Air specifically for the purpose of building aircraft with steel-tube fuselages. They were not the first when it came to personal aircraft, however. The real pioneer was WACO.

George Weaver was an early participant in the Wichita aircraft scene when he joined the Laird brothers in 1921. His stay in the city was brief, however, and he soon returned to Ohio, where he had barnstormed immediately after World War I. There, he and two friends, Elwood "Sam" Junkin and Clayton Brucker, formed the Weaver Aircraft Company, which soon became known by its trade-name formed from the company's initials, WACO. After Weaver died in 1924, Junkin and Brucker reorganized the firm as Advance Aircraft, but kept the trade name. In late 1929, following another reorganization, the company changed its name to the WACO Aircraft Company. The first aircraft built by the company was constructed of wood and fabric. However, in April, 1925, the firm introduced the WACO Model 9, constructed with a welded steel-tube fuselage. The Model 9 was a fabric-covered, three-place, open-cockpit biplane powered by an OX-5 engine. Although it originally sold for $2,500, the company built and sold thirty by August.[26]

The first decades of the twentieth century witnessed the rapid development of the Wrights' invention. Military, commercial, and general aviation uses of aircraft emerged during this period. Both the aircraft and their applications, however, remained very much in their experimental phases through the mid-1920s. This was as true in general aviation as it was in military and commercial aviation. Yet all three areas were on the verge of exponential growth. During the next two decades, general aviation would grow dramatically and enter into what many consider to have been its golden age.

A 1930 Fairchild KR-21A biplane powered by a Kinner K-5 engine.
Photo courtesy Michael G. Williams Aviation.

CHAPTER 2

The "Golden Age"

1926–39

The years between 1926 and 1939 are known as the "golden age" of general aviation. This golden age came about despite the depression and even as federal rules and regulations made the business of flying as well as of manufacturing and selling aircraft more complex. The mid-1920s marked a turning point in the history of aviation in the United States. All forms of aviation—military, commercial, and general—were affected by federal action. Congress promoted the expansion of military aviation with the passage of the Air Corps Act in 1926. The year before, Congress approved the Air Mail Act or Kelly Act. This required the transfer of the U.S. Post Office's airmail service from the government to the private sector, thus providing the spark for the organization of the nation's first important airlines. Congress also enacted the Air Commerce Act in 1926. While much of that act was directed at regulating commercial aviation, its provisions had consequences for general aviation.

Although the advent of federal regulation might have reined in some of aviation's more freewheeling elements, the late 1920s saw general aviation begin to come into its own. Much of this was due to the energizing influence of Charles Lindbergh's nonstop solo flight across the Atlantic. Suddenly, a large number of Americans wanted to find out more about flying. The market for personal aircraft, hoped for but never quite realized through the mid-1920s, finally emerged, although it never reached the scale anticipated by the more optimistic aviation boosters. Then, in the 1930s, the federal government attempted to directly stimulate the general aviation aircraft market by promoting the design and manufacture of a simple, affordable airplane. Finally, the 1930s witnessed the introduction of the first affordable, reliable engines for general aviation aircraft. Thus, despite the depression, pioneer general aviation aircraft manufacturers were in many ways responsible for the general aviation industry "boom" during the late 1920s and 1930s.

What had been experimental uses of aircraft in the early 1920s emerged as established aviation businesses in the late 1920s and 1930s. Crop dusting expanded throughout the South and by the end of the decade "dusters" were aiding farming and lumbering interests in all regions of the United States. Perhaps the most important expansion of general aviation activities occurred when America's business leaders took to the air. Although they also patronized the nation's fledgling commercial airlines, they saw the value of having personal or corporate business aircraft.

During the earliest years of powered flight, exhibition fliers had drawn large and enthusiastic crowds on the air show circuit, but air racers began to steal the spotlight in the early 1920s. By the late 1920s, air racing had emerged as a major spectator sport, and it continued to draw large crowds throughout the 1930s. Many of the aircraft used in these races were the creations of inspired aircraft designers, both amateur and professional, and they ranked among the most advanced aircraft in the world at that time.

With the general increase in flying by the mid-1920s came a concurrent demand for more and better landing facilities. The construction of thousands of airports around the country created new opportunities for those who sought a living in aviation by acting as a fixed-base operator. A number of these new airports, whether publicly or privately owned, either leased the facilities to a fixed-base operator or hired a manager to promote and develop activities at the airport—everything from flight schools to restaurants, and from oil and gas sales to pay toilets—to help provide operating revenue.

Numerous New Deal programs and other legislation enacted in the late 1930s represented both important contributions and challenges to general aviation. In addition to the affordable aircraft program, the New Deal also sponsored an air-marking campaign and the Civilian Pilot Training Program (CPTP). The Civil Aeronautics Act of 1938 further regulated general aviation activities. Federal regulations from the Air Commerce Act in 1926 through the Civil Aeronautics Act in 1938 profoundly shaped the homebuilt aircraft movement. Then, in the late 1930s, general aviation pilots organized, forming the Aircraft Owners and Pilots Association in an effort to use the strength of numbers to protect the interests of private pilots.

Women and African Americans continued to carve out a role for themselves largely within the realm of general aviation. Women worked in aircraft sales and promotion as well as participating in popular air races, and African Americans struggled to build on Bessie Coleman's successes in the 1920s.

Landmark Legislation and the Lindbergh Boom

In many ways, aviation was a very informal affair before 1926. The adventurous and mechanically inclined built and flew their own airplanes. Many of these intrepid airmen taught themselves to fly, although flight training was offered as early as 1910. Licenses were available, but they were issued by a private organization. The Aero Club of America, with the authorization of the Federation Aeronautique Internationale, administered tests and awarded certificates. Meanwhile, several states and a number of cities passed laws and regulations governing aviation. Most of these local measures concerned the control of stunt flying.[1] Aside from funding military aviation, however, the federal government played almost no role at all. That changed in 1926.

The Air Commerce Act passed that year was designed to bring a measure of order and efficiency to aviation. It also created a federal aviation bureaucracy responsible for both regulating and promoting aviation. Most of the act's provisions focused on commercial aviation. The Kelly Act, passed the previous year, aimed at helping create commercial airlines in the United States by providing them with a subsidy for carrying the mail. The Air Commerce Act authorized the creation of rules and regulations to govern the new enterprises.[2] As far as the emerging general aviation industry was concerned, the two most important provisions of the Air Commerce Act dealt with pilot licensing and aircraft certification.

The Air Commerce Act authorized the new Bureau of Air Commerce to create regulations concerning the licensing of pilots. The regulations set up two types of pilot licenses: commercial and private. In the late 1920s, private pilots were licensed to fly licensed aircraft. They were not allowed to accept pay for either carrying passengers or for instructing

students. The examinations and tests for the private pilot license included demonstrating knowledge of air traffic rules and Air Commerce
regulations and completing a flight test involving three successful landings to a full stop. This meant that pilots had to bring their aircraft to a
complete stop after each landing, rather than simply touching down,
adding power, and taking off again. Pilots were required to renew their
licenses every year and to keep accurate records of their flying time in a
logbook.[3]

The first chapter of the Air Commerce regulations was devoted to
aircraft licensing. Planes used strictly for recreational flying or for noncommercial purposes needed only to be registered, not licensed. However, anyone wishing to build and sell aircraft for anything other than
strictly recreational flying or for noncommercial purposes had to have
their aircraft licensed. There was, therefore, still a place for the makers
of homebuilt aircraft.

Licensed aircraft had to meet certain airworthiness requirements.
These requirements covered such aspects of aircraft construction and
equipment as structural strength, the power plant, propellers, and the
aircraft's general flying characteristics and qualities. Once the proper
paperwork had been submitted and an aircraft design deemed airworthy, it was awarded an Approved Type Certificate. The Bureau of Air
Commerce also issued licenses for individual aircraft, including special
licenses for racing and experimental aircraft.[4]

The end result was a more formal structure for aviation. Although
unlicensed pilots and aircraft continued to fly during the 1930s, their
days were numbered. The introduction of formal regulations could have
had a dampening effect on general aviation, particularly private flying,
but that was not the case. First, the regulations brought a measure of
order and improved safety to aviation. Second, and perhaps even more
important, the issuance of the regulations came at the same time as one
of the greatest aviation feats of all time: Charles Lindbergh's nonstop
trans-Atlantic solo flight. "Lucky Lindy's" achievement created a sensation around the world and inspired many to explore the world of flight.

The Quest for the Affordable Airplane

Private flying was limited primarily to affluent individuals through the
mid-1920s. Although a few manufacturers, including Cessna, attempted

to build a smaller aircraft for the private market, the price remained too high. Not only were the aircraft expensive, but flight training, maintenance, storage, and fueling also added to the overall cost. Still, the dream of the widespread use of aircraft for personal transportation remained, and a number of individuals—especially aircraft manufacturers and government officials—worked to make the dream come true.

By the early 1930s, a number of small aircraft appeared on the market priced under $2,000. While this was still expensive when compared to automobiles, these were the first of the so-called affordable aircraft. The most popular of the group, which included the Curtiss-Wright Junior and the American Eaglet, was the Aeronca C-2, known affectionately as the flying bathtub.

The Aeronca C-2 grew out of work begun in the early 1920s by Jean Roche, the chief of design and a technical adviser serving with the Army Air Service's Materiel Division at McCook Field in Dayton, Ohio. Roche had demonstrated an interest in aviation at an early age. He participated in glider and model clubs in the New York City area as a youth. Then, after receiving a degree in mechanical engineering from Columbia University, Roche worked for a number of aircraft firms before moving to McCook Field. While at McCook, Roche developed his aviation engineering philosophy. It centered on three tenets: sound engineering, simplicity, and functionality. While most of the aviation world was moving toward bigger and more powerful aircraft, Roche refused to accept the movement toward bigger for its own sake.

Roche's first opportunity to act on his philosophy came in 1923, when the Materiel Division asked him to design a glider for the Army Air Service. The resulting GL-2 glider was a high-wing monoplane. At about the same time, Roche began to develop plans for a light aircraft. He first searched for an airfoil superior to the one used on his glider, which employed upper wing panels from a Curtiss JN-4 Jenny. Impressed by a series of tests conducted at MIT, Roche chose a Clark Y airfoil for his proposed aircraft.

The next problem involved the power plant. As noted, power plants were both expensive and heavy. Smaller, cheaper engines were available in Europe, but the cost of importing them was prohibitive. Roche and his design partner, John Dohse, turned to another employee at McCook field for help. Harold Moorehouse, an engineer in the power plant section, had recently designed a small fifteen-horsepower engine for use on blimps, but it was too small for a heavier-than-air machine. Nonetheless, Moorehouse eagerly accepted the challenge of designing a slightly larger twenty-nine-horsepower engine, which he completed in mid-1925.

Roche, Dohse, and Moorehouse then mated the engine and airframe and took their new aircraft out to nearby Wilbur Wright Field for testing. On September 1, Dohse added too much power during a taxi test and the little airplane took to the air. Dohse, who had very little flight training, took the small craft skyward, climbed out to a distance of five miles and then returned to the field, ending the flight with a perfect landing. Throughout the following year, the trio tested their new craft more than two hundred times. The next challenge proved to be more difficult: finding a way to bring the aircraft into production.

The opportunity finally came in 1929. A group of Cincinnati businessmen had joined together to form the Aeronautical Corporation of America (Aeronca). Despite its name, however, the new company had no airplane, no designers, and no factory. A friend of Jean Roche, Conrad Dietz, suggested that the company take a look at the small aircraft designed and built in Dayton. Roche and Dohse demonstrated their aircraft, now powered with a new Poole-Galloway (a pair of McCook engineers) engine, for the Cincinnati businessmen. After making arrangements for the production of the new engine, designated the E-107A, and finding factory space at Cincinnati's new airport, the final deal was struck in the summer of 1929. Roche decided to stay with the Materiel Division and accepted an advisory position with the new company. Robert Galloway, who had helped develop the new engine, left McCook Field to become Aeronca's first chief engineer. The company also hired Roger E. Schlemmer to reengineer the plane in order to make it more suitable for factory production. The company produced its first Aeronca C-2, as the aircraft was designated, in October, 1929, and its maiden flight was made on October 20.

Despite the fact that the stock market crash came less than two weeks after the maiden flight of its first aircraft, the company aggressively moved to promote it. As the first affordable and reliable small aircraft available, the Aeronca C-2 dominated the light aircraft market in 1930. By 1931, the C-2's success led to the entry of more than a dozen competitors. All of these one- and two-place aircraft sold for under $2,000. Aeronca responded to the competition by introducing the two-place Aeronca C-3 with an improved thirty-six horsepower E-113 engine in 1931. (Although the C-2 could carry two persons, it was designed to carry only one.[5])

The deepening depression put a damper on the market for light aircraft. In addition, despite the fact that the new light aircraft were inexpensive compared to larger individual sport planes, they were still more expensive than automobiles. With the coming of the New Deal, a new effort emerged to design and manufacture a truly affordable "everyman's aircraft."

Eugene Vidal came to the directorship of the Aeronautics Branch of the Commerce Department as a "true believer" in the winged gospel. A former Army Air Service pilot and assistant general manager of Transcontinental Air Transport, Vidal was determined that the Aeronautics Branch help spearhead a New Deal for the "forgotten man" of aviation: the private flyer. He believed that if a safe and affordable aircraft were available, Americans would take to the skies in large numbers. The problem was that, despite the appearance of less costly aircraft such as the C-2, flying in the United States was still an expensive proposition. In Europe, organized flying clubs helped lower the cost of training and flying. Yet, such clubs were rare in the United States. For the most part, private flyers were on their own when it came to finding training and then purchasing and maintaining their own aircraft. Vidal hoped to use New Deal programs to promote private flying and to create a truly affordable aircraft.

Upon taking office in October, 1933, Vidal began work on two programs aimed at supporting private or general aviation. The first was an airfield construction and/or improvement program. Conducted under the Civil Works Administration (CWA), Vidal's airport program included funding for building or improving small airfields in the nation's smaller cities. While monies also went to larger municipal airports, Vidal placed great stress on expanding the number of small fields suitable for general aviation around the country.[6]

The second program involved the Public Works Administration (PWA). Vidal was promised $500,000 from that New Deal program, money he hoped to use in concert with the U.S. aviation industry to design and manufacture an all-metal, two-place monoplane. The plane would sell for $700, placing it in the same price range as automobiles. Vidal began by sending out a questionnaire to all of the licensed pilots, student pilots, and mechanics in the country (thirty-four thousand in November, 1934), asking them if they would be interested in such an aircraft. The response was affirmative. With the promise of PWA money, Vidal then created a special committee to tackle the problems of designing and promoting such an aircraft.

Although the popular press responded positively, professional and aviation trade journals proved far more guarded in their response, and the aircraft industry issued a negative appraisal of the project. Those already involved in light aircraft manufacturing feared that the promise of a $700 airplane would cause those wanting to purchase an airplane to wait until the cheaper version was available. Nonetheless, Vidal continued to move forward with his plans. Eventually, the aviation industry, not wanting to lose out on a share of the promised $500,000 PWA grant, decided to cooperate.

In the end, however, it was not the aviation industry's skepticism that killed the program, but rather congressional distrust of the aviation industry. In early 1934, while Vidal was trying to finalize arrangements for creating a new firm—owned jointly by existing aviation companies—to build the proposed aircraft, the airmail scandal rocked the Roosevelt Administration. The administration, responding to complaints over the award of airmail contracts by Pres. Herbert Hoover's postmaster general, Walter Brown, canceled the contracts. The administration had determined that the contracts involved collusion on the part of the country's larger aviation firms. In February, while the Army Air Corps was attempting to carry the mail with disastrous results, the PWA recommended canceling the promised grant for Vidal's aircraft program. It thus was suspicion of the aviation industry—a suspicion held by the federal government since World War I and the disappointing results of the military aircraft program during that conflict—that killed the program to design and manufacture a $700 airplane.[7]

With the collapse of the affordable aircraft program, Vidal turned to promoting the design and manufacture of a safer, easier-to-fly aircraft. Such an aircraft did not initially have to meet the $700 price goal, but Vidal hoped that if one could be mass-produced, prices would eventually fall to the target level. The Bureau of Aeronautics issued specifications that any aircraft designed for the new program would have to meet. It had to be of all-metal construction, seat at least two (the pilot and a passenger), have dual controls, a maximum speed of 110 miles per hour, and a maximum range of three hundred miles. It also had to be easy to control and be designed to minimize the danger of stalling and spinning. A number of aircraft were designed and built in answer to this call, the most successful of which was Fred Weick's W-1.

Fred Weick, a senior National Advisory Committee on Aeronautics (NACA) engineer, gathered together a group of fellow NACA employees to discuss the problems involved in building a safe and affordable small plane. A number of design concepts emerged, and the group built models of three. Weick's emerged as the best of the group, and construction soon began on a prototype. When Bureau of Air Commerce officials visited NACA, they were sufficiently impressed that they recommended testing of the aircraft begin as soon as possible.

The W-1 was a high-wing, pusher monoplane. The original model included a standard stick-and-rudder control system, but it had a number of other features aimed at making it both safe and easy to handle. These included a wing slat to allow for low-speed landings, and tricycle landing gear with a steerable nosewheel. The wing slat, along with several other design features, also made the airplane difficult to stall. If a plane does not stall, it will not go into a spin. After the first aircraft was damaged in a hard landing, Weick built a new prototype. The resulting W-1A, funded by the Bureau of Air Commerce, included a number of changes. The wing slat was replaced with flaps, and the standard stick-and-rudder control system was replaced with a dual-control system that eliminated the rudder pedals. Under the new system, a control wheel manipulated all three control surfaces (ailerons, elevator, rudder), automatically coordinating their operation.

Although the W-1A was a safe aircraft, it did not meet the program's specifications. It was not an all-metal aircraft and, at the time, no plans existed for putting the aircraft into production.[8] Just before World War II, Weick and his partners finally began production of an aircraft that incorporated many of the features tested on the W-1A. Called the "Ercoupe," it sold well until the war put an end to private aircraft production (see Chapter 3). A number of other aircraft appeared as a result of the Vidal program. These included the Stearman-Hammond Model Y, the Waterman Arrowplane (a roadable aircraft), and a roadable autogiro.[9]

By 1936, Bureau of Air Commerce's efforts to promote private flying were coming to an end. Although the program supported technological innovations that proved important, especially tricycle landing gear, it failed to promote the creation of a healthy market for small aircraft. The publicity generated by the program kept alive the myth of a future in which the private use of aircraft would be widespread, even commonplace. However, the light aircraft industry generally opposed the entire program. Manufacturers did not believe that small, safe, and affordable aircraft were really possible. They believed Vidal would have been more successful if he had concentrated on an airport program and supported improved weather reporting and navigation aids. In addition, Vidal became the target of much criticism, especially for his $700 airplane program, during congressional hearings in 1936. He resigned from the Bureau of Air Commerce the following March.[10]

The Homebuilt Movement

Efforts to provide pilots and would-be pilots with an affordable aircraft were not limited to established aircraft manufacturing companies and the federal government. Another avenue explored involved the do-it-yourself aircraft market. Since the early years of aviation, backyard tinkerers had been producing their own aircraft. Enthusiasts from the Baysdorfers to Clyde Cessna built their own planes either from scratch or from parts purchased from manufacturers. Beginning in the early 1920s, any number of hopeful pilots and/or manufacturers produced plans for small, affordable aircraft. By the late 1920s and early 1930s, a full-blown homebuilt aircraft "movement" was in place. However, homebuilding emerged at the same time both federal and state legislation appeared aimed at improving the safety and reliability of aircraft. Between 1926 and 1938, federal and state regulations gradually made homebuilding difficult, if not impossible. With the coming of World War II and the restrictions on private flying that came with it, the homebuilding movement temporarily disappeared.

Beginning in the early 1920s a number of aviation magazines and journals, including *Aerial Age,* published plans for small, affordable aircraft designed to be built at home and powered by automobile or motorcycle engines. As early as 1925, inspired by a light plane aircraft contest held in England and a light airplane race included in the 1924 National Air Races, Edmund T. Allen called for the creation of an organization to promote and support the activities of amateur plane builders. Allen, who later became a test pilot, was unsuccessful, but interest in homebuilding continued to increase and received a significant boost from Lindbergh's flight in 1927.[11]

Following Lindbergh's epic journey, a wider variety of magazines and journals began publishing aircraft plans. The planes depicted in these plans could either be built from scratch or from kits. One of the most popular scratch-built aircraft was the Pietenpol Air Camper. Powered by a Ford Model A engine, B. H. Pietenpol published the plans in 1930 in *Modern Mechanics and Inventions.* Edward Heath, who designed his first Heath Parasol in 1927, offered his Super Parasol in 1929 in kit form. The kit could be purchased for $199. The builder had to provide the engine, the most expensive part of any aircraft. Aircraft plans could also be found in *Science and Invention* and *Popular Aviation.* In addition to publishing aircraft plans, *Modern Mechanics and Inventions* also published a series of manuals between 1929 and 1933. The manuals offered homebuilders information and expert tips as well as additional aircraft plans.[12]

However, just as the homebuilt movement gained its initial momentum, federal and state regulations combined to gradually apply the brakes. The Air Commerce Act of 1926, as noted, called for the licensing of all aircraft except those flown strictly for recreation—which applied to most homebuilt aircraft. The regulations were also interpreted as excluding aircraft flown only intrastate rather then interstate, particularly if they were not being flown for hire. The federal government, though, was not the only level of government in the United States creating regulations for aircraft. States also perceived an interest in promoting and regulating aviation activity within their borders. Following the passage of the Air Commerce Act, state after state passed regulations based on the Air Commerce Act. Increasingly, these state regulations covered those aircraft, including homebuilt aircraft, not covered by federal regulations. As the 1930s progressed, it became increasingly difficult for homebuilders to legally fly the products of their efforts.[13]

Homebuilders responded to the increasingly restrictive regulatory environment by attempting to organize. As early as 1933, John B. Rathbun, the managing editor of *Popular Aviation,* issued a call for the creation of an organization of amateur builders. Although that particular effort failed, out of it grew a second attempt by Leslie Long of Oregon, who hoped to create an Amateur Aircraft League. Long also wrote a number of editorials for *Popular Aviation* and other magazines arguing the homebuilders' position.

Despite these efforts, state after state passed restrictive legislation. Then, in 1938, Congress passed the Civil Aeronautics Act. This act limited the issuance of airworthiness certificates to aircraft that had passed the tests necessary to receive a type certificate. There was no provision to issue an airworthiness certificate to an uncertified or homebuilt aircraft. The new law still allowed for the construction of experimental or special purpose aircraft, but the requirements for these types of aircraft made the process of gaining a needed airworthiness certificate very difficult. By the end of the 1930s, Oregon was the only state in which homebuilders could operate. The federal government, state governments, and many in the light plane industry argued that such regulations were needed to improve aviation safety. Homebuilders, naturally, viewed such regulations as unnecessarily restrictive. As a result, Leslie Long announced in 1941 that the combination of federal and state regulations, as well as restrictions on private flying initiated with the coming of war, had killed the movement. Yet, the homebuilder movement, initially led by a group of homebuilders from Oregon, would witness a resurrection after World War II.[14]

The New Deal and General Aviation

Given the results of Eugene Vidal's affordable aircraft program and the increasing federal regulation of general aviation aircraft (both manufactured and homebuilt) and of pilots, many in general aviation were ambivalent, if not hostile, to the New Deal's aviation policies. Those policies, however, were not limited to Vidal's efforts and the creation of regulations. As noted earlier, in addition to his aircraft program, Vidal also worked with the CWA to construct or improve small airports. Furthermore, the Works Progress Administration (WPA), established in 1936, had a number of aviation programs, including funding for airport improvements as well as an extensive air-marking program. Finally, the Civilian Pilot Training Program, established in 1939, provided subsidized flight training. As initially envisioned, the program was aimed at creating a large pool of pilots, both male and female, and, hence, a large potential market for private aircraft. These programs also encountered both ambivalent responses and mixed records of success.

The WPA, created as a "permanent" program to provide work for the unemployed, sponsored a wide range of projects from road and bridge construction to theater and arts programs. It also provided grants for airport construction and/or improvement and for an air-marking program. Both programs were conducted with the cooperation of the Bureau of Air Commerce and its successor organization, the Civil Aeronautics Administration (CAA). The WPA provided funding for labor, but little or none for materiel or equipment.

The WPA airport program picked up where the earlier CWA–Federal Emergency Relief Administration (FERA) program left off. (Both the CWA and the FERA were temporary programs intended to exist for a limited amount of time.) Only publicly owned airports were eligible for the program. The result was that the majority of airports receiving aid were in major metropolitan areas. These airports, while available to general aviation, focused on serving commercial airlines. However, a number of local governments saw the advantage of creating airfields for private and sport pilots in order to encourage tourism. The WPA paid for workers to help with the construction of a number of airports and seaplane bases in such areas as New England, northern Michigan, and Florida.[15]

One of the most extensive of the WPA aviation programs was the air-marking campaign. Although the instruments necessary for "blind" or instrument flying had been developed by the late 1920s, the new and expensive equipment was primarily limited to commercial airlines. General aviation pilots, especially private pilots, still operated under visual flight rules. In other words, they depended on visual cues for keeping their aircraft straight and level and to a great extent navigated by way of visual landmarks. To aid pilots, including the early airmail pilots who flew across the country before the introduction of flight and navigational instruments, small municipalities painted the roofs of buildings or water towers with town names and directions to the airport. During the mid-1930s, the WPA embarked on a program to completely air mark the nation.

The air-marking program not only provided visual navigational cues to pilots, it also provided a source of employment for women pilots. Phoebe Omlie, a barnstormer and, along with her husband, a fixed-base operator in Memphis, directed the National Air Marking Program. Omlie campaigned for Roosevelt in 1932 and his campaign managers, who worked in several ways to identify FDR with aviation technology, hired her to fly throughout the country. She flew over twenty thousand miles during the campaign and made numerous speeches. Roosevelt originally rewarded her with an appointment to the NACA as special adviser for air intelligence. When Omlie proposed the air-marking program and the WPA created it, she became its director. To help her, she hired five flying administrators, all women: Nancy Harkness Love, Helen McCloskey, Blanche Noyes, Helen Richey, and Louise Thaden. The program proved successful in that an extensive system of air markings appeared throughout the United States. However, many of the markers were removed during World War II because Civil Defense officials feared they might undermine security. After the war, a more widespread use of radio navigation aids by general aviation pilots made the markings obsolete.[16]

Many people concerned with promoting general aviation believed that two major obstacles stood in the way of the more widespread use of airplanes for private and recreational use. The first was the fact that airplanes were expensive. Vidal's aircraft program aimed at addressing that concern. The second was the fact that flight training was also expensive. A program created by the Civil Aeronautics Authority (after 1940, the Civil Aeronautics Administration) addressed that obstacle. In 1939, the CAA created the Civilian Pilot Training Program to provide subsidized flight training to young Americans regardless of race or gender.

The CPTP was essentially the brainchild of Robert. H. Hinckley, an official with the CAA. He believed that a program of subsidized flight training would accomplish several ends. First, it would create a large pool of pilots, all of whom would be potential customers for the products of the light aircraft industry. Second, it would "air condition" America's youth, preparing them for the coming "air age." Finally, it would provide initial training to a number of young men who could then be more quickly trained to serve as military aviators. The CPTP enjoyed only limited success in all three areas.[17]

Initially, the primary thrust behind the CPTP was the desire to bring a measure of recovery to the light aircraft industry. Earlier efforts by Eugene Vidal centered on the design and manufacture of a safe and affordable aircraft had failed, so the CPTP's backers hoped to succeed by focusing on the demand side of the equation. They reasoned that a dramatic increase in the number of licensed private pilots in the United States would increase the demand for small private planes. The CPTP contracted with colleges, universities, and local airport operators to provide flight training. From July 1, 1939, through June 30, 1942, when the program shifted its focus exclusively to training pilots for the military, the CPTP trained 125,762 pilots. While the number of private pilots in the United States had been growing in the latter half of the 1930s, the CPTP significantly accelerated that growth.[18]

The CPTP contained a nondiscrimination clause that made the program accessible to all citizens, and as a result, a number of women and African Americans participated in it. However, program officials had not originally considered including either group in the program and, consequently, never fully embraced the idea of training either of them. The CAA established a small segregated program to train African-American pilots, while the enrollment of women initially was even more limited. At first, only women enrolled at four participating women's colleges could receive training. When the program was opened up for women at other colleges and universities, only one woman enrolled for every ten men accepted. As the CPTP transformed from a program aimed at training civilian pilots to one focused on training future military pilots, everyone accepted into the program had to agree to enlist and undergo more advanced military pilot training. Shortly after the start of World War II, military aviation was opened to African Americans—but not to women. The enlistment requirement thus excluded them from the program. During the short time women were allowed in the program, however, the number of women pilots in the country increased from 675 to nearly three thousand.[19]

A second goal of the CPTP was the "air conditioning" of American youth. This clearly reflected the continued influence of the winged gospel, which included a vision of the future in which aviation would play a significant role in the everyday lives of Americans. Those who believed in that future also believed that America's youth needed to be trained in a way that would allow them to fully participate in that future. The CPTP program included the creation of textbooks in mathematics, science, literature, and the social sciences built around aviation themes for students in both elementary and secondary schools. It also sponsored a number of teacher training institutes. Although the CPTP air education program ended with the CPTP's demise in 1946, other efforts to develop an air age curriculum continued into the 1950s and, to a certain extent, are still visible today. However, it was clear that enthusiasm for such a program peaked during World War II and faded afterward.[20]

The program's third goal, training young men for military aviation service, became its major focus with the coming of World War II. Within a week of the Japanese attack on Pearl Harbor, an executive order transformed the CPTP from a civilian pilot training program into one providing initial training for future military pilots. In December, 1942, the program officially became known as the War Training Service (WTS). However, the military, especially the Army Air Forces (AAF), never embraced it. The AAF wanted full control over pilot training, and argued that the CPTP-WTS produced inferior pilots and allowed money to be wasted on training individuals who did not meet military standards. The navy was less hostile to the program, but it was clear that neither service viewed the CPTP-WTS as a particularly helpful program.

In fact, the CPTP-WTS never garnered the support of any of its potential constituencies. Although the general public initially favored the program, the light plane industry's response was cautious. After the failure of Vidal's efforts, the industry was unsure whether the new program would work. Many in the industry believed that the best way to stimulate private flying would be to reduce the regulations stemming from the Air Commerce Act of 1926 and, more importantly, the Civil Aeronautics Act of 1938. They believed that the new regulations favored commercial aviation to the detriment of private flying. Without the support of either the light aircraft industry or the military, the CPTP-WTS ended in 1946.[21]

Airport Managers and Fixed-Base Operators

The widespread creation of airports beginning in the late 1920s provided both opportunities and challenges for fixed-base operators. Some of the earliest of these, such as the Stinsons, owned and operated their own airports, where they conducted flight training and handled maintenance and fuel sales. Although many fixed-base operators continued to own and operate their own airports, other options appeared in the late 1920s. Following the passage of the Air Mail Act and Lindbergh's flight, local interests all over the country initiated campaigns to build airports. At first, many of these "municipal" airports were owned and operated by private interests. Others were owned and operated by cities. Regardless of ownership, however, all of them required management and on-field enterprises to generate income.

Airports, though often little more than fields of grass to begin with, never were cheap to build or maintain. During the 1920s and 1930s they became increasingly complex and, hence, expensive. Both public and private owners of these facilities needed to find ways to generate income to help with maintenance and upgrade costs. Charging landing fees was problematic. The nation's largest and busiest airports could afford to impose such fees, but many airport owners viewed themselves as part of a great competition to attract the nation's emerging airlines and their business. They feared that requiring landing fees would scare potential service providers away. Thus, much of the pressure to generate airport income fell on the fixed-base operators, many of whom also managed the airports at which they were located.[22]

A group of businessmen from the Dayton, Ohio, area joined together in 1928 to provide their city—the home of the Wright brothers—with an airport. During the mid-1920s a small private field south of the city had served as the city's "official" airport. By 1927, airmail carriers were using the facilities at nearby Wright Field. Members of the local business community decided that their city needed its own airport and they could no longer wait for it to take action. They therefore formed a corporation, raised money, purchased land near Vandalia (a small town about twelve miles north of Dayton), and built an airport, which was dedicated in late 1928. The corporation owned this "municipal" airport, and a local fixed-base operator, the Johnson Flying Service, managed it.[23]

E. A. Johnson, who became a leader in the emerging profession of airport management, had operated a flying school at another small field just outside of Dayton, and the local airport corporation contracted with his company to operate the new airport. Johnson relocated his flying service to the Vandalia field and began what would be a losing battle to make it profitable.

Johnson attended a conference for airport managers held in Buffalo, New York, in 1930. There he joined with others faced with the task of managing the nation's growing municipal airports. A major topic of conversation at the conference was how to make airports pay for themselves. In the 1920s and well into the 1930s airport managers proposed a whole range of activities to generate income. These included operating restaurants, swimming pools, and tennis courts on airport grounds, as well as renting aircraft parking space and selling fuel. Among the many moneymaking activities tried, pay toilets proved to be a good source of profits. With the crowds drawn to airports to watch airplanes, this proved to be a welcome service that generated much needed income. In Los Angeles, the managers of the private Grand Central Terminal Airport also devised a number of activities to generate income. They offered weekend "joy rides" and air shows, operated a restaurant and bar, and drew crowds by publicizing Hollywood stars' travel schedules.[24]

Although their efforts to earn profits for local airports generally fell short, the managers and fixed-base operators provided essential services for all segments of the aviation industry. In addition to providing fuel services, hangar space, and maintenance facilities, many fixed-base operators focused on flight training. As such, they were key participants in the CPTP. They were also the main source of rental aircraft for pilots unable to purchase their own machines. Overall, fixed-base operators provided needed but often overlooked services at the nation's airports—large and small, public and private.

Agricultural Aviation and Business Flying

During the late-1920s and through the 1930s agricultural aviation, or more popularly crop dusting, emerged as an important general aviation activity. Experiments carried out by the Department of Agriculture, with help from the Air Corps, proved the viability and value of spreading chemicals by air. A number of companies formed in the mid-1920s to conduct crop dusting on a commercial basis. Crop-dusting operations, though initially focused in the South, gradually spread to other regions of the country, and by the late 1930s had been established as an important aviation enterprise.

The main target for the dusters throughout the late 1920s and into the 1930s remained the cotton boll weevil and perhaps the most important of the pioneering operations remained Huff-Daland and its successor, Delta Air Service (which eventually also spawned Delta Airlines). The Huff-Daland Airplane Company entered the crop-dusting business in 1923, after early experiments at the Delta Laboratory at Tallulah, Louisiana, convinced company officials of the soundness of the idea of crop dusting and of the potential market for crop-dusting airplanes. The new company, Huff-Daland Dusters, flew aircraft manufactured by its parent company. In addition to recruiting a number of pilots, Huff-Daland Dusters also hired C. E. Woolman away from the Delta Laboratory. Woolman, an entomologist, served as the company's vice president and field manager. In 1929, when the parent company ran into severe financial problems, Woolman and a number of southern businessmen bought the dusting service and changed its name to Delta Air Service. Delta continued to be an important innovator in the crop-dusting industry, developing equipment and many of the practices that later became standard.

Crop dusting remained largely a southern business through World War II. One of the prime reasons was the lack of widely effective chemicals. The chemicals that were available were nonselective, killing both pests and beneficial insects, and there simply were no effective chemicals for many other pests. Nonetheless, dusting operations spread to the West, the Midwest, and the East Coast during the 1930s, although many of the companies involved remained small, almost experimental. The dusters did, however, discover other services they could provide. One of the most important was seeding and fertilizing rice fields from the air. They also successfully demonstrated the usefulness of the aerial application of chemicals to forested areas.

The aircraft used by the dusters were varied. Huff-Daland Dusters and its successor, Delta Air Service, flew Huff-Daland aircraft. Many other general aviation aircraft were modified for dusting. They included high-end, high-powered models such as the Stearman C3B, the WACO ASO, the Alexander Eaglerock, and the Travel Air 4000. While these larger, more powerful aircraft were preferred, other small aircraft such as the DeHavilland Moth and the Piper J-3 Cub also saw duty as agricultural aircraft. The first aircraft designed specifically for agricultural work did not appear until after World War II.[25]

While the emergence of crop dusting was important to the development of the general aviation sector (both as a business activity and as a market for aircraft), perhaps more important was the fact that corporate America had discovered aviation's benefits by the late 1920s. Many American businesses had offices, manufacturing plants, material sources, and customers located throughout the country and around the world. Although business executives and sales representatives served as an important customer base for the young airlines, "time is money" in the modern world and businesses recognized the value of being able to fly on their own schedule, rather than those of the airlines. The result was that many companies began to purchase corporate aircraft and/or make use of air taxi and charter services.

A number of aircraft manufacturers responded to the new market with planes designed for speed and comfort. The initial aircraft produced ranged from two-place biplanes with top speeds of eighty miles per hour and costing $2,000 to $2,500 to five- and six-place enclosed-cabin monoplanes with top speeds of a hundred miles per hour and ranges of five hundred to seven hundred miles with a price tag of nearly $12,000. The largest companies used customized versions of early airliners such as the Ford Tri-Motor.

Business or corporate aviation continued to grow slowly during the 1930s despite the depression, and new aircraft appeared to satisfy that

market. Clyde Cessna, who closed his aircraft company in 1931 and concentrated on building a few customized racing planes, reestablished his
company in 1934 at the urging of his nephews Dwight and Dwayne
Wallace, who soon took the lead in the newly reopened company. Under
their direction, Cessna produced and marketed its first model of the
Airmaster in 1935. The Airmaster (which went through several changes
as it moved from model C-34 to C-37 to C-38) was one of a generation
of smaller (four-place) business aircraft that helped make business flying truly economical (not to mention the fact that the Airmaster's sales
helped keep Cessna solvent). Airmasters had a cruising speed of about
150 miles per hour and a range of five hundred to seven hundred miles
(depending on the model). New Airmasters sold for just under $5,000
in the mid-1930s, but by the end of the decade the cost ranged from
$7,875 for the basic model to $11,035 for the seaplane version.[26]

Cessna's former business partner, Walter Beech, also produced aircraft for the business market. His first entry was the Beechcraft Model 17
Staggerwing, which was used not only as a business aircraft but for racing as well. Introduced in 1932, the five-place biplane had a top speed of
two hundred miles per hour and a range of close to a thousand miles. In
1935, Beech began design work on a twin-engine aircraft he hoped to sell
to companies as a high-end executive transport or to airlines for their
feeder lines. Construction of the Model 18, which appeared in 1937, involved some of the most advanced manufacturing techniques of the time.
The aircraft carried a pilot, copilot, and six passengers; cruised at 190
miles per hour; and had a range of one thousand miles. Despite its hefty
price tag—$33,000 a copy—the aircraft nonetheless found customers
all over the world, including the U.S. military. The Twin Beech stayed in
production until 1969.[27]

Sport Aviation: The Golden Age of Air Racing

Air racers began to steal some of the spotlight from the barnstormers
during the 1920s. International air races, particularly the Schneider Cup
competitions, captured the imagination of audiences in both America
and Europe. Beginning in the early 1920s, Americans could thrill to the
competition in their own National Air Races, sponsored by Joseph
Pulitzer's newspaper empire and the Aero Club of America. Military
planes and pilots dominated the early contests. With the end of the

Pulitzer races in 1925 and the withdrawal of military involvement, interest in air races temporarily waned. In the late 1920s, however, Los Angeles area automobile dealer Clifford Henderson revitalized the competition. From then until the late 1930s, the National Air Races ranked as the
nation's premiere aviation event and provided an opportunity and a
showcase for civilian pilots and their often specially designed racing aircraft.

Henderson drew large crowds and attention to the National Air Races
in 1928, when Los Angeles hosted the event. The following year, race
officials asked him to manage the races to be held in Cleveland. Henderson turned the Cleveland National Air Races into a nonstop aerial
spectacular featuring thirty-five different air competitions, of which the
Women's Air Derby proved to be one of the most popular. Although
military pilots and planes participated, civilian pilots and their racing
planes outclassed them. Doug Davis, flying Walter Beech's specially designed, high powered Mystery Ship, took first place. Roscoe Turner finished third in a Lockheed Vega, a six-passenger plane designed to carry
people and airmail.

Following the success of the Cleveland National Air Races, Henderson
convinced local manufacturer Charles Thompson to sponsor a closed-
circuit speed race. Then in 1931, Vincent Bendix offered to sponsor a
long-distance race. Although many of the men behind the racers were
more or less established aircraft manufacturers, a number of the successful designers are best described, like many of the homebuilders, as
inspired amateurs.

Walter Beech's Mystery Ship, which won the 1929 race against military aircraft, finished second in the inaugural Thompson Trophy race
the following year, but Beech was back on top in 1936. Beech's new aircraft company, Beechcraft, produced one of the most popular business
aircraft of the 1930s, the sleek Staggerwing biplane. When Beech offered
his former salesperson Louise Thaden the opportunity to compete in
the Bendix Trophy race in a stock version of the Staggerwing, Thaden
flew the aircraft to victory. Another woman pilot, Laura Ingalls, finished
second in a Lockheed Orion.[28]

In addition to Walter Beech, another aircraft designer with Wichita
connections involved in air racing was Emil "Matty" Laird. Challenged
by Beech's Mystery Ship, Laird offered his own "Solution" in 1930. Seven
aircraft competed against Laird's creation for the first Thompson Trophy. Piloted by Charles "Speed" Holman, the Solution took first place

with an average speed of 201.9 miles per hour. A Mystery Ship piloted by Jimmy Haizlip finished second. In 1931, legendary pilot Jimmy Doolittle won the Bendix Trophy in an improved Laird Super Solution. Roscoe Turner, perhaps the most successful air racer of the golden age, turned to Matty Laird in 1937 and asked him to help refine the design of his racer. The Turner-Laird Special was favored to win the 1937 Thompson race, but Turner missed a pylon, had to circle it again, and ended up finishing third. In 1938 and 1939, however, Turner and his Turner-Laird Special won the Thompson Trophy.[29]

An inspired amateur, Benny Howard, finished third in the 1930 Thompson Trophy race. Howard began his aviation career as a rigger on reconditioned Curtiss Jennies in 1923. After learning to fly, he became one of the nation's first multirated pilots. In the late 1920s he decided to become involved with air racing. Howard's first aircraft was a tiny monoplane powered by a ninety-horsepower Gypsy engine. Although the other entries had more power, the streamlined design of Howard's "Pete" allowed the small aircraft to slip past most of its competition and finish third in 1930 with an average speed of 162.8 miles per hour. It truly lived up to its designation DGA-3: "Damn Good Airplane-3." Five year's later, Howard-designed aircraft dominated the National Air Races. His high-wing, enclosed-cabin monoplane "Mister Mulligan" won both the Thompson and Bendix Trophies, and his smaller racer, "Mike," won all three of the limited class races it entered.[30]

Other inspired amateurs included Zantford D. "Granny" Granville and his brothers. They produced the infamous series of Gee Bee aircraft. Built for speed, the Granville racers were both fast and unstable. The aircraft gained the nickname "Flying Silos." They had big, round radial engines; short, round fuselages; almost nonexistent vertical stabilizers; and thin wings. All seven aircraft built by the Granville brothers crashed, and the pilots of the 1931 and 1933 National Air Races entries died. Granny Granville died in the crash of one of his airplanes in 1934.[31]

The last, and the most successful of the inspired amateurs, was the team of Jimmy Wedell and Harry Williams. Wedell barnstormed during the 1920s before joining forces with the wealthy Williams to establish the Wedell-Williams Air Service, which operated an airline between New Orleans and Houston. Williams provided the money and Wedell provided the intuitive engineering skill when the pair decided to compete in air races. The racers they produced were the most successful of the

1930s and were flown by some of the most successful air racing pilots, including Roscoe Turner. Flying his own aircraft, the Wedell-Williams 44, Jimmy Wedell won the 1933 Thompson Trophy. The following year, Doug Davis won the Bendix Trophy in the same aircraft. Flying the Wedell-Williams 57, Turner won the 1933 Bendix and the 1934 Thompson Trophies. The Wedell-Williams era came to a close in 1936 following the deaths of Jimmy Wedell, his brother, and Harry Williams in flying accidents.

By the time Roscoe Turner won his third Thompson Trophy in 1939, public interest in the National Air Races was in decline. Between 1925 and 1939, the winning speeds advanced only thirty-four miles per hour, from 249 to 283. More than a third of the pilots winning the Thompson and Bendix races died in air crashes. Furthermore, almost all of the aircraft entered were single-copy, special-purpose craft designed specifically for the races. Only Howard's Mister Mulligan was produced for commercial use. As war began to spread across Europe and the depression came to an end, the American public turned its attention elsewhere.[32]

AOPA: The Aircraft Owners and Pilots Association

In the late 1930s, a group of Philadelphia area pilots came to the conclusion that private pilots needed to form an organization in order to protect their interests. Other private pilots' organizations existed, but the Philadelphia aviators believed they needed a more professional organization to lobby on their behalf. They believed that in the absence of such an organization, the airlines' interests would prevail when it came to aviation regulations and legislation—much to the detriment of private pilots.

The five men behind the creation of the new private pilots' organization were all members of the Philadelphia Aviation Country Club. They were John Story Smith, Alfred L. Wolf, Philip and Laurence Sharples, C. Townsend Ludington, and Joseph B. Hartranft Jr. They began meeting in 1938 and resolved to found an organization to lobby for the interests of private pilots and improve what they perceived to be private pilots' poor image in the eyes of the general public.

They signed an agreement with the Ziff-Davis Publishing Company in 1939 calling for the publisher to provide the soon-to-be-established organization with funds ($500 to start and then $1,000 monthly) to help build a membership base. It also provided space for the organization to publish information in *Popular Aviation*. In return, *Popular Aviation* would serve as the new group's official publication. The bargain also stipulated that the new organization had to acquire seventy prominent corporate or private sponsors. (The publishing company wanted the sponsors to have names with advertising value.) Finally, the new organization had one year in which to build its membership to twenty-five hundred. The five founding members held their first formal organizational meeting in April and adopted the name Aircraft Owners and Pilots Association (AOPA).[33]

Founding member Joseph Hartranft, serving as the first executive secretary, worked out of an office in a Chicago building owned by another founding member, C. Townsend Luddington. The "AOPA News," written initially by Gill Robb Wilson (see Chapter 3), appeared in the September issue of *Popular Aviation*. The four-column feature soon grew to a nine-page "AOPA Section," and the AOPA began vigorously lobbying for the interests of private pilots. It not only represented the interests of its membership in the halls of Congress, it also engaged in talks with the NACA and with aircraft manufacturers. By April, 1940, the AOPA's ranks had swelled to four thousand pilots, far exceeding its initial membership goal.[34]

Women and General Aviation

While women continued to engage in exhibition flying after 1926, they also carved out expanded roles in general aviation as air racers, record setters, and aircraft sales representatives. Just as they had before World War I, the top women fliers during the "golden age of aviation" gained as much fame as their male counterparts. Furthermore, they repeatedly proved themselves to be just as skilled by winning a number of prestigious air races. However, society's general attitude toward women—the roles they could play and the jobs they could hold—continued to restrict their involvement in aviation to the general aviation sector.

Air racing and record setting, as already noted, had captured the American public's imagination by the late 1920s, and women were full, if sometimes segregated, participants. Before 1929, most air records were absolute records, meaning that no distinction was made between men and women pilots. However, the Federation Aeronautique Internationale set up a separate category for records set by women pilots that year. Although this new distinction in some ways implied that records set by women were different and perhaps inferior to those set by men, it nonetheless created an immediate opportunity for women to gain attention as they vied to set endurance, altitude, distance, and speed records.

Women also participated in the air races of the 1920s and 1930s. In 1929, the National Air Races promoters held a separate Women's Air Derby. Designed to take place over a period of eight days, the race involved a flight from Santa Monica, California, to Cleveland, Ohio, home of the National Air Races. One leg was flown each day. The time between each point was recorded, and the pilot with the lowest total elapsed time was declared the winner. This event marked the beginning of women being seen as serious air racers.[35]

Many of the 1930s' air races, especially those involving distance flights, eventually included both men and women contestants. Women were particularly successful in the Bendix Trophy Race, an unlimited transcontinental air race. In 1936, the second year women were allowed to compete, the Bendix Trophy went to Louise Thaden and Blanche Noyes. Another woman, Laura Ingalls, came in second. Two years later, Jackie Cochran took the trophy, then went on to set an absolute world speed record in 1940.[36]

Air race victories and successful record-setting attempts brought women pilots fame and, to a few at least, some fortune. No matter how glamorous it may have seemed, even the best women pilots found it difficult to earn a living from these activities. A number of women, including some of those who had managed to gain fame as air racers and record setters, earned their living in aviation as aircraft company representatives—a role that in many ways reflected the contemporary prejudices concerning women pilots. The dangers associated with barnstorming and the early airmail flying had created something of a negative view of aviation in the minds of the American people. To many, flying was simply too risky. General aviation aircraft manufacturers, hoping to calm the public's fears, hired women to act as sales representatives. These women pilots demonstrated their employers' aircraft to potential buyers. The reasoning was that if a woman could fly an airplane, it really could not be that difficult or dangerous. Many women recognized the role they were being asked to play, but they accepted it as part of the price they paid for participating in aviation and promoting it to the American public.[37]

One of the earliest female sales representatives was Louise Thaden. Thaden was born in Bentonville, Arkansas, in 1906. Her father, who apparently wanted sons rather than the two daughters he had, encouraged her to develop her athletic and mechanical talents. She attended college for a time, but did not graduate. While on a break from college, she was hired as a sales representative for a coal company in Wichita, Kansas. Once there, she began to frequent the factory and flying field operated by the Travel Air Company. The firm's president, Walter Beech, realizing the potential value of a female sales representative, hired her and taught her how to fly. Thaden then began to set records while flying a Travel Air plane. Her victory in the 1929 Women's Air Derby brought fame to herself and her company. Thaden married in the early 1930s and for the rest of the decade alternated between concentrating on her family and participating in aviation events. She set a new endurance record in 1932, and won the Bendix Trophy in 1936. She also worked as a sales representative for Beechcraft, a corporate successor to Travel Air, and for the WPA's air-marking program. She withdrew from aviation in the late 1930s to focus on her family.[38]

Like Katherine Stinson, whose effort to break the gender barrier in the Post Office's airmail service had failed, Helen Richey, despite the more sustained nature of her efforts, also failed to break the barrier in commercial aviation. Richey was a successful air racer and record setter during the early 1930s, and in 1934 her fame and ability as a pilot brought her to the attention of Central Airlines. The company, which had just been awarded the Washington-to-Detroit airmail route, hoped to ensure the success of its new venture by hiring Richey as a copilot that year. It was obvious from the start, however, that Central Airlines was more interested in using Richey for publicity purposes than as a copilot, as she made only a dozen flights in the ten months she worked for the airline. In addition, her fellow pilots were very hostile toward her. This not only reflected the prejudices many held about women pilots, but also the circumstances of the 1930s. Many women worked during the depression, but primarily at jobs not traditionally held by men. Piloting a commercial airliner, although a new job, was already seen as a male occupation. Richey thus was viewed as preventing a male pilot from working. That was unacceptable. Furthermore, for some reason never articulated, the Bureau of Air Commerce strongly suggested that Central Airlines restrict Richey to daytime flights in clear weather. The disgruntled Richey resigned in October, 1935, proof once again that women had been relegated to general aviation.[39]

African Americans and General Aviation

Although they did not participate in air racing or record setting for the most part, African Americans played an increasing, albeit segregated, role in general aviation during the 1930s. Racism barred blacks from commercial aviation entirely, and from military aviation until World War II. Nonetheless, a number of pioneer African-American pilots saw aviation as a possible path toward greater equality in American society. By organizing their own air shows and conducting well-publicized long-distance flights, pioneer African-American aviators worked hard to promote aviation among blacks.

As the nation thrilled to Charles Lindbergh's historic flight, African Americans seeking to participate in aviation continued to find the door largely barred. Immediately following World War I, Bessie Coleman had been forced to travel to France to receive flight training. In the late 1920s, a few African-American aviators managed to find a small number of flight schools and individual instructors willing to train them. As late as 1932, however, there were fewer than twenty licensed African-American pilots—although there may well have been others who flew without a license. This handful of dedicated aviation enthusiasts spent much of the 1930s trying to bring the thrill and potential of flight to their fellow African Americans.[40]

One of the most prominent of those promoters was William J. Powell, a college-trained engineer who had served in World War I. Inspired by Lindbergh's trans-Atlantic solo flight, Powell set out to learn to fly. It took him a long time to find anyone willing to train him, but the Warren College of Aeronautics in Los Angeles finally accepted him as a student. He earned his license in 1930, and the following year organized the Bessie Coleman Aero Club, which sponsored an air show that drew fifteen thousand spectators. The organization then fulfilled Coleman's dream by establishing the Bessie Coleman School for training African-American aviators.

Powell was a true believer in aviation. He also believed that African Americans could improve their position in American society and the economy by becoming pilots, engineers, and mechanics, as well as participating in other flying-related professions. In 1934 he published his autobiography, *Black Wings*. In it, he predicted that wealthy whites would soon abandon their automobiles for airplanes. Just as African Americans had been serving as chauffeurs for whites in their automobiles,

Powell believed they could get a start in aviation by serving as chauffeurs in the skies. Powell clearly did not yet see aviation as creating new, more equal roles for African Americans. However, by 1938 he had a different vision of the future. He called for the creation of African-American aircraft manufacturing and transportation companies. Like Marcus Garvey, who in the 1920s promoted the creation of separate economic enterprises, Powell believed that black-owned and black-controlled companies would provide tremendous opportunities to African Americans. Once they had proven their abilities by successfully operating these companies, white Americans would come to have greater respect for blacks. Thus, participation in aviation held the promise of a future with greater interracial harmony.

Thanks to Powell's efforts, Los Angeles emerged as an important center of African-American aviation. Another important center was Chicago, where a number of African-American aviation enthusiasts inspired by the legacy of Bessie Coleman formed the Challenger Air Pilots' Association. Finding themselves barred from airports in the Chicago area, the group built a black-owned and -operated airport in the Chicago suburb of Robbins in 1933. After a storm destroyed the Robbins Airport's hangar, the group moved its operations to what was known as the Harlem Airport, also in the Chicago suburbs. Harlem Airport housed the Coffey School of Aeronautics, founded to provide flight training to African Americans. The Challenger Air Pilot's Association also sponsored air shows. Through the efforts of the organizations in Los Angeles and Chicago, as well as scattered organizations in other parts of the country, the number of African-American aviators, both male and female, began to rise during the 1930s.[41]

In addition to founding clubs and schools, a number of other pioneer African Americans also sought to promote aviation by participating in well-publicized (at least in the black press) long-distance flights. In 1932, James Herman Banning and his mechanic, Thomas C. Allen, made the first transcontinental flight by African Americans. The following year, C. Alfred "Chief" Anderson and Dr. Albert E. Forsythe flew their plane from Atlantic City, New Jersey, to Los Angeles and back again, thus making the first transcontinental round-trip flight by African Americans. The duo planned an even more ambitious journey in 1934. Dubbed the Pan-American Goodwill Flight, they planned to fly from the United States to the Caribbean in an airplane they named the "Spirit of Booker T. Washington." As initially envisioned, the flight would have covered more than twelve thousand miles. The trip began with a flight from Miami to Nassau in the Bahamas—the first such flight by any land plane. Although they successfully completed the first few legs of the flight, mechanical problems and a mishap on takeoff in Trinidad brought the effort to a premature end. Anderson and Forsythe had hoped that their flight would help dispel many of the negative stereotypes held by white Americans. While it did receive a great deal of attention, it probably did little to change attitudes. However, it is telling that these two pilots believed that a demonstration of their aviation skills would improve the image white Americans had of members of their race.[42]

In 1939, the National Airmen's Association (founded to promote African-American aviation) and the *Chicago Defender* sponsored a flight from Chicago to Washington, D.C. The purpose of the flight, piloted by Dale L. White and Chauncey E. Spencer, specifically was to convince the U.S. government to open up greater opportunities for African Americans in aviation. In terms of achieving its goal, this was perhaps the most successful of the distance flights of the 1930s. The publicity surrounding the journey helped pressure Congress to open up the new Civilian Pilot Training Program to African Americans.[43]

As noted, although the CPTP was created to offer affordable flight training to Americans, it initially failed to include women and African Americans. When the African-American pilots' efforts prompted Congress to include a provision forbidding discrimination in the program on the basis of race, creed, or color, the CAA did not challenge the action. Reflecting the attitude of American society as a whole in the late 1930s, the CAA created a small, racially segregated program for African-American flight training within the CPTP. The CAA initially funded training programs at six historically black colleges: the West Virginia State College for Negroes, Howard University, Tuskegee Institute, Hampton Institute, the Delaware State College for Colored Students, and the North Carolina Agricultural and Technical College. The program was later extended to a number of other schools. By the time it ended in 1946, the number of African-American pilots had increased to approximately two thousand. Participation in the CPTP not only increased the number of black pilots, it also opened the door for black men to enter the military as pilots as the CPTP helped create a core of trained pilots and instructors for the military pilot training program established at Tuskegee in 1942. In many ways, African-American males gained far more from the CPTP than did women of any race. While as late as 1945 a woman's place in aviation remained in general aviation, African-American males had carved out a permanent role for themselves in military aviation. Both, however, were still excluded from the airlines and commercial aviation.[44]

Planes and Power Plants

A number of important developments transformed the appearance of general aviation aircraft, particularly light aircraft, between 1926 and 1939. The most significant was the introduction of more reliable and, eventually, affordable engines. Nonetheless, engines remained high-cost items into the early 1930s. Their power and greater reliability helped create a group of important sport and utility aircraft. Gradually, engine manufacturers began to turn out smaller, more affordable and reliable engines. A near revolution in the light plane market finally came with the appearance of the Continental A-40 engine.

The period also witnessed important changes in aircraft design and manufacturing techniques. In the second half of the 1920s, aircraft manufacturers began their movement away from the open-cockpit biplane to the enclosed-cabin monoplane. Although enclosed-cabin monoplanes had been built earlier, most notably the Bellanca CF, the war-surplus aircraft that dominated the entire aircraft market in the early twenties were all open-cockpit biplanes. More efficient airfoils and an emphasis on pilot and passenger comfort helped spur a shift in aircraft design.

Manufacturing techniques also changed. With the Air Commerce Act's safety regulations basically outlawing the old stick-and-wire construction used on war-era trainers such as the Standard and the Jenny, the shift toward steel-tube fuselages was completed. Although the use of metal in aircraft construction was greatly increasing, most general aviation aircraft remained covered with fabric, and wing structures (spars and ribs) continued to be made of wood. However, the entrance of the Lockheed Vega into the market in 1927 meant commercially viable semimonocoque construction had entered the field as well. By the end of the decade, the first "all-metal" general aviation aircraft appeared.

The Power Plant Revolution

The first important new aircraft engine introduced was the Wright Whirlwind in 1926. The evolution of the Wright Whirlwind dated back to 1921.

Charles Lawrance, owner of a small engine company, built a nine-cylinder, 180-horsepower radial engine. The J-1 was a good engine, but Lawrance lacked the capital necessary to further improve the engine and bring it into large-scale manufacture. The navy, looking for a powerful, lightweight engine for its carrier-borne aircraft, played a pivotal role in supporting further development of Lawrance's engine. Backed by strong encouragement from the navy, Lawrance's company merged with Frederic Rentschler's newly organized Wright Aeronautical.

Wright Aeronautical had the engineering talent, including that of Samuel D. Heron, to produce a new and better engine. That engine, the J-5—a nine-cylinder, 220-horsepower engine—appeared in 1926 and soon demonstrated its high degree of reliability. Charles Lindbergh's "Spirit of St. Louis" was designed specifically around the J-5. Though modified somewhat to allow for longer-term continuous operation, the J-5's basic reliability made his epic flight across the Atlantic possible.

The Wright Whirlwind's success soon invited competition. Frederic Rentschler, after leaving Wright Aeronautical, soon formed a new air-craft engine company, Pratt and Whitney—which took the name of the machine-tool firm that formed the core of the new venture. Rentschler lured many of the talented designers from Wright Aeronautical to Pratt and Whitney. He also maintained his contacts with the navy. In answer to the navy's continued need for more reliable, lightweight, higher horse-power engines, Pratt and Whitney soon introduced the 450-horsepower Wasp.[45]

The military and commercial airliner manufacturers were the pri-mary market for the Wright Whirlwind and the Pratt and Whitney Wasp. However, both engines also found their way into general aviation air-craft. The Wright Whirlwind powered one of the most popular versions of the best-selling WACO Model 10. The Wasp powered the Ford Tri-Motor and the Lockheed Vega.

The WACO Model 10 was an updated and improved version of its Model 9. Improvements included the first shock-absorbing landing gear offered on a light aircraft, more wing area, more room in the cockpit, and an adjustable stabilizer. Initially powered by an OX-5, OXX-6, or Hispano Suiza, once the aircraft sported the new Wright Whirlwind, it became the most popular aircraft in America.[46]

The high cost of aircraft engines continued to act as a brake on the general aviation industry. Beyond making the cost of an aircraft high—engines alone could account for up to 50 percent of the total price—the

lack of a low-cost, reliable engine also increased the cost of flight training. In order for a fixed-base operator offering flight training or airplane rentals to make money, operating costs needed to stay low. By
the end of the 1920s, the supply of war-surplus OX-5 engines was finally
running out. Although expensive to operate, the OX-5 had been inexpensive to purchase. To answer the need for small, more affordable,
and reliable engines, several companies introduced new products in
the late 1920s and early 1930s. Though superior to their 1920s predeces-
sors, these new engines were still expensive to procure and had relatively high operating costs due to their fuel and oil consumption.
Wright, Pratt and Whitney, Warner, and Lycoming all produced smaller
radial engines, while Fairchild/Ranger and Menasco turned out air-
cooled inline engines.

Pratt and Whitney introduced its alternative to the OX-5 and Whirlwind in 1929. The Wasp Junior was a seven-cylinder, three-hundred-
horsepower engine. By 1932, refinements and upgrades raised the horsepower rating to 450. Considered the best of its class, the Wasp Junior
powered a number of general aviation aircraft—including Stearmans,
Howards, and versions of the Beech Staggerwing. Two Wasp Juniors provided the thrust for Lockheed and Beech light twin transports. They
also appeared on military trainers by the end of the 1930s. Lycoming
also produced an engine in this class, introducing its nine-cylinder, 220-
horsepower R-680 in 1929. Because Lycoming was part of the great aviation empire created by E. L. Cord, R-680s primarily found their way
onto planes produced by the aircraft-manufacturing component of this
giant conglomerate, Stinson. Lycoming R-680s were found on Stinson
Tri-Motors, Detroiters, and Reliants.

A third producer in this class was Jacobs. It introduced two engines
in 1930: a three-cylinder, fifty-five-horsepower radial, and a seven-cylinder, 150-horsepower radial. Although the smaller engine did not find a
market, the seven-cylinder radial not only found a market, it also improved its yield first to 150 horsepower, then 170 horsepower, and, finally, by 1932, 195 horsepower.

The final important producer in this class was Warner, whose seven-
cylinder Scarab engine appeared in 1928. The company introduced its
Super Scarab, generating 145 horsepower, in 1932. By 1938, a 165 horsepower version was available. The Super Scarab powered a number of
general aviation aircraft, including the popular Cessna Airmaster, and
was available as an alternative to the Ranger engine in the Fairchild 24.

While the round radial engines proved very popular, inline engines also found a market. Fairchild Aircraft introduced its 6-370, a six-cylinder engine generating 122 horsepower, in 1928. Fairchild renamed its engine division Ranger two years later, and throughout the 1930s improved versions of the Ranger engine appeared, eventually reaching two hundred horsepower. Ranger was the in-house engine source for Fairchild, and its engines were used only on Fairchild aircraft. The other important inline engines from this era were those produced by Menasco. Menasco built an inverted four-cylinder inline engine in 1929 known as the A-4 Pirate. The following year, however, the company shifted production to the B-4—another four-cylinder engine—and the B-6, a six-cylinder engine that originally generated 160 horsepower. The B-6 became a very popular engine for racing aircraft, and refinement eventually raised its output to 315 horsepower.[47]

However, in large part because of the continued expense of reliable engines, flying remained the purview of the wealthy and major corporations. Not until the end of the 1920s did a widely affordable aircraft with a reliable engine appear: the single-seat Aeronca C-2, powered by the Aeronca E-107 engine, which appeared in 1930. As noted, the C-2 ushered in the age of private aviation for many, if not for the masses.

The two-cylinder Aeronca series culminated in the E-113 series of thirty-six-horsepower engines that, when combined with the two-place Aeronca C-3 aircraft, set the initial pace at the lower end of the consumer market. Following its introduction, other firms quickly followed with low-power engines, including the Szekley and LeBlond/Ken Royce. However, these engines all had limited growth potential, long-term reliability problems, or continued higher-than-optimal costs.

The real revolution in low-cost, reliable engines for light planes came with the introduction (and, more importantly, the perfection) of the four-cylinder Continental A-40. The A-40 powered the early Taylor and Piper E/J-2 Cubs, the early Taylorcrafts, and, after 1937, even powered Aeronca's K model, which originally was equipped with the E-113C engine.

The A-40's eventual success led to something of a power-plant war. Continental's competitors, Lycoming and Franklin, quickly went to work on fifty-horsepower engines. Continental responded with its own fifty-horsepower model, the A-50. Each company then went on to build and introduce models with ever increasing horsepower. By World War II, these second generation motors, which boasted between sixty-five and eighty horsepower, provided the core engine technology that remains with us today. They also powered some of the most successful general aviation light aircraft of the late 1930s.[48]

The emergence of the small, affordable aircraft engine contributed significantly to the appearance of the most popular light aircraft of the late 1930s: the Piper J-3 Cub. The J-3 Cub could trace its lineage back to the design work of C. G. Taylor in the late 1920s. Taylor taught himself aeronautical engineering, and he and his brother, Gordon, who was responsible for sales and marketing, founded the Taylor Brothers Aircraft Corporation. Gordon died in 1928, and members of the Bradford, Pennsylvania, Chamber of Commerce invited C. G. to move his company to their city the following year. The company soon produced its first aircraft in Bradford: the two-seat "Chummy," which was powered by a ninety-horsepower engine and sold for $4,000. Unfortunately, the onset of the depression in late 1929 doomed aircraft sales, and Taylor Brothers Aircraft went bankrupt in 1931.

A local oilman and investor with a seat on the Taylor Brothers board of directors, William Piper, bought the company for $600. Among the assets he purchased was a prototype of a small plane designed to sell for $1,500. The prototype, which soon became known as the Taylor Cub, first flew in September, 1930. The problem continued to be finding a suitable, affordable power plant. In June, 1931, Piper and Taylor decided to go with the new Continental A-40, which generated thirty-seven horsepower. The new Taylor Aircraft Company bet its future on its E-2 Taylor Cub.

The E-2 sold in small numbers between 1931 and 1933. Sales finally picked up in 1934, when the company sold seventy aircraft. The original E-2 had an open cockpit, but the company added a cockpit enclosure in 1935. Also in 1935, the company added Walter Jamouneau to its design team. He introduced several changes to the Cub, and the company debuted its new model, the J-2. Although the J-2 enjoyed great sales success (210 were sold in 1935) conflicts between Taylor and Piper over design changes and other issues led to C. G. Taylor's departure in December, 1935. Taylor moved to Alliance, Ohio, where he founded Taylorcraft and continued to produce small, light aircraft.

Piper, now the sole owner of Taylor Aircraft, continued to experience sales success with the J-2. The company sold 550 aircraft in 1936, and experienced two important milestones the following year. First, the Bradford factory burned to the ground—a disaster that proved to be an opportunity because it prompted Piper to expand. He moved the company to a new facility adjacent to the Lock Haven, Pennsylvania, airport, and, despite the fire, the company sold 687 Taylor Cubs that year. The second milestone came in November, 1937, when Piper changed the company's name to Piper Aircraft Corporation.

The new Piper Aircraft Corporation introduced its latest design, the J-3 Piper Cub, in 1938. Initially powered by the Continental A-40, the company soon brought out models with higher rated (up to sixty-five horsepower) Continental, Lycoming, and Franklin engines. Not only did the more powerful engines improve the J-3's performance, the later engines also cost less than the original A-40. With the more powerful engines, the J-3 became the best-selling aircraft of any type by the end of the decade.[49]

New Paths in Light Aircraft Construction

Despite the onset of the depression in late 1929, general aviation and general aviation aircraft advanced during the 1930s. Manufacturing techniques continued to evolve at both the high and the low end of the general aviation spectrum. By the end of the decade, the first "all-metal" general aviation aircraft appeared. Two of the most important figures in the movement toward all-metal light aircraft construction were Don Luscombe and Fred Weick.

Don Luscombe had a decidedly ground-based job during World War I: he was an ambulance driver. However, he took every opportunity he could to fly as a passenger and he returned home enamored with aviation. After several years working in advertising, Luscombe purchased an OX-5–powered Jenny and learned to fly. Despite the fact he was finally airborne, Luscombe was unhappy with the flying experience in his Jenny. He began to think about what an ideal aircraft would be like. He eventually settled on a lighter, stronger, more responsive plane with a high-wing and an enclosed cabin. When he was unable to find such an aircraft available on the market, Luscombe decided to go into the airplane business and build his own.

In 1926, Luscombe and a group of Iowa investors formed the Central States Aero Company. The company then hired a local homebuilder who had taught himself to fly in his own aircraft. Clayton Flokerts, following Luscombe's suggestions, developed the prototype Monocoupe in 1927. The high-wing, two-place monoplane flew with both an Anzani sixty-horsepower engine and a Detroit Air-Cat sixty-horsepower engine. The company received Air Transport Certificate (ATC) 22 in January, 1928, and production soon began. The early Monocoupes sold for $2,285 to $2,375 and quickly found a number of buyers. This success attracted new investors. These included Willard L. Velie, a Moline, Iowa, automobile manufacturer, who bought Central States and absorbed it into the new Mono-Aircraft Company that same year.

Mono-Aircraft continued to produce aircraft after Velie's death and the onset of the depression—both in October, 1929. Air racers especially favored a number of Monocoupe models. However, the company was in receivership by the end of 1930. The following year, a St. Louis businessman bought the company and moved it to Lambert Field, that city's municipal airport. Luscombe initially stayed with the firm, but was ready to move on in 1933.

By then, Luscombe had developed an entirely new version of his ideal airplane: an all-metal aircraft that could be mass-produced. It is perhaps worth noting that an all-metal aircraft is one in which the major structural elements are made of metal. Despite the name, an all-metal craft could and did have surfaces such as wings, ailerons, and the rudder, which were fabric covered. To realize his vision, Luscombe hired a group of engineers to develop the new aircraft. His charge to them included a call for no wood, no nails, and no glue. The prototype "Phantom" they came up with flew in 1934. It was a high-wing monoplane with an enclosed cabin, powered by a Warner Super Scarab 145-horsepower engine. The wings were still fabric covered. After receiving ATC 552, Luscombe moved his new company from Kansas City to Trenton, New Jersey.

The Phantom was a good airplane, but it did not lend itself to mass production. Instead, each aircraft had to be largely handcrafted, which resulted in a hefty price tag: over $6,000. Sales, as might be expected, were steady but slow. To help the company stay afloat, Luscombe, always more a promoter than anything else, came up with the idea of sponsoring an "Apprentice Program." For $500, a student could go to work for the company, earning a salary of $15 per week for twenty-six weeks. During the half-year course, the students were taught skills associated with building an all-metal aircraft.

Luscombe still wanted an all-metal aircraft that could be produced with mass-produced, interchangeable parts. He moved closer to that goal with the Luscombe 90 or Model 4. It was a two-place aircraft powered by a ninety-horsepower Warner Junior Scarab engine. The production process still demanded a great deal of handcrafting, however, and the engine cost brought the sales price to $4,000. The Luscombe 90, like its predecessor, was still too expensive for its market.

Luscombe came closest to achieving his goals with the Luscombe 50 or Model 8. Like the Luscombe 90, it was a two-place aircraft. There were important differences, however. First, Luscombe and his engineers managed to further simplify the production process, moving closer to mass production and interchangeable parts. Second, although the prototype used the Continental A-40, the production model boasted the equally affordable A-50 engine. This allowed the Luscombe 50 to sell for the more competitive price of $1,895. Finally, even the wings were eventually covered with aluminum. The aircraft sold well until the outbreak of World War II.[50]

Fred Weick, as noted earlier, developed a spin-proof airplane in response to Eugene Vidal's safe aircraft program. In 1936, the head of the Engineering and Research Corporation (ERCO) invited Weick to join the company as chief engineer. Weick accepted the invitation. His first goal was to take the ideas developed for the W-1 and W-1A and use them to design a new airplane that could be commercially produced and sold at an attractive price for private use.

The experimental prototype for the new airplane first flew in October, 1937. It was a two-place, all-metal aircraft featuring tricycle landing gear. The wings were fabric covered. A Continental A-40 powered the prototype, but that was considered temporary as Weick was waiting for an affordable sixty- to sixty-five-horsepower engine with which to replace it. The company conducted a number of test flights, many of which centered on reconfiguring the aircraft to work with the unconventional dual-control system developed by Weick.

Following the completion of the test flights, redesign work intended to prepare the aircraft for production began. Weick, still unable to find a suitable sixty-five-horsepower engine, convinced ERCO to hire a Continental engineer to design an engine for the aircraft. In January, 1940, the company was awarded certification for the aircraft with a new sixty-five-horsepower ERCO engine. Continental came out with a sixty-five-horsepower engine of its own at about the same time. That engine proved to be far less expensive than the ERCO engine, so the company decided to go with the Continental A-65 in an effort to hold production costs down. The "Ercoupe," as it came to be called, received certification with the new engine in the spring of 1940.

The Engineering and Research Corporation moved quickly to begin production. Many of the metal workers came to ERCO via Don Luscombe's training school in New Jersey. They built the Ercoupe in both dual- and triple-control models. Depending on the control system, the airplane sold for between $2,265 and $2,290. The company built 112 planes before the war buildup siphoned off its supply of aluminum, bringing an end to production.[51]

The 1920s and 1930s were an era of celebrity pilots, both male and female. Air racing captured the nation's attention. Many aircraft designs now considered classic made their appearance during this period. Furthermore, general aviation had strong advocates in federal government, even though some questioned the value of a number of the programs they proposed and many more bridled at some of the new regulations. A number of general aviation businesses gained a firm footing. This so-called golden age came to an end with the advent of World War II. As general aviation companies struggled to make the traumatic switch from peacetime to a wartime economy, new challenges and opportunities quickly presented themselves.

A U.S. Army Piper L-4 (J3C-65) powered by a Continental A-65 engine. Photo courtesy Michael G. Williams Aviation.

CHAPTER 3

For the Duration

1939–45

As war spread through Europe and the Far East in the late 1930s, light aircraft manufacturers—along with most of American industry—anticipated participation in war preparedness and then war production. Although it was not clear as late as 1938, general aviation manufacturers and pilots would play a number of military and civilian roles involving both powered and nonpowered aircraft during World War II, and come out of that conflict with optimistic dreams of the future.

Civilian general aviation pilots and planes both found new roles and continued in old ones during the war. Although wartime restrictions grounded much of the general aviation fleet, many civilian pilots joined the Civil Air Patrol (CAP) and continued to fly throughout the war, performing a number of missions that contributed to the nation's defense and well-being. Aviation gained a larger role in fighting forest fires with the creation of the "smokejumper" program, whereas agricultural aviation was perhaps the most challenged by wartime conditions. Women attempted to break out of general aviation during the war years and, for a short period, managed to carve out a small role in military aviation. They remained civilians, however, and the government discontinued the program that employed them before the end of hostilities.

Aviation of all kinds has played an important role in the history of Alaska. Before World War II, aviation, though important, operated under very primitive conditions in what was then still a U.S. territory. During the war, however, Alaska gained many of the aviation infrastructure improvements that would foster the postwar expansion of both commercial and general aviation throughout the frozen north.

As the war neared its end and Americans looked to the future, aviation enthusiasts envisioned a future in which many of the promises of the winged gospel would be realized. They saw an aircraft in nearly every garage. That, in turn, meant greatly expanded production of light aircraft. General aviation anxiously anticipated a bright new postwar world.

General Aviation Aircraft and the Aerial Observation Post Program

It seemed at first as though general aviation manufacturers and their airplanes would play only a small role in America's war effort. Expecting to be asked to use their skilled workforce to produce war materials, especially parts and components to support the fifty-thousand-airplane program Pres. Franklin D. Roosevelt announced in 1940, manufacturers began retooling to do just that. William Piper, for example, reported that his company's largest wartime contract was for radar masts. However, many manufacturers and some in the military believed that general aviation airplanes could play a role in the coming conflict.

After President Roosevelt announced his aircraft production goal, all of the nation's aircraft manufacturers headed to Washington to meet with the military. The military representatives at that meeting made it clear that small planes did not figure into the fifty-thousand-plane figure. Military leaders—especially in the Army Air Corps—wanted faster, more powerful airplanes. They could conceive of no use for small, light aircraft in modern mechanized warfare. The general aviation manufacturers, however, had some allies within the armed forces. These allies envisioned light aircraft being used in a variety of roles, including liaison and courier missions, medical evacuation, and aerial artillery spotting. Light aircraft employed as artillery spotters played a crucial role in bolstering the army's argument that some aviation assets must remain organic to the ground forces.[1]

The idea of using light aircraft for liaison, artillery spotting, and other tasks had been circulating in the army for a number of years. Not all of the army's pilots were in the Air Corps: a number of officers and enlisted men had private pilot licenses, and they were in the ranks of those who came to believe that light aircraft could perform several important missions. Procuring aircraft, however, was the Air Corps's responsibility. Within the limited budgets available during the 1930s, the Air Corps was reluctant to purchase aircraft it did not view as suitable for airpower's primary missions. The Air Corps focused on procuring strategic bombers and tactical fighters. The service's main criteria in judging aircraft were power and speed. When elements within the army finally convinced the Air Corps to buy lighter aircraft, the models purchased were faster, heavier, and more complex than necessary for the desired missions. Army artillery officers in particular came to believe that the aircraft most suited for the mission they envisioned—aerial artillery spotting—would have the size and performance characteristics of a small personal aircraft like the Taylor/Piper Cub.

Between 1939 and 1941, a number of determined army artillery officers pushed a plan for the creation of a program to provide artillery units with organic aviation support. With the support of general aviation aircraft manufacturers, proponents proved the value of small aircraft for aerial observation in a number of field training exercises. Despite strong opposition from Air Corps/Army Air Forces leaders, the service authorized a formal test in late 1941 that led to the creation of the Air Observation Post Program in June, 1942. For the most part, the army's aerial observers flew modified versions of a number of light aircraft, the most common being a military version of the popular Piper Cub.[2]

Most of these light aircraft earned the nickname "grasshopper" because of their small size and the methods used by their pilot observers, who were trained to fly close to the ground, pop up quickly to make observations, and then duck back down to treetop level. Six different fixed-wing light aircraft, designated L-1 through L-6, were employed during the war. The L-1 Vigilant was a Vultee-Stinson two-place aircraft. One of the larger, more powerful aircraft used by the field artillery, it sported a 295-horsepower Lycoming engine. The L-2 Grasshopper was a two-place Taylorcraft equipped with a 65-horsepower engine, although one version had a 50-horsepower Franklin engine. Acronca provided the L-3 Grasshopper, a two-place, 65-horsepower plane. The most popular (both in terms of numbers purchased and of pilot preference) was the Piper L-4 Grasshopper. The army acquired 5,671 of these aircraft. Several versions were equipped with 65-horsepower engines, but others boasted more powerful 75- and even 100-horsepower Lycoming engines. Vultee-Stinson also manufactured the L-5 Sentinel. Like the L-1, it was larger and more powerful than most of its competitors: all but the G model (which had a 190-horsepower engine) came equipped with

185-horsepower Lycoming engines. The L-6 Interstate was also a two-place aircraft. The army purchased one experimental model with a 100-horsepower Franklin engine. The 250 additional aircraft acquired came with 102-horsepower Franklins. At the very end of the war, the army bought five Piper L-14s. These aircraft could carry four—the pilot, an observer, and two passengers—and came with a 130-horsepower Lycoming engine. The end of the war with Japan brought the cancellation of the primary order for 845 of these aircraft.[3]

These light aircraft, plus a small number of rotary-wing aircraft, provided the army with the ability to test and prove the value of organic aviation. While most of the army's aviation assets (personnel, planes, and infrastructure) separated from the parent service in 1947 with the creation of the U.S. Air Force, other aviation assets remained. The World War II experience with light aircraft marked the institutional origin of today's army aviation branch.

General Aviation and the Army Air Forces Glider Program

While general aviation's participation in the Aerial Observation Post Program was marked by success and a long-term legacy, its experience with the AAF's combat glider program was less favorable. Although the industry provided the AAF with both training and combat gliders, the service never embraced the glider program, never developed a clear doctrine for the use of gliders, and abandoned the program shortly after the war. One company in particular, WACO Aircraft, suffered due to its participation in the military glider program.

The AAF glider program began in early 1941 when Maj. Gen. Henry H. "Hap" Arnold called for studies concerning the use of aircraft-towed gliders for delivering troops and equipment to the battlefield. At the time, in the United States at least, the idea of airborne warfare was quite new. The army's Command and General Staff School did not address the topic until 1938, and studies conducted there focused primarily on the use of parachutists. Over the next few years, while the AAF worked to shape its fundamental doctrine, it failed to develop anything more than a training circular dealing with airborne warfare. Despite the fact that a glider development and procurement program was under way, airborne doctrine lagged behind. However, with General Arnold's support, the glider program moved forward and general aviation manufacturers responded.

Gliding was an elite sport in the United States with fewer than two hundred licensed glider pilots at the time General Arnold initiated the military's program. Those responsible for the new initiative thus had to provide not only for the development and production of gliders to be used in combat, but also had to provide training gliders. For small, two-place training gliders, the military turned not only to those few companies that had built gliders during the 1930s, but also to the nation's general aviation manufacturers. In addition to modifying their products for use by the Aerial Observation Post Program, a number of general aviation firms modified their light aircraft for glider training by removing the engine and propeller and replacing them with a weighted nose section. Piper produced what became known as the TG-8, Aeronca the TG-5, and Taylorcraft the TG-6. All of these aircraft could be reconverted to powered models simply by removing the nose section and reinstalling the engine and propeller.

The design and production of the requested combat gliders proved more complicated. Eleven companies responded to the initial call, but only one company's gliders proved successful in testing. These were the XCG-3 (later significantly modified to become the XCG-4), an eight-place glider, and the XCG-5, a fifteen-place glider, both designed by the WACO Aircraft Company of Troy, Ohio. In the late 1920s, WACO ranked first in the nation in aircraft production. The company's "Taperwing" model proved extremely popular with sport pilots, stunt pilots, and air racers, and it continued to produce its trademark fabric-covered biplanes throughout the 1930s. Near the end of the decade, it succeeded in gaining a contract to deliver six hundred of its UPF-7s to the Civilian Pilot Training Program. The army and navy air arms were moving toward all-metal monoplanes, however, so if the company wanted to win military contracts, it needed to develop a new product. It soon found its opportunity with its glider designs.

Although WACO was able to produce winning designs, it could not produce combat gliders fast enough to satisfy the AAF. As a result, glider contracts were awarded to a number of other firms. Many of those firms were, in essence, paper companies, created solely to gain contracts and having little or no experience with aircraft construction. Due to that circumstance, plus the lack of a clear doctrine for procurement policies, the glider program was marked by a great deal of fraud, waste, and abuse. Yet WACO, despite its relatively small size, was able to nearly match the production performance of the Ford Motor Company, one of the larger subcontractors, in terms of cost. Ford produced 2,418 CG-4As at a unit cost of $14,891, compared to WACO's 999 CG-4As built at a unit cost of $19,367.

Despite the fact that the military failed to embrace the glider program or develop a clear doctrine for their use, WACO saw great promise for the future. This was exemplified by the way the company changed its logo during the war. Initially, the company's symbol was a set of wings with "Waco Airplanes" engraved between the wings, and the slogan "Ask Any Pilot" appearing underneath. The wings and engraving remained during the war, but a drawing of a CG-4A was added above the wings, and the slogan underneath was changed to: "All Army Cargo-Transport Gliders Are Waco Designed." In late 1945, WACO's president, Clayton Bruckner, clearly signaled that he saw the company's future in terms of military gliders.

The armed services, however, had a different future in mind—one that did not include gliders. The newly independent U.S. Air Force dropped the glider program in 1947, and all references to the glider-borne delivery of troops disappeared from air force doctrine in 1950. Stunned by this development, WACO tried to reenter the general aviation aircraft field. Its proposed product—a high-wing, nonspinnable aircraft with a pusher-type propeller, called the Aristocraft—was radically different from the elegant biplanes that had made the company famous. First flown in March, 1947, the Aristocraft was doomed by development problems, increased costs, and the collapse of the private aircraft market. Unable to recover from this setback, WACO withdrew from aircraft manufacturing that same year.[4]

Gliding in the United States to World War II

Many of the earliest experimenters in flight in the United States, including the Wright brothers and Octave Chanute, first took wing in gliders. In fact, the famous Wright patent is based on the control system perfected in their 1902 glider, not their more famous 1903 Flyer.[5] Once the Wrights achieved powered flight, gliders faded into the background. However, there was a resurgence of interest in nonpowered flight after World War I. This was particularly true in Germany, where conditions imposed by the Treaty of Versailles strictly limited powered flight activities. In the 1920s, Germany and England both became centers of gliding activity. Although published records are somewhat scarce, it is clear that interest in gliding began to increase in America in the late-1920s and 1930s.[6]

Charles Lindbergh's nonstop New York to Paris flight in 1927 apparently inspired interest in all kinds of flight—both powered and nonpowered. In fact, the Lindberghs helped spur the emergence of nonpowered flight when Anne Morrow Lindbergh became the first American woman to earn a glider pilot license in 1930.[7] Enthusiasts wishing to take up the sport formed the National Gliding Association in 1928. It got off to a rough start, however. Pilots believing that their skill in handling a powered aircraft would easily translate into an ability to fly a nonpowered aircraft discovered they were mistaken. Crashes were commonplace and that, at least in part, led to the disbandment of the National Gliding Association in 1930.[8]

Despite the early difficulties they encountered, many gliding enthusiasts still wanted to pursue their new sport. They received a big boost in 1929 when Alexander Lippisch and Robert Kronfeld, two pioneer glider pilots, invented the variometer, a cockpit instrument designed to measure the rising and/or falling of the air mass in which a glider is moving. With this instrument, even inexperienced pilots could enjoy the sensation of prolonged gliding or, more properly, soaring. The following year witnessed the founding of the Soaring Society of America, an organization that worked to bring order and safety to the sport.[9]

Elmira, New York, the initial home of the Soaring Society of America, emerged as the center of soaring activity. The ridges in that area provided the lift needed by early gliders. It is perhaps worth noting here that there is a difference between gliders and sailplanes. Gliders, very simply, are nonpowered aircraft designed to glide through the air once launched. A sailplane is a lightweight glider designed to use air currents to gain and maintain altitude. The earliest gliders made simple straight-ahead flights of limited length and duration. By the 1930s, primitive sailplanes were used to make flights of eight or more hours' duration, and covering hundreds of miles. However, the Federal Aviation Administration (FAA) has always used the single term glider for both gliders and those craft that are technically sailplanes. For the sake of simplicity, this work will follow the FAA convention.

During the prewar years, the gliders involved in competitions were launched from the ridges near Elmira in one of two ways: motorized winch or automobile tow. It did not become common until after World War II for civilian gliders to be towed into the air by a powered aircraft.

Elmira was also the home of an important pioneer in the construction of gliders, the Schweizer Aircraft Company. The Schweizer brothers—Ernie, Paul, and William—built their first glider in 1929. Later designated the SGU-1-1(Schweizer Glider Utility—single seat, first model), it first flew in 1930. The brothers—especially the older two, Ernie and Paul—continued to build gliders throughout the 1930s. Once the older brothers graduated from college with engineering degrees, they set up the Schweizer Metal Aircraft Company in the barn on their family farm. They hoped that their glider, built with an aluminum frame, would find a market among competitive glider pilots. Although the craft they built were high-performance gliders, sales were slow. In 1939, with their youngest brother still in college, the brothers moved their operation to Elmira and renamed their newly incorporated company the Schweizer Aircraft Company. A local businessman had encouraged the move with the notion that the "Glider Capital of America" ought to be home to a glider manufacturer.

With the coming of war and the decision to establish a military glider program, the AAF purchased all of the licensed gliders in the United States—a move that effectively put an end to sport gliding for the duration. It then turned to the few glider manufacturers and to some aircraft manufacturers for both training gliders and military troop gliders. As noted, WACO Aircraft took the lead in the design of troop gliders. In February, 1942, Schweizer provided the AAF with a static test model of its training glider, the TG-3. Upon the successful completion of the tests, the AAF ordered seventy-five TG-3s.

As the glider program grew, the demand for trainers outstripped Schweizer's ability to produce, and, as noted, the AAF eventually turned to light aircraft manufacturers to meet its requirements. The high demand for the Schweizers' product, plus subcontracting work done by the company, resulted in rapid, frequently uneven, growth. In fact, the subcontracting work proved crucial as the company actually lost money on its training gliders. As the war came to a close, Schweizer Aircraft began planning for the postwar period. Like their counterparts in the light plane industry, they predicted a boom in sport gliding.[10]

The Civil Air Patrol

Even before the outbreak of war in Europe in 1939, some general aviation pilots, sensing the coming conflict, began to think about how the
nation might utilize its private pilots in a civil defense scheme. Widespread action began in 1940 when the Aircraft Owners and Pilots Association, founded in 1939, organized its members into what it called the
Civil Air Guard. The AOPA operated a pilot registration program during the war. Pilots registered by AOPA were allowed to continue flying,
often performing missions in support of the war effort. A similar organization calling itself the Civil Air Reserve appeared in Ohio. It was an
organization founded in New Jersey, however, that evolved into the Civil
Air Patrol. Gill Robb Wilson, a reporter and pilot, gained the support of
that state's governor as well as that of Air Corps chief General Arnold,
and Robert Hickley of the Civil Aeronautics Authority. Wilson envisioned
the creation of a group that would help protect airports, provide small
aircraft for liaison work, and use light aircraft to patrol the nation's coastal
areas. By 1941, governors in a number of states followed the New Jersey
governor's example in authorizing the creation of general aviation civil
defense groups in their states. In June of that year, representatives of
these various state organizations went to Washington, D.C., hoping to
gain the War Department's support and make the organization a part of
the Office of Civilian Defense. On December 1, 1941, a formal announcement marking the birth of the Civil Air Patrol was issued.

A volunteer civilian organization, the CAP included general aviation
pilots, mechanics, and others willing to give their time to the organization and its goals. While much of the general aviation fleet of the United
States was grounded "for the duration," CAP planes and pilots flew missions in support of the defense of the United States. Despite the civilian
nature of the organization, military personnel, as well as military uniforms and rank structure, played a role in the CAP. From the beginning,
the AAF detailed officers to help organize and train CAP members. The
men and women volunteers wore modified army uniforms and, depending on their jobs within the organization, were assigned military rank
titles (lieutenant, major, colonel, and so forth). They also drilled and
received weapons training. On April 29, 1943, the CAP, which included
seventy-five thousand members nationwide, became an AAF auxiliary.

One of the CAP's first missions was to conduct antisubmarine patrols along the East Coast, where German submarines were wreaking

havoc on coastal shipping. Beginning in March, 1942, CAP pilots flew their small planes in search of enemy submarines. Equipped with radios, the CAP pilots reported the positions of any subs sighted to military authorities. It was reported that oftentimes the mere presence of a CAP aircraft was enough to force subs to submerge and break off their attacks. The mission could also be dangerous. Not only were CAP aircraft fired upon, unfortunate pilots and observers forced to ditch in the Atlantic off the northeastern coast of the United States often died in the frigid winter waters. The CAP's records indicate that twenty-six men lost their lives while flying coastal patrols. For that reason, coastal patrol missions were limited to men. Women pilots also served with the CAP, however, flying a number of other missions assumed by the group, including forest-fire patrols, liaison flights, search-and-rescue missions, and humanitarian flights.

News of the CAP's actions reached the American public not only through standard news reporting outlets, but via newspaper comics as well. Zack Mosley, the creator of the "Smilin' Jack" comic strip, served in the CAP, rising to the rank of lieutenant colonel. When Mosley joined the CAP, his cartoon hero signed up, too. The adventures of "Smilin' Jack" thus mirrored the experiences of actual CAP pilots and kept the organization in the public eye throughout the war.

The CAP's wartime role began to wind down in 1944. The decreased need for its services did not, however, bring an end to the organization. Beyond its flying missions, the CAP created a physical legacy. During the war, the CAP had maintained and improved much of the general aviation infrastructure in the United States. Volunteers helped build 81 airports by 1945, and made improvements to 108 others. Many others worked to keep a large number of smaller airports open during the war years, as well. Nationwide 1,600 airports remained open for civilian flying. Studies indicated that up to a third of those airports would have closed had it not been for the CAP volunteers who guarded them (a requirement during hostilities), cut the grass, and even provided airport management. By early 1945, the CAP owned, operated, or managed 215 airports.

With the end of the war, the CAP shifted its emphasis from wartime missions to training and education. In July, 1946, the CAP received a congressional charter that outlined the organization's primary purposes during peacetime. These included the promotion of aviation, both civilian and military, and the provision of education and training especially to young people. The peacetime CAP did not give up all of the missions it had performed during the war. Fire-spotting and search-and-rescue missions continued to be part of the CAP experience. However, providing education and training for CAP members and cadets became and remained the heart of the CAP mission during the postwar years.[11]

Aerial Fire Fighting: From Fire Spotting to Fire Fighting

The use of aircraft in fighting forest fires actually dated to the end of World War I. It remained experimental and an activity supported by the military until the late 1930s. In 1938, the U.S. Forest Service purchased its first aircraft and in 1940 deployed the first "smokejumpers": firefighters who arrived at the scene by parachute. During World War II, a number of those working as smokejumpers were conscientious objectors. By the end of the war, the use of smokejumpers to fight fires was firmly established.

Congress created the Forest Service in 1905. Reflecting the conservation ethic of the time—which emphasized efficiency and the elimination of waste—two of the main tasks taken on by the new agency were fire prevention and fire fighting. Forest fires destroyed untold acres of trees every year. A particularly devastating fire in 1910 helped spur the passage of the Weeks Act, which offered federal aid to any state that would underwrite a fire prevention program. Fighting fires once they started was only part of the challenge. A key element of containing fires was spotting them while they were still small, before they had a chance to grow into a major conflagration.

In 1918, the Chief Forester Henry S. Graves, head of the U.S. Forest Service, believed he had part of the answer. He contacted the chief of the Army Air Service (which became the Army Air Corps in 1926) and asked for his help in providing aerial fire detection. The initial aerial forest-fire patrols, flown in 1919, focused on the western states. Both the Air Service and the Air Corps aggressively sought opportunities for military fliers, particularly reservists, to gain practical experience. By 1925, the Air Service had loaned two DH-4s to the Forest Service for use on fire patrols. For the first few years, Air Corps reserve pilots flew the planes.

Once the Forest Service gained its initial wings, it began to explore other uses of the airplane. In 1929, aircraft were used to drop supplies to firefighters, and by the mid-1930s such cargo drops had proved their utility. The Forest Service established the Aerial Fire Control Experimental Project in 1935. At first, the project focused on developing the means and procedures for dropping water or chemical "bombs" on fires, but by the late 1930s the Forest Service had determined that this was impractical, given the state of the art of the equipment. Another experimental program initially dismissed as too dangerous, but which later proved quite valuable, involved the aerial delivery of firefighters by parachute.

Many forest fires begin in remote areas. Simply getting personnel and equipment to the site of a fire can be as great a challenge as fighting it. In 1934, a Forest Service employee hired a professional parachutist to make a number of demonstration jumps. He hoped to show the practicality of getting firefighters to remote forested areas by airplane. The effort was labeled a stunt, and the Forest Service refused to reimburse the employee for the cost of the experiment. In 1939, following the discontinuation of the "water bombing" trials, the Aerial Fire Control Experimental Project, acting on a recommendation from David P. Godwin, the assistant chief of fire control, decided to reconsider the aerial delivery of firefighters.

The Forest Service contracted with the Eagle Parachute Company of Lancaster, Pennsylvania, to provide parachutes and protective clothing as well as professional riggers and parachutists. In October and November of 1939, following a number of dummy drops, both civilian and Forest Service personnel made trial jumps in the Chelan (now Okanogan) National Forest. The parachutists jumped into both open and forested areas, experiencing no serious injuries. During the course of the trials, the Forest Service also developed what became the standard equipment package for early smokejumpers (a name coined by one of the early aerial firefighters). It included a main and reserve parachute, a two-piece felt-padded suit, a football helmet with a wire-mesh facemask, athletic supporter, ankle braces, and heavy logging boots. The experimental program proved to be such a success that the operational use of smokejumpers began the following year. The first fire jump was made on July 12, 1940, in the Nez Perce Forest.

During World War II, young men participating in the Civilian Public Service (CPS) program enlarged the ranks of the early smokejumpers. Formed by three antiwar churches and a number of peace groups, the CPS provided a way for conscientious objectors to serve their country during wartime outside of the military. The CPS's smokejumping program began in 1943 with sixty young men. By 1945, some 260 had participated in the program, making roughly five thousand jumps during the two years of the program's existence.[12]

Agricultural Aviation

The crop-dusting industry faced a number of challenges during World War II. First and foremost, the need for experienced pilots and flight instructors disrupted the operations of many companies, especially the smaller ones. Agricultural pilots filled a number of roles, both civilian and military, during the war. The thinking during the early years of the war was that these pilots and their skills were best used in military and military-related activities. As the war continued, however, many began to realize that crop dusting was essential to the war effort because it helped assure steady food production. Agricultural pilots eventually were exempted from military service, and many of those who had been called to serve as instructor or ferry pilots in the armed forces returned to crop dusting.[13]

General Aviation and Alaska: Modernization

If anywhere in the United States came close to meeting the dreams of those who believed in the winged gospel, it was the territory of Alaska. In a land where many settlements could be reached only by water or dogsled, the airplane offered a much-valued boost in mobility. Alaska's first, and for many years only, road—the Richardson Highway between Valdez and Fairbanks—did not carry its first automobile traffic until 1913 and was not paved until 1957. During the early decades of the twentieth century it was open only three months out of the year. The territory could boast of only one rail line. However, despite the airplane's obvious utility, flying in Alaska remained a very primitive adventure until the late 1930s. As war loomed, the United States realized Alaska's strategic value and began to invest in the modernization of its aviation infrastructure.

The most celebrated pioneer Alaskan aviator was Carl Benjamin Eielson. A former Air Service pilot and World War I veteran, Eielson left

Georgetown Law School and headed to Alaska in 1922. While teaching high school in Fairbanks, he convinced a number of local businessmen to invest in aviation. Soon afterward, Eielson went to work as the only pilot for the newly formed Farthest North Aviation Company. Flying an army-surplus aircraft, Eielson ferried passengers, supplies, and mail between Fairbanks and the interior mining camps. In 1924, he won a temporary postal contract to carry the mail between Fairbanks and McGrath, Alaska, a distance of three hundred miles. When the post office canceled the contract at the end of six months, Eielson left Alaska and returned to the military.

The chance to fly on exploratory expeditions, however, soon brought Eielson back to Alaska. In 1926, he served as the pilot for an expedition lead by Sir Hubert Wilkins. Although the expedition as a whole failed, Eielson became the first pilot to cross the Arctic Ocean. A second expedition failed in 1927, but Eielson and Wilkins finally accomplished their planned mission the following year by flying the twenty-two hundred miles from Alaska's North Slope over the polar ice cap to Spitzbergen, Greenland. As a result, Eielson received the Harmon Trophy in 1928. He died in 1929 while flying a rescue mission to a freight ship trapped in ice off Siberia.[14]

Eielson was not the only adventurous pilot who saw the potential for aviation in Alaska. Others followed and pioneered a number of routes and air services throughout the territory. They carried mail, food, and construction supplies, ferried miners to distant claim sites, and transported sick or injured individuals from remote outposts to places where they could receive modern medical care. They did so, however, in the most primitive conditions. Until 1937, Alaska had no paved airstrips, no lighted fields, no radio beacons, and no en route weather reporting. Pilots could fly only under visual flight rules. A few communities and other outposts served by the pioneer aviators managed to carve out small, primitive landing areas, but Alaska's bush pilots, as they came to be known, generally landed wherever they could: sandy beaches, open tundra, and even on glaciers. Large "tundra tires" and skis became standard equipment on planes. Pilots often had to make do with whatever they could find when repairing and maintaining their airplanes. Although federal inspectors from the Bureau of Aeronautics did make their way to Alaska, aviation in the territory remained an informal affair limited to the hearty and adventurous.

The threat of war and the recognition of Alaska's strategic value finally brought federal aviation funds to the territory in the late 1930s. In 1939–40, the CAA established the first federal airway in the region, connecting Fairbanks, Anchorage, Ruby, and Nome. In April, 1940, the government published a defense plan for Alaska that included the construction of more than a dozen airfields throughout the territory. The military soon concluded, however, that the fields being built by the CAA would not work for military aircraft because they generally did not have hard-surfaced runways and were usually under five thousand feet in length. By late 1941, the War Department had decided to play a larger role in the construction of Alaskan airfields. Shortly after war was declared, army engineers began work on a number of fields throughout the territory.[15]

Both the CAA and the Corps of Engineers faced incredible challenges. Many of the proposed airfield sites were located far from any settlements. In addition, similar to the settlements themselves, the sites could only be reached via boat or by air. Throughout the war, a number of Alaska's pioneer aviators hauled people, construction materials, and other supplies in support of the defense effort. In turn, the government improved flying conditions in Alaska not only by building new airfields, but also by installing aerial navigation aids. While this often required Alaskan pilots to purchase larger, better-equipped aircraft, the increased safety measures and the business generated by the war provided an important boost that would help launch a number of postwar aviation enterprises in Alaska.[16]

By the end of the war, the territory could boast of fifty new airports, with approximately one major airport every 130 miles. In addition, the CAA had completed the construction of eighty-three hundred miles of airways. Pilots were able to receive important flight-planning information from 150 weather-reporting stations. Overall, the war years provided for the vital modernization of Alaska's aviation equipment and infrastructure. The improvements made would contribute to the continued growth of both commercial and general aviation in the territory during the postwar years.[17]

Women: Opportunity Lost

African-American males were able to expand their participation in aviation during World War II because, under pressure from Congress, the military was forced to train and employ black combat pilots. After the war, when an executive order desegregated the military, African-American military pilots found a permanent role in aviation beyond general aviation. Women also sought to expand their participation in aviation during World War II, but they were less successful than African Americans. Although some women played a role in the Civil Air Patrol, and others flew temporarily for the military as civilian contract pilots, the women's military flying program was never without controversy and was eliminated even before the war ended. The skills and experience women brought to the Women's Auxiliary Ferrying Squadron (WAFS) and, later, the Women's Airforce Service Pilots (WASP) programs demonstrated their wide-ranging aviation activity. Yet, though their flying abilities often matched those of men, America still was not ready to accept a role for women outside of general aviation.

As noted earlier, the Civilian Pilot Training Program was originally designed to increase the number of trained pilots in the United States. The new pilots it trained (though only the males in the first case) would both serve as a trained reserve in time of war and as an expanded market for general aviation aircraft manufacturers. African Americans and women were allowed to enter the program in limited numbers, but the CPTP quickly changed from its broader initial focus to one concentrated on providing pilot candidates for the military. Women thus found themselves excluded as students.

Still, women played another role in the CPTP: they worked as instructor pilots. Women had few options when it came to careers in aviation. Many participated in sales and marketing. Still others became air racers or barnstormers. A third avenue open to women was service as an instructor pilot. Although jobs were scarce (and some jobs associated with certain ratings, such as Air Transport Pilot, were closed to women), women did have the option of acquiring an instructor rating. With the establishment of the CPTP, many flight schools were in need of qualified instructors, and a number of women found their first steady aviation employment serving in that capacity.[18]

Evelyn Sharp, a young pilot from Nebraska, was one such woman. After earning her license in 1936, she was one of only eight women pilots in the state—and, at seventeen, the youngest. The people in the small community of Ord took great pride in having their own aviatrix and even went so far as to help her purchase her first airplane. She spent the first few years of her flying career making demonstration flights at county fairs and other local celebrations throughout the state. All the while, she honed her flying skills and attended the Lincoln Airplane and Flying School in order to gain her commercial license. In June, 1940, she earned her instructor rating and worked at CPTP flight schools in Nebraska, South Dakota, and California. With hundreds of flying hours and several ratings to her credit, Evelyn Sharp was typical of the type of woman pilot who would soon be sought to ferry military aircraft.[19]

Two women, Jacqueline Cochran and Nancy Harkness Love, were most responsible for the creation of a women's flying program during World War II. Cochran was one of the most visible women pilots of the time. An accomplished air racer, she won the Bendix Trophy in 1938 and twice won the Harmon Trophy, the highest award given to an American aviator. Love had flown as part of the WPA's air-marking program. She and her husband, Robert Love, ran a successful aviation company in Boston known as Inter-city Airlines. She also acted as a safety pilot for the Bureau of Air Commerce. Only twenty-eight years old in 1942, she had been flying for more than a decade.[20]

Even before Pearl Harbor, Cochran approached authorities in Washington with a plan to train women pilots for the military. Rebuffed, she instead organized a group of America's most experienced women pilots (those with a minimum of three hundred flying hours) to serve in the British Air Transport Auxiliary (ATA). By February, 1942, Cochran and the first group of American women recruited for the ATA were on their way to England. In the meantime, the shortage of pilots available to ferry aircraft from factories to training bases grew steadily more apparent. Nancy Harkness Love, who with her husband was working for the Air Transport Command (ATC) in Washington, approached Col. William Tunner of the ATC in June. She insisted that there were plenty of women pilots in the United States available to take on ferrying duties. Although the idea once again met resistance, the pilot shortage soon made it a more attractive option. In September, Maj. Gen. Harold George, the ATC commander, announced the formation of the Women's Auxiliary Ferrying Squadron (WAFS). The first women hired for the WAFS averaged over eleven hundred hours flying time.[21]

One of the original WAFS pilots was Cornelia Fort. The daughter of an elite family from Nashville, Tennessee, and a 1939 graduate of Sarah Lawrence College, Fort grew restless in her life as a society belle and took up flying in 1940. Within a year she had her commercial pilot license, an instructor rating, and had moved to Hawaii to work at a flying school. On December 7, 1941, while flying with a student pilot out of John Rogers

Airport next to Pearl Harbor, she and her student witnessed the attack. Fort returned to the mainland and in September, 1942, answered Love's telegram seeking women pilots for the newly formed WAFS.

Another member of the first group of WAFS pilots was Betty Huyler Gillies. Also from a wealthy family (Long Island, New York), she began her flight training at eighteen after meeting her future husband, Bud Gillies, a navy aviator. One year after earning her license, Gillies attended the organizational meeting of the Ninety-Nines, the International Organization of Women Pilots. One of only 117 licensed women pilots in 1929, Gillies spent the 1930s working as a demonstration pilot with Curtiss Aviation. In 1942, having just completed a term as president of the Ninety-Nines, Gillies, married and the mother of two, helped Love organize the WAFS.[22]

Upon hearing of the establishment of the WAFS, Jackie Cochran immediately returned from England. Furious that Love and not she would head the first group of women pilots to fly for the U.S. military (albeit as civilians), Cochran demanded that General Arnold do something about the situation. In response, his office announced the creation of the Women's Flying Training Detachment (WFTD) under Jacqueline Cochran's leadership. Eventually, the WAFS and the WFTD merged to form the Women Airforce Service Pilots (WASP) program, headed by Cochran.

The minimum requirements for the original WAFS pilots were five hundred flying hours and a two-hundred-horsepower rating. The first group of pilots hired numbered twenty-five. At first, women wanting to join Cochran's WFTD—in order to gain the training needed to join the ferry squadrons—had to have already logged two hundred flying hours. The requirement eventually was lowered to fifty hours. The women pilots were initially restricted to flying only primary training and liaison aircraft, but by the time the program was deactivated, WASPs had flown every plane in the AAF's inventory.

Just over a thousand women served as WASPs during World War II, of whom thirty-seven, including Evelyn Sharp and Cornelia Fort, died. Congress, goaded by the American public's continued reluctance to accept women in any kind of military flying role, finally terminated the program in December, 1944. Although a few former WASPs went on to serve in the U.S. Air Force, they did so in nonflying roles. Most returned to civilian life, where those who continued to fly engaged in the same kinds of general aviation activities they had pursued before the war.[23]

Visions of the Postwar General Aviation World

The general aviation industry survived the Great Depression and, in fact, experienced growth in the late 1930s. With the coming of World War II, the industry found a number of new opportunities: producing small aircraft for military use or acting as subcontractors for companies producing military fighter, bomber, and transport aircraft. Even before the war's end, many in the industry began to dream of a postwar world in which general aviation would see the fulfillment of the promises embodied in the winged gospel. Though popular belief in the gospel had begun to fade by the mid-1940s, many still clung to a vision of the future in which flying would be almost if not as common as driving. Such a future world was dependent upon a large number of pilots, a large number of airplanes, and a large number of small airports.

The government and the military would provide the pilots. The Civilian Pilot Training Program continued during the war years. By 1944, four hundred thousand trainees—many of whom went on to flying duty in the military—had participated in the program. Nearly two hundred thousand men completed military flight training during the war. By war's end, the United States had nearly 350,000 pilots—male and female, black and white. Forecasters in the government and private sectors assumed that many, if not most, of the pilots would want to continue to fly after they returned to civilian status. In addition, a large number of Americans had been introduced to flight as aircrew, maintenance personnel, or as passengers in air transports. Forecasters also assumed that many of those who had been exposed to flight during the war would want to take up flying themselves afterward. All of those new pilots, of course, would want their own airplanes.[24]

The general aviation industry would provide the planes. Many of the companies founded in the late 1920s and 1930s to meet the demand their owners believed would come in the wake of Lindbergh's flight, survived the depression and war years and planned to continue to produce during the postwar years. The same forecasters who predicted that there would be hundreds of thousands of pilots in the postwar air age also predicted that the nation would soon need hundreds of thousands of private aircraft. The numbers ranged from one hundred thousand to five hundred thousand. Regardless of whether the actual numbers turned out to be nearer the lower end of the range or the higher, this represented a tremendously expanded market for private aircraft. Private aircraft manufacturers planned for sustained and expanded production in the postwar period.[25]

Cities, states, and the federal government would provide the airports. From the late 1930s and through the war years, airport advocates at the local and federal levels foresaw the need both for more commercial airports and for more small airports serving the private flyer. During the war, military training needs led to the improvement of airports large and small throughout the country. Those focused on the future of private flying envisioned a need for thousands of small airports in and around the nation's cities and towns. In the Minneapolis and St. Paul area, for example, aviation proponents predicted in 1943 that the number of planes and pilots would increase dramatically in the postwar period. They estimated that 10 percent of all those owning automobiles in 1943 would become airplane owners after the war. Based on that estimate, they foresaw twenty-five thousand private aircraft flying in and around the Twin Cities. To accommodate all those aircraft, they believed that twenty to forty additional small airports would have to be built.[26]

The airports those aviation enthusiasts envisioned would be smaller and less complex than those needed by commercial or military operations. The term *airpark* frequently was used to describe such facilities. Advocates emphasized that airparks would be like the early airports: small, simple, and inexpensive. They would operate with shorter grass runways, small hangars that could be sold or leased, and minimal fuel and service facilities.[27]

With all of the pilots, planes, and airports envisioned, the postwar general aviation world looked bright and promising. Many believed that the promises of the winged gospel would at last be realized. The reality proved to be far different.

A 1955 Cessna 310 powered by a Continental O-470 engine at Moraine Airpark in Moraine, Ohio. Photo courtesy Michel G. Williams Aviation.

CHAPTER 4

Up from the Ashes

1945–80

The hopes many aviation enthusiasts had for a coming air age following World War II were soon dashed. After selling what remains an all-time record number of aircraft right after the war, the general aviation manufacturing industry immediately entered a steep decline from which many companies never recovered. In addition, the postwar period witnessed increased federal regulation. The relationship between the general aviation sector and the federal government became quite tense in the 1950s and continued so into the 1960s.

On the other hand, the general aviation manufacturing sector began a slow but steady recovery in the early 1950s thanks to the strength and growth of the business aircraft sector. It was in this sector that general aviation entered the jet age. In addition to jets, helicopters also became a part of general aviation. Although they failed to live up to some of the extravagant early promises made by certain enthusiasts, helicopters found general aviation roles in agricultural aviation, public safety (primarily medical evacuation), aerial fire fighting, and a host of other small but significant roles. Meanwhile, glider pilots, though relatively few in number, continued to soar despite the serious competition from European imports that plagued glider manufacturers. The postwar period also witnessed the rebirth and remarkable growth of the homebuilt aircraft movement.

Although African-American men found both military and commercial aviation open to them after World War II, the ban against women serving as pilots in military and commercial aviation remained in place until the 1970s. The result was that they continued to be confined primarily to general aviation, although the number of women serving as leaders in aviation and aerospace companies increased during the period.

The winged gospel had suggested that aviation could be used for the public good, and during the postwar years a number of new ways were found to use aviation to support the good works performed by a variety of organizations. Missionary groups in the United States and elsewhere, for example, began to use aviation on a regular basis to reach remote and isolated parts of the world. In terms of the public good, many surplus World War II aircraft were used as water and chemical "bombers" in aerial fire fighting and as crop dusters in support of agricultural aviation.

The latter witnessed significant growth and faced significant challenges after World War II. New chemicals revolutionized the industry, and the postwar period saw the introduction of the first aircraft designed specifically for agricultural aviation. However, the new chemicals that at first seemed so promising proved to be extremely controversial. By the early 1960s, environmentalists and others began to warn the nation of the harmful consequences of many of the new chemicals. In the face of this and other challenges, the agricultural aviation industry organized and has worked to survive within an increasingly complex federal regulatory environment.

The Boom That Went Bust

Even before the end of World War II, many aviation enthusiasts in both the government and private sectors began making wildly optimistic predictions about the future of general aviation. Some claimed that hundreds of thousands of aircraft would have to be manufactured by 1950 to meet the demand. This mass market would in turn bring down the price of the average aircraft to around $1,000. Light aircraft manufacturers placed advertisements not only in aviation journals, but also in mass circulation magazines such as *Better Homes and Gardens, Business Week,* and *Fortune.* At first it seemed that the hopes and dreams of aviation enthusiasts would be realized. The general aviation industry sold a record high 33,254 aircraft in 1946. This represented an increase of several hundred percent over prewar sales levels. As it turned out, however, it also represented a several hundred percent increase over postwar sales levels.[1]

The contraction in general aviation aircraft sales came about suddenly and violently. In 1947, the number of aircraft sold dropped to less than half the 1946 total, then dropped by more than half again in 1948. The number continued to drop until 1951, when the total number of general aviation aircraft sold reached a low of 2,302.[2] The reasons for the precipitous drop in sales were many and varied. First, the typical light aircraft, which flew at ninety-five to one hundred miles per hour, did not appeal much to former military pilots routinely accustomed to flying three or four times that fast. If these veterans continued to fly at all—and the vast majority did not—they were far more likely to do so in the readily available and relatively inexpensive surplus military aircraft that came on the market. Second, most of the light aircraft produced right after World War II were limited to visual flight rules (VFR) conditions. They were not well suited to cross-country flying, and they did not have the instrumentation needed for flying when instrument flight rules (IFR) conditions were in effect. Moreover, in terms of both price and comfort, the typical light aircraft compared poorly to automobiles being produced in Detroit.

The rapid postwar contraction caught the entire industry by surprise. Both traditional and nontraditional light aircraft manufacturers suffered. Lured by the promises of a major market for light aircraft, both Republic and North American Aviation, for example, attempted to fill the void caused by the cancellation of military contracts with the production and sale of light aircraft models. Neither company had previous experience building light aircraft, and both experienced heavy losses.[3]

The contraction forced a major shake out among traditional light aircraft manufacturers. Many companies, even those that had been industry leaders before the war, simply could not survive as aircraft manufacturers in the harsh new environment. Among those that failed was WACO, which had been an extremely successful aircraft manufacturer in the late 1920s and 1930s. During the war years, WACO designed the army's CG-4A glider and focused its efforts on producing it and other glider models. The company initially planned to continue producing gliders for the military after the war. However, when the army decided that all of its airborne troops would reach the battlefield by parachute in future conflicts, the newly created U.S. Air Force canceled its glider procurement program. Although the company took another stab at designing and manufacturing a new small aircraft, its Aristocraft never made it past the prototype stage. WACO soon ceased manufacturing aircraft and eventually faded away entirely. Aeronca left the light plane industry and reoriented itself to the production of aviation subassemblies. Luscombes continued to be built for a number of years with various corporate owners, but they, too, eventually faded out of existence. Such was the fate of most of the pre-war light aircraft manufacturers.[4]

Three companies emerged as the major general aviation aircraft producers: Piper, Cessna and Beech. Through a combination of luck, sound financial management, corporate reorganizations, and diversification, these companies managed to survive the immediate postwar crisis in the industry and were in place and ready to take advantage of the recovery that began slowly but surely after 1951. Yet, despite the improving market conditions, these companies and others faced a situation in which the relationship between the general aviation industry and the federal government often proved to be tense and problematic.

Who Owns the Skies? General Aviation versus Federal Regulation

Not only did the general aviation sector face a severe contraction in manufacturing, there also seemed to be a contraction in the amount of support offered by the federal government. By the 1950s, general aviation felt as though it was under siege as relations between the industry and pilots, on one hand, and government regulators, on the other, soured. If general aviation had enjoyed at least a modicum of support from the federal government in the 1930s and early 1940s with Eugene Vidal and his programs as well as the advocacy of Theodore Wright at the CAA, it seemed that the general waning of belief in the winged gospel brought an end to any sense of a supportive atmosphere in Washington.

Many factors led to the discontent felt by those in general aviation. For example, the Republican congress elected in 1952 focused a great deal of attention on cutting the federal budget. Among the items that fell prey to the budget ax were the CAA's general aviation programs. These included low-frequency radio navigational aids and other services, such as low-altitude flight information, weather reports, and flight tracking. More importantly, however, the federal government sought to come to grips with the increasingly crowded skies of the postwar world, which included not only small piston-engine aircraft, but also increasingly larger, multiengine passenger airliners and military jets. Furthermore, federal regulators faced the imminent introduction of commercial jet airliners at the end of the decade. Finally, government efforts to improve air safety seemed to many in general aviation to come at their expense.

America's skies were still very much a VFR environment in the late 1940s and 1950s. Commercial and military aircraft could and did fly under IFR rules when warranted. However, when conditions allowed for VFR flight, planes were required to follow "see and avoid" rules. VFR flight conditions assumed in most cases three miles of visibility. Pilots flying under VFR rules were expected to engage in a continuous scan of the skies for other air traffic. It was the pilot's responsibility to see and avoid any conflicting traffic. These rules were put in place when most airplanes flew at speeds under two hundred miles per hour and many at speeds less than a hundred miles per hour. Pilots in planes traveling at those lower speeds could, for the most part, see traffic in time to take evasive measures. With the dawn of the jet age, however, planes began traveling at much higher speeds, reducing the pilot's reaction time. In 1958, for example, an air force jet descending rapidly from twenty-eight thousand feet to twenty-one thousand feet collided with a United DC-7 near Las Vegas. The sky was clear and cloudless, but the jet was traveling too fast to take evasive action.[5]

Both the greater mix and the greater number of planes in the air, particularly around major airports, made for a very dangerous environment. Beginning in the late 1940s and continuing throughout the next decade, midair collisions became the all-too-frequent subject of banner newspaper headlines. Solutions proved elusive because flight-control technology (particularly radar) had not yet advanced to the point that it could provide a clear answer. The technology that was available was expensive and, before the invention of the transistor, very large and heavy.[6]

Within the context of the limits of the available technology, the CAA attempted to impose minimum flight and equipment standards that it hoped would improve flight safety. These included proposals not only for increasing the amount of controlled airspace (airspace in which aircraft were under the positive control of CAA air traffic controllers), but also requirements that pilots flying in such areas have instrument ratings and that their aircraft be equipped with a two-way radio and a transponder. General aviation pilots and the organizations that represented them fought the implementation of these proposed minimum standards throughout the 1950s. The bottom line was that general aviation pilots, especially private pilots, saw the standards as an attempt to restrict their freedom. Many, inspired by the winged gospel, had pursued aviation as an avocation because it offered them a sense of freedom—freedom from the bonds of gravity, freedom of movement, and so on. They saw the CAA's efforts as an unconstitutional restriction of their right to use the nation's airspace, which they equated with public lands—and like those lands, they believed the airspace should be open to all users.[7]

The arguments against the proposed new regulations varied among the organizations representing general aviation's interests. The National Business Aircraft Association and the National Pilots Association tried to set a moderate tone. However, the Aircraft Owners and Pilots Association (AOPA), soon took the lead, giving the debate a more strident and uncompromising tone throughout much of the 1950s and into the early 1960s. Founded in 1939, the AOPA was by far the largest pilots' organization in the country. By the mid-1950s it had eighty thousand members, about a quarter of all those holding a private pilot license. It saw the CAA measures as potentially sounding the death knell for general aviation. Furthermore, it believed that if anyone should be reined in, it should be the military and commercial aircraft sectors. It seemed to general aviation pilots that commercial airliners and military jets were causing most of the problems, and by the late 1950s, they and many others in the industry had grown suspicious of the motives of the regulators in Washington. Moreover, they were convinced that Washington saw those in general aviation as second-class citizens and, as such, expected them to pay the highest price for the advent of the jet age.[8]

The relationship between general aviation and federal regulators reached its nadir in the early 1960s following the establishment of the Federal Aviation Administration (FAA) as the successor to the CAA, and the appointment of Elwood "Pete" Quesada as its first chairman. Quesada served in the Army Air Corps and the postwar air force, rising to the rank of lieutenant general before retiring. During the 1950s, he served as an aviation adviser to President Eisenhower. When the FAA was created, the legislation specifically required that the administrator be a civilian. Many, including general aviation advocates, believed that the military already exercised too much authority over the nation's airspace and its use, thus making a civilian perspective important. Nonetheless, Eisenhower insisted on nominating Quesada. In order to accept the post, Quesada had to resign his commission, which meant losing his retired pay and other privileges afforded military retirees. Subsequent legislation restored Quesada's commission and pension when he resigned as head of the FAA.[9]

Quesada thus came to the job with a military background that immediately made him the object of suspicion on the part of many in general aviation. Although both sides initially tried to work together, any chance of cooperation soon vanished. General aviation organizations, the AOPA in particular, argued that the FAA was not moving fast enough to open airspace for the use of general aviation pilots. Furthermore, they did not think the FAA was moving sufficiently aggressively to deal with what they saw as a major hazard to general aviators: the construction of tall broadcast towers across the county. The final insult came when the FAA required that FAA-approved physicians conduct all pilot physicals. Previously, rules concerning flight physicals, at least when it came to general aviation pilots, had been either laxly enforced or waived. The new FAA effort to tighten the issuance of medical certificates seemed to those in general aviation as the final and most intrusive effort to restrict their ability to fly. The AOPA launched a strident anti-FAA campaign, calling the administrator, among other things, capricious and a dictator. The bad blood and suspicions born in the 1950s and early 1960s lingered for years, and the relationship between the general aviation sector and Washington regulators continued to wax and wane.[10]

The AOPA and others in general aviation welcomed Quesda's departure from the FAA in 1961. His replacement, Najeeb Halaby, began his term by working to repair relations between the FAA and the general aviation sector. Halaby initiated a series of meetings with general aviation advocates around the country. He also created three studies (Project Horizon, Project Tightrope, and Project Beacon) aimed at addressing long-standing concerns of general aviation pilots. The various studies examined such issues as the need to create federal programs to promote the growth of general aviation, the revision of the process used by the FAA for identifying and making final rulings on regulatory violations, and the future use of transponder technology—which general aviation pilots at first opposed.[11]

Challenges remained, however. Budget problems led to the elimination of twenty-one flight service stations by 1965, and in 1964 the FAA again moved to increase the positive control of aircraft flying in the vicinity of the nation's major airports. Limits to technology, however, once again postponed the widespread implementation of the plan. In the late 1960s, another series of midair collisions created public pressure for action, but by that time secondary radars and transponders had improved to the point that technology limits were no longer a factor. The AOPA protested the implementation of the new type of airspace (terminal control area) with its requirements for two-way radio communication and the use of a transponder. In the end, however, the drive for greater safety led to the creation of the new airspace and the implementation of the new requirements. Coincidentally, advances in electronics made the required equipment lighter weight, more affordable, and, thus, more acceptable to general aviation pilots.[12]

During the 1970s, the AOPA and the FAA continued to clash. However, it seemed that while the AOPA remained a strong advocate for general aviation, the tone of the exchange between it and the FAA changed somewhat. The AOPA and its Safety Foundation began to work to protect the interests of general aviation within a stricter regulatory environment rather than attempting to block completely new measures, especially those aimed at increasing air safety. Nevertheless, the AOPA, which by then boasted 245,000 members, continued to aggressively insist that general aviation interests be considered in the formation and implementation of all new regulations.[13]

The Recovery of the General Aviation Manufacturing Sector

Although relations between the general aviation sector and Washington became and remained tense through most of the immediate postwar period, general aviation manufacturing experienced a resurgence beginning in 1952. The postwar recovery in general aviation was the result of a number of factors. Perhaps most important was the decentralization of U.S. industry. During World War II, much of the nation's manufacturing had moved out of the major cities to smaller towns and rural locations, many of them in the South and West. The dispersal of industry was seen as key to keeping production safe from enemy bombers. It also meant the distribution of jobs and industrial activities to previously underdeveloped areas of the nation. After World War II, industry continued to decentralize—driven not only by Cold War considerations, but also by the search for cheap land and inexpensive labor. Many of the new manufacturing plants were established in smaller cities and towns with irregular or nonexistent commercial air service, and keeping these remote plants in contact with headquarters and suppliers required the

use of corporate aircraft. In addition, American general aviation manufacturers were able to capture much of the world's light aircraft market
due to the wide variety of quality aircraft they offered.[14]

Cessna, Beech, and, to a lesser extent, Piper turned their corporate
focus away from personal and sport aircraft to the manufacture of aircraft best suited for use by business people and corporations. (Piper
tapped the business market, but it also continued to provide low-cost
aircraft for personal and training uses.) The new business aircraft produced by these companies included both single-engine aircraft and a
new generation of light twin-engine planes. All of these aircraft benefited from the development of lightweight and affordable avionics that
allowed them to more easily fly cross-country and under IFR conditions.

The light twin-engine aircraft designs also brought significant advances in performance. Grumman introduced the first business aircraft
with twin turboprop engines and a pressurized cabin. First sold in 1959,
the $1 million Gulfstream I proved to be popular despite predictions
to the contrary.[15] Beech, which had dominated the market for corporate
twin aircraft, responded with its Queen Air and King Air models—the
former an unpressurized piston-engine aircraft and the latter a pressurized turboprop plane. Aircraft such as these allowed business people to
travel at 350 MPH at altitudes of up to thirty thousand feet.[16]

The growth of the business aircraft market led the general aviation
recovery. By 1960, the number of aircraft sold had increased to 7,588,
and peaked at 15,768 in 1966. The economic problems of the late 1960s
and early 1970s cut into sales, however, and by 1972 the number of aircraft sold had dropped to 7,466. Despite the stagflation of the 1970s,
recovery in the general aviation sector began the following year and continued steadily until 1978, when a post-1946 high of 17,811 general aviation aircraft were sold.[17]

William Lear and the Business Jet

The market for business aircraft clearly signaled a demand for performance. Corporate flyers wanted speed and comfort. That demand helped
bring general aviation into the jet age. Lockheed and North American
took the first stab at producing a jet aircraft that could be used for both
corporate travel and military training. Introduced in 1961, with price

tags of between $1 million and $1.5 million, neither company's product experienced much success in the civilian market.

While some thought that there simply was no market for a corporate jet, others believed that the market was just waiting for a more afford-able model. William Lear fell into the second category. Before World War II, Lear, whose background was in electronics, designed and mar-keted a radio for use in automobiles. His company built radio and navi-gation equipment for the military during the war, and in 1949 he won the Collier Trophy for his autopilot design. Lear entered the aircraft modification business in the 1950s as head of a company that converted Lockheed Lodestars into executive transports known as Learstars. By the end of the decade, he was thinking jets.[18]

Lear, hoping to design and build a small, affordable jet, traveled to Switzerland, where the Swiss government had canceled a program to build its own military jet. Lear and his team used the wing designed for use on that aircraft as the starting point for their corporate jet design. Lear originally planned to build his aircraft in Switzerland, thinking that he could capitalize on its location in the heart of Europe. However, the difficulty of dealing with a number of suppliers from various countries led him to transfer the project to the United States. He chose Wichita, Kansas, as the location for his new enterprise because of its long asso-ciation with the aviation industry. In addition to putting him in touch with the necessary suppliers, the city helped him finance the new fac-tory by giving him tax advantages. The first Learjet took to the skies over Wichita in 1963.[19]

The new Learjet could carry six passengers with a crew of two and fly at up to five hundred miles per hour at forty-five thousand feet. Most importantly, the Learjet sold for between $600,000 and $750,000. At that price, it sold quite briskly. This rapid success strained the company's resources and in 1967 Lear sold out to the Gates Rubber Company. Un-der new management, Gates Learjet soon enjoyed healthy sales. The cor-porate jet age had arrived.[20]

Helicopters and General Aviation

Images of the forerunners of what we today know as helicopters or rotary-wing aircraft date back nearly as far as humankind's imaginings about flight. Leonardo DaVinci's drawings are perhaps among the most famous. In the late eighteenth century, two Frenchmen demonstrated a small, powered rotary-wing toy. Although experiments with rotary-wing aircraft were undertaken contemporaneously with the late nineteenth and early twentieth century efforts to develop a successful fixed-wing aircraft, the true advent of the helicopter age did not come until several decades after the dawn of the airplane age.

Both Igor Sikorsky and Alberto Santos-Dumont, important pioneer airplane designers, tried unsuccessfully to build and test helicopters in the first decade of the twentieth century and a number of other individuals continued to experiment with them during the 1920s. It was not until the 1930s, however, that the world witnessed the first successful helicopter flights. Among those designing and constructing those first helicopters was Igor Sikorsky. Sikorsy left his native Russia for the United States in the wake of the communist revolution and by the mid-1920s had successfully established an aircraft manufacturing company specializing in large, multiengine airplanes. In the late 1930s, Sikorsy once again had an opportunity to work on his early dream of a helicopter. In September, 1939, Sikorsky test flew his first successful rotary-wing vehicle, the VS-300. During the months that followed, he worked to perfect a prototype. Sikorsky was rewarded in early 1941 when his company received a contract to provide the U.S. Army with its first helicopter, the XR-4. Based on the VS-300, the XR-4 first flew in January, 1942. Problems remained, however, and Sikorsky spent most of the war years continuing to perfect his new machine. As a result, the army purchased only sixty-five helicopters during the war. The development work paid off, though, and by war's end, Sikorsky and other pioneer helicopter manufacturers such as Frank Piasecki, Larry Bell (who, like Sikorsky, was also involved in the design and manufacture of fixed-wing aircraft), and Stanley Hiller Jr., were ready to take America into the helicopter age. The promise, however, much like that in general aviation, proved somewhat distant from the reality.[21]

As early as 1943, while Sikorsky and others were working to produce the first successful helicopter designs, some began dreaming of a new air age in which the helicopter would finally allow Americans to realize the dream of personal aerial transportation. If there would not be a personal fixed-wing aircraft in every garage, perhaps there could be a personal rotary-wing aircraft. Department stores offered customers visions of a future in which they would use helicopters to travel from their suburban homes to downtown flagship stores. The stores themselves would use helicopters to deliver goods to far-flung customers and to move goods between store branches. In 1947, Filene's in Boston actually set up a helicopter retail parcel delivery service using a Bell Model 47. That same year, G. Fox and Company, a Connecticut retailer, used a helicopter to move goods from store to store. In 1952, McCreery's in New York City held a helicopter fashion show, displaying what a well-dressed suburban, helicopter-flying woman would wear on a trip downtown.

These dreams of a future helicopter air age proved as illusive in reality as many of the more expansive notions associated with the winged gospel in general. The military became the primary consumer of helicopter technology and the nation's helicopter manufacturers for the most part focused on developing products for that market. Despite improvements during the postwar years, helicopters were and remained relatively more expensive than fixed-wing aircraft and far more complicated to maintain. Helicopters only made sense where their particular characteristics gave them a clear advantage over fixed-wing aircraft. Thus, despite extensive efforts on the part of helicopter manufacturers to promote the public use of their products, the civilian (general aviation) helicopter market remained small. There were areas, however, in which helicopters did find relatively widespread use.[22]

First and foremost, helicopters became part of the agricultural aviation industry. Bell Helicopter designers recognized early on that the downwash from the helicopter's main rotor made it a potentially effective delivery vehicle for spraying operations. Helicopters were first used in the agricultural aviation industry in 1947 after Bell developed spray bars and hoppers for spraying pesticides and defoliants. They proved especially helpful to cranberry growers. The use of helicopters to seed and tend cranberry bogs eliminated the need for cranberry farmers to laboriously walk through the bogs.

Helicopters were also put to use in a number of special commercial applications. In many cases, helicopters proved to be just as or even more effective than fixed-wing aircraft. Aerial photographers, for example, found helicopters made excellent platforms for both still and motion picture photography. Helicopters allowed movie directors to film certain types of shots that had previously been physically impossible. Local broadcasters found helicopters useful for providing traffic reports and on-the-scene reporting of major events such as fires and other natural disasters. Helicopters also came into use in the air-charter industry. However, despite many attempts, most helicopter taxi services failed in the long run due to the expensive operating costs. Helicopters proved much more successful in the sightseeing industry. Power companies used helicopters to fly power-line patrols and the petroleum industry used helicopters for pipeline patrols and for conducting geological surveys in remote locations.[23]

Law enforcement, public safety, and emergency medical services also turned to helicopters in the 1960s and continue to use them. Broadcasters use helicopters to monitor traffic conditions, as do law enforcement officials. Law enforcement agencies and fire departments use helicopters to quickly transport personnel and equipment to emergency sites. In the western United States, helicopters are employed as aerial water tankers, helping to fight brush and forest fires in remote locations. Perhaps the most familiar civilian use of helicopters is as aerial ambulances, rushing medical personnel to the site of accidents or disasters, and transporting critically ill or injured people rapidly to medical facilities.[24]

Soaring: Bust, Boom, and Bust

The nation's glider community also anticipated a boom in activity following World War II. Like their counterparts in the world of powered aircraft, they were soon disappointed—particularly the nation's largest glider manufacturer, Schweizer. The military sold off the training gliders it had acquired during the war, flooding the market and severely depressing the demand for new gliders and sailplanes. Moreover, the war had transformed both the method of launching gliders and the method of training pilots. Before the war, gliders were launched with the aid of a motor-driven winch or while being towed by an automobile. Afterward, aero towing became the primary means of launching gliders. The glider community in turn shifted from single-seat training gliders to two-seat trainers that allowed for dual instruction. By their own admission, the Schweizers responded slowly to these significant changes. However, despite the depressed conditions, they entered the postwar period determined to stay in the glider business and slowly introduced a number of new products. These included a kit version of one of the firm's existing models and, eventually, a two-place trainer.[25] To survive, however, the Schweizers had to aggressively diversify. In addition to their glider business, they became an important subcontractor for a number of larger aviation firms, including Bell, Grumman, and Piper.

Glider sales began to improve in the early 1950s, but the market remained small. By 1953, Schweizer was the only commercial glider manufacturer in the country, and the Schweizer brothers—still in control of the company they had founded in the 1930s—remained determined to continue in the business. They stayed out of a love of soaring, however, and not because it represented a good business decision. The company continued to introduce a few new models throughout the decade, becoming especially well known for the high-performance gliders it built for competition pilots. Schweizer also became the supplier for the glider program established at the U.S. Air Force Academy outside Colorado Springs in the late 1950s. Although business remained steady at the company's glider school, annual glider sales reached only the low thirties throughout the decade.

The long-anticipated market for gliders finally emerged in the 1960s, yet it never grew as large as some of the more enthusiastic members of the soaring community, including the Schweizers, had hoped or expected. As that decade dawned, the Schweizer Aircraft Company's annual glider sales rose steadily into the fifties, and by 1963 reached seventy-seven units, including forty-two single-seat training gliders, twenty two-seat basic trainers, and six high-performance gliders. However, European glider manufacturers began to capture more of the domestic market in the mid-1960s. European gliders used fiberglass in their construction, whereas Schweizer continued to build all-metal gliders. The company complained that FAA regulations did not allow for the extensive use of fiberglass in the domestic manufacture of gliders. The sleek, lower-priced, and lightweight European gliders proved increasingly popular. Despite that, Schweizer's sales continued to grow, reaching a peak of 130 in 1968.

The glider market began to contract at the end of the decade. Sales dropped from their 1968 peak to only seventy-nine in 1969. Although Schweizer's sales recovered a bit the following year, they fell to sixty-four in 1971. The role of European imports was clear: the entire U.S. glider market that year was about 150 units—of which sixty, mostly from Germany, were imports. Schweizer found the competition most stiff in the area of high-performance gliders. Schweizer sales rose a bit after 1972, to 120 units in 1974, but the late 1970s saw another period of steep decline. In 1978, the company sold only forty-five units. At that point, the Schweizers decided to concentrate on trainers and sport gliders, leaving the high-performance market to the Europeans. By 1980, company sales were down to twenty-two units. The Schweizers attributed the drop in sales to high interest rates, the strong dollar (which made European imports affordable), and the fact that the market generally favored the new fiberglass ships over the Schweizer's all-metal models. The only bright spot remained the company's glider school.[26]

The EAA and the Growth of the Homebuilt Movement

Although general aviation manufacturers had begun to cater primarily to business customers, the demand for affordable personal aircraft did not go away. Piper and a few smaller companies continued to produce affordable models aimed at the personal aircraft market, but the homebuilt movement also helped meet the demand. Despite the fact that the general aviation industry felt it was coming under siege by the federal government, homebuilders were able to work with the CAA to create a new category covering their amateur designs.

As noted earlier, the homebuilt movement faced its greatest challenges during the 1930s, when a combination of state and federal laws and regulations severely restricted the ability of individuals to build and fly their own aircraft. Homebuilders finally began to organize to protect their interests in the late 1930s, but the war soon intervened. Activity was light during the war years, but as soon as it was over, leaders in the homebuilt movement began to reorganize and push for needed federal regulations.

In 1946, George Bogardus, a homebuilder in Oregon, took over the leadership of the existing homebuilding organizations following the death of Leslie LeRoy Long, who had led the movement in the 1930s. Bogardus's efforts to reorganize resulted in the creation of the American Airmen's Association. Although the new organization's membership came largely from Oregon, it had a number of members located elsewhere in the United States. The group's magazine, *Popular Flying*, kept the far-flung membership informed on issues of importance to homebuilders.[27]

The same year he helped created the American Airmen's Association, Bogardus traveled across the country by automobile to meet with the CAA. Along the way, he visited with a number of members of his new organization. His goal was to convince the CAA to create a new, permanent, homebuilt aircraft category. Although he was unable to get the new category established in 1946, he managed to convince CAA officials to allow homebuilt planes constructed before World War II to operate with an experimental certificate. This certificate, though helpful, had to be renewed every six months.[28]

Bogardus traveled to Washington again in 1947, carrying with him a proposal for the new category of homebuilt aircraft. As envisioned, aircraft qualifying for the new category would initially fly under an experimental certificate for the first fifty to one hundred hours. Either the owner/builder or an associate with a private pilot license would perform the test flights. If the plane proved airworthy, the CAA would issue a certificate for it based on the proposed new category. Aircraft capable of carrying passengers would be required to bear a placard informing them that they were in a homebuilt aircraft. Owners could sell their aircraft, but the new owner would have to repeat the test period before gaining the new type certificate. These aircraft would fly under the same restrictions covering other aircraft flying under an "X" certificate. One of the most important restrictions involved the prohibition of flight over heavily populated areas.

Building on the proposal from Bogardus and the American Airmen's Association, the CAA moved forward with the process to create the new aircraft category. In early January, 1951, new CAA regulations governing experimental aircraft became effective and the organization worked to develop more detailed rules and regulations. The CAA issued its final procedures for certifying homebuilt aircraft in September, 1952.[29]

That same year, a group of aviation enthusiasts interested in building their own airplanes began planning for a new organization. Led by a Wisconsin Air National Guard pilot, Paul Poberezny, thirty-one people in the Milwaukee area joined together in January, 1953, to found what became the Experimental Aircraft Association.

During the first years of its existence, the EAA operated out of the basement of the Poberezny home. By September, the small group was ready to host its first convention. Held in conjunction with the Milwaukee Air Pageant, the EAA drew twenty-two airplanes to the local Curtiss-Wright Airport (now Timmerman Field). Once news of the new organization began to spread, its membership grew quickly. By 1959, the annual convention had grown so large that the EAA had to relocate to Rockford, Illinois. Within a decade it had outgrown its second home, so the EAA moved its convention to Oshkosh, Wisconsin, in 1970.[30]

As the conventions and other activities grew, so did the task of running the organization. After eleven years of operating out of the Poberezny's basement, the EAA opened a new headquarters in Franklin,

Wisconsin, in 1964. It eventually outgrew its Franklin facilities and transferred its headquarters to Oshkosh in 1984.

At the heart of the EAA was the homebuilt movement. However, by the late 1960s other groups of general aviation enthusiasts began to come under the EAA's umbrella. In 1967, the newly formed Warbirds of America affiliated with the EAA. This organization, founded in Reno, Nevada, in 1964, focused on the restoration, preservation, and flying of former military aircraft. Although originally intended to include only owners of World War II–vintage aircraft, the group soon expanded its membership to include the owners of other military aircraft. In 1971, the EAA founded its Antique/Classic Division (now known as Vintage Aircraft). Members of this organization are dedicated to restoring, preserving, and flying vintage civil aircraft. Aircraft manufactured before 1946 were classified as antiques, and those built between 1947 and 1960 as classics. The group now has a Contemporary Division for aircraft built since 1960. The EAA also established divisions dealing with aerobatic pilots and aircraft, and ultralight pilots and aircraft.

In addition, the EAA has a separate, nonprofit entity, the EAA Aviation Foundation. Founded in 1962, it was established to manage a varied collection of aircraft, including both flying aircraft and aircraft for museum display. The EAA Aviation Foundation also focuses on promoting aviation education, preservation, and research.[31]

African Americans, Women, and General Aviation

African-American males broke the color barrier in military aviation during World War II. Following a landmark Supreme Court ruling in *Green v Continental Airlines,* they gained entry to commercial aviation in 1955, although their numbers have remained small. Other African-American aviators remained within the general aviation sector. A number of entrepreneurs established fixed-base operations (FBOs) at local airports. These FBOs offered both flight instruction and charter services. Through the 1970s, however, FBOs owned and operated by African Americans remained limited and were mostly confined to smaller airports. Examples included Ulysses "Rip" Gooch, in Wichita, Kansas. As proprietor of the largest black-owned FBO in the country, he offered flight instruction, had a Mooney Aircraft dealership, rented and leased aircraft, and performed helicopter maintenance for the U.S. Army.[32]

Neal V. Loving operated a flight school at the Detroit City Airport in Michigan during the late 1940s and 1950s. Developing a passion for aviation as a young child, Loving, like many of his generation, became a model aircraft builder. He joined a flying club after finishing high school and, using the money he earned from a WPA job, designed and built his first glider. Although he took lessons in powered aircraft and soloed in a Piper, he continued to favor gliders. He worked for the Ford Motor Company during World War II and made plans to study engineering. In July, 1944, while flying in a glider he had designed and built, he was in a catastrophic accident that resulted in the amputation of both his legs.

Neal Loving's physical disability could not keep him from his first love, flying. After a lengthy recovery, Loving and a number of his friends at the Detroit City Airport founded and operated their own flight school, the Wayne School of Aeronautics. They hoped to capitalize on the fact that returning veterans could use their GI Bill benefits to pay for flight training. The new school welcomed both black and white students. Despite the fact that Loving and his fellow African-American aviators faced countless examples of discrimination, the Wayne School of Aeronautics remained open until the mid-1950s, when Loving decided to attend Wayne State University to earn an engineering degree. After completing his degree, Loving was hired as a civilian engineer and went on to a career at Wright-Patterson Air Force Base near Dayton, Ohio.

While he was still serving as an instructor at his flight school, Loving once again looked at designing, building, and flying his own aircraft. This time, however, instead of a glider, he decided to build a racing plane. After World War II, as part of an effort to reignite interest in air races, the Professional Racing Pilots Association and the National Aeronautics Association created a new category of racer. To qualify, aircraft had to be relatively simple in design and were limited to an eighty-five-horsepower engine. Loving designed and built his "Loving's Love" to compete in the new category. Although a crash at the 1951 Air Races ended his career as a racing pilot, Loving rebuilt the "Love" and traveled throughout the United States and the Caribbean in it.

Loving then became one of the early members of the EAA. He joined in November, 1953, after meeting Paul Poberezny, and attended the organization's second annual convention in 1954. In 1958, Loving decided to build an aircraft to compete in the EAA's Roadable Airplane Competition and began work the following year. The completed aircraft won a design award from AIAA in 1960. However, neither the

WR-2 nor the other three entries built for the contest met the minimum requirements for the Roadable Airplane Competition. By the late 1960s, Loving had completed the design and construction of a second roadable aircraft, the WR-3. The WR-3 remained in Loving's garage and he used it as his personal aircraft. The WR-1, "Loving's Love," went on display at the EAA museum in Oshkosh.[33]

Neal Loving accomplished all he did in aviation despite the fact that he and others of his race continued to face discrimination and were often discouraged from even attempting to realize their dreams. Yet in the face of these continued obstacles, African Americans, both male and female, continued to embrace aviation. In 1967, a group of black aviators joined together to promote aviation and aviation careers. Edward A. Gibbs, a lawyer and pilot, spearheaded the effort to form an organization for African-American pilots. After learning to fly in the CPTP, Gibbs earned a commercial pilot certificate and a flight instructor rating. During the war, he helped train other African Americans assigned to the U.S. Aviation Cadet Program at Tuskegee, Alabama. After the war, he founded his own FBO in Wilmington, North Carolina. However, the difficulties he faced as a minority business owner soon led him to use his training as a lawyer to enter the field of public housing. He eventually became the assistant commissioner of federal code enforcement for the New York City Housing and Development Administration.

Gibbs never lost his love of flying, though, and after moving to New York, he helped found the Stick and Rudder Club of New York. In 1967, recognizing the continuing difficulties African Americans faced in aviation, he called together a group of fellow pilots and others concerned with aviation whom he had come to know while at Tuskegee. Together they founded Negro Airmen International (NAI). The NAI has the stated purposes of promoting aviation among African Americans and pushing for greater African-American participation in the aviation industry. Gibbs died in 1969, shortly after founding the West Indies Air Line and Air Service on the island of Saint Thomas. In 1973, NAI established its Summer Flight Academy. This program brought young people together for a two-week course in which they were introduced to the field of aviation.[34]

Women, unlike African-American males, were unable to fly for the military or break into commercial aviation throughout the 1950s and 1960s. It was not until 1973 that a commercial airline hired the first woman pilot since Helen Richey's short tenure with a commercial airline in the

1930s. Shortly thereafter, first the navy and the army and finally the air force opened flight training to women.

Not all of the women involved in general aviation were pilots. Perhaps one of the most prominent women in general aviation was Olive Ann Beech. She and her husband, Walter Beech, cofounded Beech Aircraft in 1932. As her husband's health faded during the 1940s, Mrs. Beech took over more and more of the responsibility for the company's operations, finally assuming full leadership as president and chairman of the board following his death in 1950.

Under Olive Ann Beech's direction, Beech survived the severe postwar slump in general aviation. During the 1950s, she diversified the company's product line and activities, including establishing a research and development facility that soon was producing cryogenic systems for the emerging space program. The airplane product line also expanded during the 1950s and 1960s, including general, commercial, and military vehicles. In 1969, Beech entered the jet age when it teamed with Hawker Siddeley in England to produce a corporate jet. Although Mrs. Beech stepped down as president in 1968, she remained chairman of the board. When Beech merged with Raytheon in 1980, she joined the parent company's board of directors while continuing to serve as the chairman of the board of Beech. She retired in 1982 and died in 1993.[35]

While women found a way to stay involved with aviation through nonpiloting activities, the vast majority involved in general aviation were licensed pilots, increasing their participation throughout the postwar period. By 1960, 12,471 women (3.6 percent of all private pilots) had earned a private pilot license. Their numbers more than doubled by 1970—to nearly thirty thousand—representing 4.3 percent of all private pilots. A small number of women became helicopter pilots. They formed their own organization, Whirly Girls, in 1955, and by 1969 it had a membership of 140. (Whirly Girls was an international organization, however, so not all of them were Americans.)[36]

The largest organization of women pilots, the Ninety-Nines, worked to encourage female participation in aviation. The Ninety-Nines also sponsored a number of air races to highlight and promote women in aviation. Once women broke into military and commercial aviation in the 1970s, their horizons broadened. In response, the Ninety-Nines broadened its reach, moving beyond being an organization of women general aviation pilots to being one that represents the interests of both professional and nonprofessional, commercial, military, and general aviation women pilots.[37]

Women gained a voice in Washington with the 1964 formation of the FAA's Women's Advisory Committee on Aviation. While it did attain a certain profile in Washington, the group primarily afforded an opportunity for the women appointed to it to network with one another. Membership included the nation's most prominent and accomplished women pilots. It achieved only limited results, and the Carter administration eliminated it in 1977.[38]

Throughout the postwar period, even after breaking into commercial and military aviation in the early 1970s, women found employment as pilots in general aviation. They flew as instructor pilots—some owned and operated flight schools—they worked in the agricultural aviation industry, they performed in air shows, they acted as corporate sales representatives for both airplane and helicopter manufacturers, and they worked as bush pilots in Alaska, one of America's most challenging general aviation environments. Basically, women with a passion for flying always managed, through persistence and hard work, to find ways in which to earn a living doing what they loved.[39]

Humanitarian Aviation

The end of World War II opened up a new avenue for women pilots. As early as 1938, the idea of using aviation to support missionary work was first raised in relation to the work of George Fisk, a missionary with the Dyak tribe in Borneo. In 1944 (though some sources say 1945), pilots from Australia, the United Kingdom, and the United States founded the Mission Aviation Fellowship to realize their vision. The organization's first field pilot was a former WASP named Betty Greene.

Betty Greene earned her pilot license at age sixteen. She joined the WASPs during the war and flew a number of military aircraft, including the four-engine B-17 Flying Fortress. Like other WASPs, she also towed targets during live-fire gunnery practice. In 1946, Greene began a thirty-year career with the Mission Aviation Fellowship flying the organization's WACO biplane on a mission into Mexico in support of the Wycliffe Bible Translators. During her career, she became the first woman to fly over the Andes in Peru. She also flew in Nigeria, Sudan, Ethiopia, Uganda, Kenya, the Congo (Zaire), and Dutch New Guinea (Irian Jaya).[40]

As noted in the section on aviation in Alaska, humanitarian missions were a part of general aviation even before World War II. The CAP also flew a number of humanitarian missions during the war. These included flood relief, flying sick or injured patients to medical facilities, and dropping supplies to snowbound farmers and ranchers. Following the war, however, a number of organizations, in addition to the Missionary Aviation Fellowship, arose, providing an organizational structure for men and women who want to use general aviation aircraft for the benefit of others.

Aerial Fire Fighting

During the 1930s, the Forest Service experimented with new methods to fight remote forest fires. Experiments dealing with the so-called smokejumpers succeeded to the point that by the 1940s smoke jumping had become a regular part of fighting forest fires. Experiments using aircraft to drop water or chemicals on fires proved less successful, however, and the introduction of air tankers did not occur until the postwar period.

In the mid-1950s, the state of California and the U.S. Forest Service initiated a joint program to develop air tankers. They began with surplus military trainers—primarily Stearman PT-17 and N3N biplanes—but soon other surplus military aircraft came into use, including the B-17 Flying Fortress, the PBY Supercat, the A-26 Invader, the TBM Avenger, the P2V Neptune, and the C-119 Flying Boxcar. Military aircraft were favored for a number of reasons. First and foremost, they were affordable. Second, most had been designed to fly great distances. Third, they had been designed for hazardous work. Finally, they could easily be modified to carry tanks with heavy loads of water or fire-retardant chemicals. Eventually, helicopters were also added to the fleet. Despite the fact that government-sponsored programs led to the development of these fire-fighting aircraft, much of the nation's air-tanker fleet is owned and operated by private companies working under contract to the government.[41]

By the mid-1960s, the use of aviation in fighting fires had become so large and complex that the Bureau of Land Management and the Forest Service established the Boise Interagency Fire Center (now the National Interagency Fire Center [NIFC]). The NIFC's job is to improve aerial fire-fighting support, especially in the Great Basin and Intermountain West. Shortly after the establishment of this center, other federal agencies concerned with fire-fighting efforts on public lands joined in, including the National Park Service, the Bureau of Indian Affairs, and the Fish and Wildlife Service. In the early 1970s, the Department of the Interior established the Office of Aircraft Services to manage the department's (including the Bureau of Land Management's) aerial operations.[42]

Agricultural Aviation

In Rinker Buck's recent work *Flight of Passage,* which recounts the transcontinental flight he and his brother undertook as young teenagers in the mid-1960s, the author relates how his father's tales of aviation adventure did much to shape their desire to make the trip. One image of the colorful world of aviation their father drew for them was of pilots he considered the great "Stearman men": rough but welcoming individuals working as crop dusters, flying surplus Stearman aircraft. He strongly encouraged his sons to find and visit with as many of them as possible as they made their way across the country. Although the Buck brothers found reality to be somewhat different than their father's stories had led them to believe, they encountered a number of crop dusters flying Stearman's from small airfields throughout the Midwest and South.[43]

Just as the firefighters had, crop dusters benefited from the release of surplus aircraft following the war. The Air Corps had adopted Stearman aircraft for use as primary trainers in the mid-1930s, and by the end of the decade the standard Stearman military trainers were the 225-horsepower PT-13 and the 220-horsepower PT-17. More than ten thousand of these models were built by 1943. Although the Boeing Company built many of them, the aircraft were known simply as Stearmans. With the end of the war, thousands of these aircraft entered the surplus market at prices ranging from $250 to $870. The crop-dusting industry bought as many of the planes as possible, and after a few modifications the Stearmans became the backbone of the rapidly expanding crop-dusting fleet in the immediate postwar period.[44]

While the Stearman aircraft undoubtedly contributed to the industry's growth, it required the development of new equipment for the planes to make them work. For example, the Mississippi Valley Aircraft Service introduced a new spray unit in 1947 designed specifically for use on Stearmans. The new Aero Mist-Master consisted of a 140-gallon tank, stainless-steel wing booms, and an engine-driven Pacific Marine pump. The spray booms fit inside the plane's lower wing and were activated by a control valve in the cockpit. This equipment, and other designs like it, was soon standard in the industry.[45]

More importantly, the postwar period witnessed the introduction of new agricultural chemicals. On one hand, these new chemicals were far more effective than those available before the war. On the other, their use often resulted in harmful consequences for human health and the environment. During World War II, the U.S. government sponsored research into the use and development of effective chemicals to fight disease-carrying insects and to kill unwanted vegetation. The most important—and eventually most controversial—chemical was dichloro-diphenyl trichloroethane (DDT).

First produced in 1874, DDT was not widely used for the control of insects and weeds until the 1940s. The military made use of DDT around the world during the war, and other chemicals soon followed, including the hydrocarbons toxaphene, aldrin, dieldrin, endrin, heptachlor, chlordane, and benzine hexachloride. The agricultural aviation industry made widespread use of these chemicals throughout the 1950s and into the 1960s—not only in agricultural areas, but urban areas as well. In 1947, the Chamber of Commerce and the town of Gettysburg, Pennsylvania, hired the Aerial Crop Service to spray it with DDT in order to control mosquitoes. Townspeople were told that the material (a mixture of light diesel oil and DDT) would leave a film on all areas sprayed, but that the film could easily be washed off. They were also told that the spraying would not hurt the quality of the drinking water supply. Before the consequences of its use were fully explored and understood, towns across the country hired dusters to spray DDT in order to control mosquitoes and other pest insects.

In 1963, the agricultural aviation industry came under fire following the publication of Rachel Carson's *Silent Spring*. This pioneering work alerted the American public to the widespread and often indiscriminate use of chemicals as well as the dangers associated with their use. The industry came under pressure for both the use of chemicals and the methods it employed to apply them. Fearing overreaction, especially by the FAA, in the wake of *Silent Spring*, the industry decided to organize.

The agricultural aviation industry was part of the National Aviation Trades Association, and that group helped the industry respond—especially to a flurry of new rules and regulations proposed by the FAA. Although successful, the effort was seen as disorganized. Furthermore, some industry leaders had come to accept the necessity of reasonable changes to the rules and regulations. In November, 1965, representatives from state organizations met in Oklahoma City, Oklahoma. That meeting—

and a subsequent meeting in February, 1966—led industry leaders to conclude that they needed to form a new national organization. The result was the establishment of the National Aerial Applicators Association (later the National Agricultural Aviation Association [NAAA]). The new organization established its headquarters in Washington, D.C., and held its first annual convention in Dallas, Texas, in December, 1967. It soon achieved true national reach as more and more state agricultural aviation organizations joined. The NAAA also cultivated international members. Since 1967, the NAAA has helped the agricultural aviation industry respond to and work within an increasingly complex regulatory environment.[46]

Although the war-surplus Stearmans certainly contributed to the agricultural aviation industry's initial growth, the appearance of the first aircraft specifically designed to spray crops was also important. Fred Weick, designer of the Ercoupe, became involved with agricultural aviation shortly after World War II. In 1949, Weick served as the director of personal aircraft research at Texas A&M University. With funding from the CAA, Weick began work on the design and construction of an airplane specifically for use in the agricultural aviation industry. Weick and his staff completed the prototype in November, 1950, and a CAA test pilot took it up for the first time on December 1. Testing of the aircraft, designated the AG-1, continued into the summer.

The AG-1 had low, thick wings, a Continental E-225 engine, and built-in dispensing equipment. The plane cruised at 100 MPH, could operate at between 60 and 90 MPH, and had a landing speed of 45 MPH. It could cover four hundred miles with a twelve-hundred-pound payload. By October, 1951, Weick was ready to take the plane on a cross-country tour. More than 650 pilots tried out the new craft and the reports they sent in were highly favorable. The AG-1 was never intended to be a production aircraft, only a development and demonstration model. Following the successful testing of the AG-1, Weick went to work for the Piper Aircraft Company, where he built on the lessons learned from the AG-1 to help Piper produce the AG-3 Pawnee, introduced in 1954.[47]

Weick and Piper were not alone. A number of new airplanes designed specifically for use by the agricultural aviation industry appeared in the early 1950s. Included among them were Leland Snow's S-2 Thrush. Between 1960 and 1965, his company built and sold more than three hundred S-2s. He then sold his company to Rockwell-Standard, which continued to build the Thrush. Snow left Rockwell and returned to

manufacturing in 1972 as the founder of Air Tractor, Incorporated. The
Transland Company, a manufacturer of equipment for the agricultural
aviation industry, also moved into aircraft production in the 1950s. Designed and built by individuals who had gained experience with the
AG-1 at Texas A&M, the Transland AG-2 first flew in October, 1956. Although never a big commercial success, the AG-2 nonetheless represented another example of the important postwar development of aircraft specifically designed for use in the agricultural aviation industry.[48]

Although it specialized in military aircraft, Grumman Aircraft designed a commercial agricultural aircraft, the Ag-Cat, in 1957. Because
of its military specialization, some in the company thought it might be
best if Grumman subcontracted for the construction of the G-164, as
the prototype was known. Grumman approach the Schweizer Aircraft
Company, which had already done some contract work for it. Schweizer
jumped at the opportunity and began tooling up in January, 1958.
Grumann retained responsibility for managing the program and marketing the aircraft; Schweizer agreed to produce it according to a schedule set by Grumann. Sales began slowly, but grew, albeit a bit unevenly,
over the next two decades. The Ag-Cat became a very important component of the Schweizer Aircraft Company's business. Over the years,
Schweizer worked with Grumann to modify and improve on the basic
model. In the late 1970s, however, Ag-Cat sales slumped along with the
rest of the general aviation market. In 1978, Grumman sold the division
responsible for the Ag-Cat, Grumann American. Gulfstream, the new
company, moved to terminate the Ag-Cat contract in late 1979 after fail-
ing to sell the program to Schweizer. The two companies negotiated again
in late 1980 and this time Schweizer purchased all rights to the Ag-Cat. It
continued to build the airplane through 1993.[49]

Rotary-wing aircraft also found a niche in the agricultural aviation
industry. As noted earlier, America's fledgling helicopter industry began
modifying its products for agricultural use shortly after World War II.[50]

Planes and Power Plants

As noted earlier in this chapter, the introduction of light, twin-engine
business aircraft, the application of the gas turbine engine to general
aviation and the appearance of the first affordable business jet, the development of the first aircraft specifically designed for agricultural avia-

tion, the debut of a general aviation helicopter, and the emergence of the homebuilt movement all stood as important developments in terms of planes and power plants in the period 1945–80. Beyond those important developments, the period 1945–80 witnessed the maturation and then stagnation of airframe and power plant technology and the emergence of avionics as the significant player in general aviation progress. Light aircraft manufacturers for the most part completed the transition to all-metal construction in the early 1950s. Air-cooled, horizontally opposed piston engines produced by Continental, Lycoming, and to a lesser extent Franklin powered most light aircraft, while small gas turbine engines gradually replaced radial engines in general aviation aircraft needing more than four hundred horsepower. Finally, the appearance of avionics designed and built to meet the needs of the general aviation fleet made it possible for more pilots to benefit from the advances made in the radio navigation technology fielded in the military and commercial airline sectors. Overall, the 1950s and 1960s were characterized by improvements in airframe and power plant technology, but by the 1970s—especially in the manufacturing sector—the advances slowed nearly to a halt.

Aircraft

The majority of general aviation aircraft produced in the immediate postwar period (1945–50) incorporated minor improvements made to prewar designs. Piper, Aeronca, Luscombe, Ercoupe, Stinson, and others began the postwar years producing the same type of airplanes they had before World War II. Moreover, as noted earlier, many firms had expanded their production capacity during the war and were counting on the tremendous market forecasted for their products to sustain them. Unable to cope with the harsh postwar realities, a number of firms shifted their focus to other production fields or began a rapid decline that eventually led to closure. Companies that survived did so by diversifying their product line, developing new designs, or finding their own niche in the marketplace.

Those factors certainly help to explain the long-term survival of Cessna and Beechcraft. Piper, on the other hand, followed a slightly different, albeit successful, path by focusing on the civilian market. The firm came out of World War II with a surplus of cash and aircraft raw materials. However, the rapid fall-off of orders soon drained its surplus and

placed Piper in a critical cash-flow position. In order to generate des-
perately needed capital, William Piper ordered the company's designers
to develop a low-cost, marketable aircraft that would allow Piper to con-
vert the raw material on hand into a quickly salable product, thereby
staving off creditors by refreshing the corporate coffers. The end result
was the Piper Vagabond: a small two-place aircraft with side-by-side
seating, a wing shorter than the one on Piper's venerable Cub, but still
employing a fabric-covered steel-tube fuselage. During its one-year production run, Vagabond sales rescued Piper from bankruptcy and provided the design basis for the many "short-wing" aircraft that became
the cornerstone of Piper's product line through 1960: the Clipper, Pacer,
Tri-Pacer, and Colt.[51]

In the fall of 1952, Piper introduced its first significant postwar product shift when it introduced the Tri-Pacer, its first tricycle-geared aircraft. In 1954, the company entered the light twin market with the PA-23
Apache. The latter program came about as a result of the late 1940s downturn in the light aircraft market. In late 1948, faced with slumping sales
and a bleak outlook, Convair sold its Stinson aircraft division to Piper
in order to focus on the more lucrative military and commercial airliner
market. Included in this transaction was the prototype "Twin Stinson,"
a mixed construction (sheet metal and welded tube) light twin. Piper
developed the Apache from this design. Highly successful, the Apache
became the basis for a product line that remained Piper's mainstay twin
during the 1960s and remained in production until 1981.

During the 1960s, Piper, while continuing to aim to a great extent at
the lower end of the general aviation market, completed the transition
to all-metal aircraft with the introduction of the PA-28 Cherokee. The
Cherokee proved to be a highly adaptable basic design from which grew
new designs for the single-engine Warrior/Archer series and the
multiengine Seneca aircraft.[52]

Unlike Piper—a company that diversified, but stayed basically with
prewar design technology (steel tube, fabric covered) into the 1960s—
Cessna and Beechcraft both rapidly made the transition to all-metal aircraft. Cessna, which had survived the depression by successfully marketing its aircraft to the corporate sector, began the postwar period by
aiming at the middle range of the aircraft market. Although it produced
the large, radial-engine-powered, all-metal 190/195 series with limited
success, this design was more a modernized follow-on to the prewar
Airmaster series than a leap into the future. Based on the market inter-

est, Cessna developed its more affordable all-metal 120/140 series to compete with the Luscombe. Designed along similar lines, these successful aircraft inspired the four-place 170 series in 1948. In 1956, after losing sales to the easier landing, tricycle-geared Piper Tri-Pacer, Cessna modified a 170 to incorporate a tricycle landing gear. This match led to the 172 series, which became the world's most-produced light aircraft during the postwar period. Additionally, in the mid-1950s, Cessna re-entered the business market with its first postwar twin, the 310, variants of which remained in production into the 1970s.[53]

Although its first postwar civilian single was the 450-horsepower G-model Staggerwing, Beechcraft had taken notice of the technological progress in opposed piston engines and the production benefits of all-metal construction during the war years. Beechcraft designed and produced the Bonanza expressly for the savvy businessman. The first successful postwar high-performance general aviation aircraft, it was vastly different from the company's classic steel tube, fabric, and wood Staggerwing. The Bonanza also served as the baseline for the Beechcraft-produced T-34 military trainer and the TravelAir/Baron series of light twin-engine aircraft. Variants of the Bonanza are still in production.[54]

The postwar period also saw the initial flight of the Aero Design and Engineering Corporation's Aero Commander, a "business class" twin-engine aircraft specifically designed for the corporate traveler. Neither a converted "warbird" nor a "baby" airliner, the Aero Commander represented a "middle of the road" approach to meeting corporate America's air transportation needs. The Aero Commander became the smallest "Air Force One" during the Eisenhower years, when one was used to transport the president from Washington, D.C., to Camp David, Maryland.[55]

Hoping to reach an extensive market, Bell introduced the first successful general aviation helicopter, the Model 47 Ranger. Although it failed to fulfill the dream that many had of helicopters finally providing a great number of people with personal aerial transportation, the Ranger nonetheless found both military and civilian, including general aviation, uses. The Model 47 remained in continuous production until 1973.[56]

New classes of general aviation helicopters appeared in the mid-1960s. Turbine engines entered the field, benefiting from the military's light observation helicopter program. Civil spin-offs included the Bell JetRanger and the Hughes series of turbine-powered helicopters. Both served as the basis for turbine power in general aviation rotary-winged aircraft.[57] While sales to the civilian market remained limited, one bright spot in the 1970s was the introduction of the Robinson R-22, a small, affordable helicopter. Its "clean-sheet" design focused on providing a two-place helicopter at the cost of a light, four-place, fixed-wing aircraft like the Cessna 172. The R-22 became the best-selling light piston helicopter and, with its four-place R-44 stable mate, continues in production in the new millennium.[58]

Power Plants

Immediately after the war, a number of light piston engine manufacturers produced several new, albeit, evolutionary designs. After a number of delays during the war years, Lycoming, whose major prewar product was the 65–80 horsepower O-145, introduced the four-cylinder, 100-horsepower O-235 and 125-horsepower O-290. Likewise, after its wartime hiatus, Continental debuted its C-series 75-, 85-, and 90-horsepower engines. These engines continue to power the Beech, Piper, and Cessna lines to this day. The Franklin aircraft engine line, however, never gained strong ties to the "Big Three" survivors. Instead, the firm's products were installed in Stinson Voyagers, Republic Seabees, and the Tucker automobile—all casualties of the postwar market collapse. Franklin struggled as a minor power-plant provider for numerous helicopters and small producers of niche-market aircraft until it declared bankruptcy. In 1975, PZL, the aerospace conglomerate owned by the Polish government, purchased the company's assets to support PZL's licensed production of Piper light twins.

The 1950s witnessed the maturation of the product lines of the major producers of small aircraft engines. Lycoming, expanding on the general design of the O-290, introduced the 150- to 160-horsepower O-320 and 180- to 200-horsepower O-360 series. These engines remained in production through the end of the century with only minimal changes. Likewise, Continental grew its four-cylinder C-series variants to the O-200, providing the 100-horsepower engine need to support Cessna's highly successful Model 150 trainer introduced in 1959. In addition, Continental brought out the O-470, a 200-plus-horsepower descendant of the E-185 and its O-520 sibling, both of which stayed in production into the new millenium.[59] These engines continue to power the Beech, Piper, and Cessna lines to this day.

Fixed-wing aircraft benefited from the introduction of the Pratt and Whitney PT-6 Turboprop. Initially designed as an alternative for radial engines when over 450 horsepower was needed, the PT-6 helped to completely replace this class of piston engines by the mid-1960s. Allison produced the 250-series Turboshaft, which was initially used to power helicopters and later witnessed fixed-wing applications.[60] No new radial engines were being produced in the United States by the 1970s. However, large stocks of components and spares and a large store of engines that had been declared government surplus allowed new aircraft—primarily those produced for agriculture aviation—to use remanufactured units.

During the 1970s, Continental made an unsuccessful attempt to design and produce a clean-sheet engine for general aviation. The Continental Tiara, however, was doomed by a combination of early developmental problems, the fact that it still represented only marginal improvements over existing engines, and the lack of a production airframe for its utilization.[61]

Avionics

Affordable avionics finally became available to general aviation in the 1960s. The CAA, the military, and commercial airlines had all pushed for new and improved radio navigation aids. The onboard equipment necessary to use the new aids, however, remained heavy and expensive during the 1950s, helping to fuel general aviation's resistance to the new technologies. In the late 1950s, companies such as Narco, Lear, King, and others began to provide systems focused on the needs of the general aviation fleet. Although expensive at first, the revolution in electronics during the 1960s and beyond eventually made such equipment more lightweight and more affordable.[62]

By the 1970s, general aviation had made the transition to all-metal aircraft, horizontally opposed piston engines powered most light planes, and business aircraft had begun to use small gas turbine engines. The new avionics initially developed for commercial and military aviation finally filtered down to the general aviation market with the introduction of smaller, more affordable models. At this point, general aviation manufacturers (and to a certain extent the homebuilders who depended in many ways on the power plants and avionics developed for the manufacturing sector) reached a maturation point. They also entered a period of stagnation. While the homebuilt sector witnessed the introduction of composite materials in airframe construction, general aviation technology for the most part failed to advance after the 1970s. The only exception to that rule came in avionics, in particular the introduction of Global Positioning Satellite (GPS) technology in the late 1980s and early 1990s.

General aviation experienced recovery and growth between 1945 and 1980. Although the number of companies producing light aircraft fell, the number and type of aircraft manufactured increased. General aviation also entered the jet age. New uses for light aircraft emerged as missionary organizations took to the sky. New fire-retardant chemicals and war-surplus aircraft gave birth to the aerial tanker, a new weapon in the war against wildfires. The period was not without challenges, however. The rapid proliferation of federal regulations governing aviation precipitated increasingly heated debates between the regulators and the regulated, and agricultural aviation in particular came under intense fire from environmentalists. Signs of change were visible by the late 1970s. The last two decades of the twentieth century would prove to be some of the most difficult years in the history of general aviation.

A 1965 Cessna 172 powered by a Continental O-300D engine. Photo courtesy Michael G. Williams Aviation.

CHAPTER 5

Dreams Once Again Deferred

Post-1980

The dawn of the 1980s brought with it a sustained crisis in general aviation. The last two decades of the twentieth century saw a second significant decline in the general aviation manufacturing sector. While the sector began a long term recovery within five years of the 1946–47 collapse, the recovery during the second period of decline occurred more slowly and with great uncertainty. In addition, the number of individuals holding a pilot license and those training to become pilots both also dropped significantly. Despite well-publicized efforts on the part of the AOPA and the EAA, those numbers were able to recover only modestly by the dawn of the twenty-first century.

There were some bright spots, however. The homebuilt movement continued to expand, especially with the introduction of some revolutionary aircraft types. Moreover, both the EAA and the so-called type clubs (organizations focused on certain types of aircraft) encouraged and supported the restoration of older aircraft. Glider activity seemed to be in a holding pattern, but a new form of heavier-than-air craft found a foothold: ultralights. While following a somewhat rocky path, ultralight flying was firmly established by the end of the century. The AOPA continued to represent general aviation's interests in Washington. During the 1980s and 1990s, the AOPA and its political action committee handled a number of issues and pushed forward a number of initiatives.

Women, who finally found roles as pilots beyond the general aviation sector in the 1970s, were encouraged to enter all sectors of the aviation/aerospace industry: military, commercial, and general aviation. However, while the number of women in aviation expanded modestly in the 1980s and 1990s, the growth was far less significant than had been hoped.

The use of aircraft for humanitarian purposes also expanded in the 1980s and 1990s. American-based missionary organizations continued to use aircraft to reach remote and isolated areas of the world. In addition, a number of general aviation pilots in the United States—and elsewhere to a certain extent—organized to more effectively offer the use of their planes to fly needy patients and/or patients from remote, isolated locations to places where they could receive proper medical care.

Finally, although the 1980s and 1990s witnessed few advances in airframe and power plant technologies—with the exception of the homebuilt arena—advances in avionics helped inspire renewed dreams for the future. Despite the fact that the twentieth century passed without realizing the dream of widespread personal aerial transportation, supporters of several new National Aeronautics and Space Administration programs hoped the dream would come true early in the twenty-first century.

The Collapse of the General Aviation Manufacturing Sector

Beginning in 1980, the general aviation manufacturing sector underwent a precipitous and sustained decline. The sector reached a post-1946 high of 17,811 units shipped in 1978. The number shipped declined modestly the following year, then in 1980 dropped to 11,877. In 1983, the number of units shipped fell to 2,691, and in 1987 to 1,085. After a short, choppy period of recovery, the numbers of units shipped fell below 1,000 in 1992. Recovery came only after 1995, and by the end of the decade the number of units shipped had increased to 2,504.[1]

Despite the overall decline, the business aircraft market remained fairly healthy throughout the last two decades of the twentieth century. Corporations and aircraft manufacturers developed new and innovative programs to encourage the ownership and/or use of business aircraft. Aircraft leasing, for example, became more common. Also, a new form of ownership that in some ways mirrored a practice in the real estate industry began attracting smaller businesses interested in having access to an aircraft. Such companies have found flying affordable through a plan that allows them to "own" an aircraft on a timesharing basis, a practice known as fractional ownership. Depending on the number of timeshares (or fractions) held, each company involved in the arrangement is guaranteed the use of a pilot and aircraft for a certain amount of time per month or year, depending on how the arrangement is structured. This lowers costs for smaller businesses and encourages them to use business aircraft. The aircraft themselves are owned and operated by companies specifically organized to offer fractional ownership arrangements, such as Executive Jet, the company that pioneered the practice in 1986 and is now owned by investor Warren Buffett. In 2002, Executive Jet changed its name to NetJets, a name the company had used since 1986 for its fractional ownership program. The fractional aircraft-ownership market has grown steadily since 1998 and predictions are that it will continue to grow in the early twenty-first century.[2]

The manufacturing slump primarily involved a sharp decline in the market for aircraft designed and built for the private recreational pilot. The reasons were many. First, the large number of aircraft produced in the 1970s had in many ways saturated the market. Instead of buying increasingly expensive, newly manufactured aircraft, pilots could purchase used aircraft. Furthermore, the size of the potential market itself declined beginning in the 1980s with the drop in the number of pilots.

Aircraft produced in the 1980s increased significantly in price, which many attributed to the increased cost of liability insurance. As early as the 1970s, light aircraft manufacturers experienced a series of costly liability suits. Although many argued the validity of the claims made, courts nonetheless decided the cases increasingly in the favor of the plaintiffs and multimillion-dollar settlements began to drive up manufacturers' liability insurance expenses. They had to cover the cost of the new, higher premiums by raising the price of new aircraft. Soon, a vicious cycle ensued. As premiums went up, the cost had to be covered by the sales price of new aircraft. Yet, the number of new aircraft sold declined, forcing manufacturers to further increase their new aircraft price tags, thus further helping to drive down sales. Many believed the only solution was product liability reform. Also contributing to the bear market in general aviation aircraft was the cost of aviation fuel, which escalated with fuel prices generally.[3]

Additionally, there has been little change in the technology of light aircraft. Aircraft produced in the 1970s, 1980s, and 1990s were basically the same as those produced in the 1960s and, in some cases, the 1950s. Neither the airframes nor the engines advanced much, further increasing the attractiveness of the used aircraft market. Why buy a new aircraft when you could essentially purchase the same one on the used market for considerably less? Finally, those seeking "recreational vehicles" had many choices by the 1980s. Instead of airplanes, they could purchase campers, boats, jet skies, all-terrain vehicles, or a host of other machines designed for recreational purposes. As a result, both Cessna and Piper eventually suspended the production of single-engine aircraft. Beech did maintain production of its updated Bonanza, while both Mooney and Maule continued to produce a modest number of aircraft for their niche markets.

Once again, the long-held dream of the widespread use of small aircraft for recreational and commuting purposes faced a challenging reality. Although the FAA introduced a Special Airworthiness Certificate for Primary Category Aircraft (Part 21.24) as a simplified method to obtain certification for a four-place or smaller aircraft weighing less than twenty-seven hundred pounds, only one production aircraft, the Quicksilver, appeared as a result of this action.[4] The late 1990s recovery therefore was based primarily on the sale of business aircraft, not small, single-engine light aircraft.[5]

Where Are the New Pilots?

As the number of general aviation aircraft produced declined in the 1980s, so too did the number of people seeking and holding pilot licenses. Yet, despite concerted efforts on the part of many to reverse the trend, the number of new and active pilots had recovered only slightly by the late 1990s.

The number of people holding an active pilot license (certified and having a valid medical certificate) peaked in 1980, when the United States boasted 827,071 active pilots. The peak year for student pilots was 1979. In that year, 210,180 people were actively working toward certification. The number of active and student pilots declined sharply during the next decade. By 1990, the number of pilots had dropped to 702,659 (a 15 percent decline) and the number of student pilots to 128,663 (down nearly 40 percent). Both numbers continued to drop. By 1998, the active pilot population had fallen to 618,298 (down 25 percent from its all-time high), while the student pilot group shrank to 97,736 (down 53 percent). However, those numbers represented a slight improvement as the number of pilots bottomed out in 1997 at 616,342 and the number of student pilots hit a low of 94,947 in 1996. In 2000, there were 625,501 pilots and 93,064 student pilots.[6]

The modest improvements in the number of pilots in the late 1990s was disappointing, especially in light of the intense efforts of a number of organizations, including the AOPA and the EAA, to encourage more people to learn to fly. The AOPA launched Project Pilot in 1994 and the EAA established its Young Eagles program in 1992. Unlike the AOPA program, which is aimed primarily at adults, the Young Eagles program focuses on young people between eight and seventeen years of age. It is based on the belief that getting young people interested in aviation as they enter their late teens will prompt them to pursue that interest as either an avocation or a vocation. The EAA set a goal of getting a million young people into the air by December 17, 2003. The Young Eagles program reported that it had provided introductory flights to more than 786,000 young people by June, 2002.[7]

Despite the massive recruiting programs conducted by the AOPA and the EAA, the number of pilots and student pilots increased only marginally in the late 1990s. A number of theories have been offered in an attempt to explain the steep, relatively steady decline. First and foremost, the cost of flying has increased. Newly manufactured aircraft routinely cost over $100,000. Even older aircraft with modest performance characteristics now sell for more than $15,000. Sought-after antique and classic models can cost $20,000 to $50,000. Moreover, aircraft, both old and new, are expensive to maintain. Hangar rentals of up to $100 per month or more add to the cost. Second, flight instruction can also be costly and time consuming. The cost of the instruction needed to earn a private pilot license is between $2,000 and $3,000. Although the prosperity of the late 1990s may have provided many with the necessary means, the busy lifestyle associated with the booming economy did not leave much time for safe recreational flying. Additionally, while the salaries paid to many professional pilots reach well into the six-figure range, the road to the rank of captain at a major airline is generally a long one. Moreover, a number of observers claim that much of the glamour associated with flying has disappeared. Airliners, for example, are no longer considered to be an elegant form of transportation. They are often referred to as "aerial Greyhounds," and some consider their pilots to be on a par with bus drivers. Those factors, coupled with the lure new technologies present to those interested in being on the cutting edge, have further stunted pilot training. The decline in the number of pilots trained in the United States affects not only general aviation, but commercial aviation as well. It also concerns military leaders, who can do little to

compete with commercial airlines offering salaries and working conditions that are enticing a growing number of experienced pilots to leave
the armed forces.

The Homebuilt Phenomenon

Although the number of general aviation aircraft being manufactured
was in sharp decline, the homebuilt aircraft movement grew and thrived
in the 1980s and 1990s. The FAA did not provide a separate category for
homebuilt, experimental aircraft before 1993. Their numbers were simply included with the appropriate types of manufactured aircraft (piston engine, turboprop, rotary wing, and so forth). In 1993, however, the
FAA created a new category: experimental aircraft. It in turn has three
subcategories: amateur-built, exhibition, and other. In that first year, the
FAA counted 6,171 amateur-built aircraft. These aircraft, both plan and
kit built, captured much of the existing light aircraft market. They cost
less and generally have higher performance characteristics than the
manufactured products available.[8]

Kit aircraft account for the lion's share of the expanded market for
amateur-built aircraft. The early plan-built aircraft required a certainly
level of mechanical ability. The first kit aircraft were designed for relative ease of construction and the use of fewer, more common tools. Many
of the later kits also employed materials new to aircraft, including fiberglass and other composites that simplified construction even more. With
the support and encouragement of the EAA, the number of experimental, amateur-built aircraft increased from 6,171 in 1993 to 11,231 in 1996.
While the total number of general aviation aircraft increased in the 1990s,
experimental, amateur-built aircraft accounted for the most significant
relative growth.

One arguable aspect of the homebuilt movement is that it fostered
the kit aircraft industry's efforts to incrementally achieve the capability
required to achieve full FAA certification of designs and manufacturing
processes. Although kit aircraft endeavors had once been largely a side-
line "hobby" involving a comparative handful of enthusiasts, they are
now the mainstay of established businesses with the requisite focus on
sound business and financial practices, including liability concerns. Basic design concepts and materials were "proven out" via the amateur
aircraft movement, a method that allowed designers to generate the cash

needed for further development. Unlike the earliest kits, which generally consisted of raw material and a select number of complex components, later examples included all of the components, subsystems, and finished parts needed to assemble a complete aircraft. Once a homebuilt firm had "debugged" the basic design and had the processes in place to track and maintain the industrial endeavor needed for a complete kit, the stage was set for it to more easily obtain FAA design and production certification. This general approach was recently followed by Cirrus Aircraft, which introduced its basic four-place VK-30 composite design to the amateur-built kit market in the late 1980s. It then proceeded to develop its SR-20/22 designs for the general market, achieving full Part 23 FAA design certification in late 2000.[9]

Burt Rutan: Achieving the Impossible Dream

Most U.S. glider manufacturers saw no need to employ new fiberglass and composite materials in the construction of their craft, but Burt Rutan was impressed with European glider manufacturing techniques and began making plans to follow them in the construction of his own aircraft. The result was that the Rutan Aircraft Factory introduced a number of innovative, even revolutionary, aircraft designs for the homebuilt market. Rutan also used his expertise with the new construction methods to design an aircraft that would capture the last, great powered aircraft record: a nonstop around-the-world flight without refueling.

Burt Rutan received his degree in Aeronautical Engineering from the California Polytechnic University in 1965. Upon graduation he went to work for the U.S. Air Force as a flight test project engineer at Edwards Air Force Base, California. In 1968, while still at Edwards, Rutan began work on an aircraft of his own design that became known as the VeriViggen. Built using conventional methods, the VeriViggen nonetheless was something of a path-breaking aircraft. By choosing to employ a canard configuration, Rutan in many ways showed the way to the future by invoking the past.[10]

Most of today's conventional aircraft have a fixed horizontal stabilizer and movable elevator located at the rear of the fuselage. Many of the early glider pioneers such as Lilienthal, Chanute, and Pilcher placed their movable stabilizers at the rear of their aircraft. The Wright brothers, on the other hand, employed a canard configuration with their first gliders and then with their first flyers. Given the canard configuration's controllable stall characteristics, the Wrights were able to avoid serious injury as they tested their early aircraft and gradually taught themselves to fly. The canard configuration also meant that Wright aircraft would be "pushers." Most conventional aircraft have a tractor configuration, with their propellers up front, pulling them through the air. In the pusher configuration, the propeller or propellers are located at the rear of the aircraft, thus pushing the aircraft through the air.[11] Rutan's new design, therefore, harkened back to the earliest days of powered flight because he adopted a canard and pusher configuration for his VeriViggen in order to produce a safer, stall-resistant aircraft.

The prototype VeriViggen first flew in 1972. After demonstrations at a number of air shows, including the EAA's annual show in Oshkosh, Wisconsin, Rutan began selling plans for it in 1974. By the following year, his company reported that at least 150 homebuilders were hard at work on their own versions of the aircraft. The plane's superior stall/spin characteristics, which helped make it a safe aircraft to fly, found wide appeal. Soon, however, Rutan was at work on another aircraft design, one that proved truly revolutionary.[12]

The Rutan Aircraft Factory was based at a small airport in Mojave, California, that also was the home of a glider repair facility. The owner of that facility introduced Rutan to the glass composite materials being used by European glider manufacturers. Rutan reasoned that if the materials were strong enough for gliders, they ought to be strong enough for powered aircraft. Although the methods the Europeans used were quite complex, Rutan believed that he could simplify the process so that homebuilders could employ it. After some experimentation, he developed a construction method that involved a shaped foam core overlaid with glass composite and epoxy. He first used this method to create new high-performance wings for the VeriViggen. In 1975 he introduced an entirely new aircraft design: a two-place pusher aircraft with a canard configuration built entirely using the new composite construction method. He called it the VeriEze (pronounced "very easy").[13]

Rutan introduced the new craft to homebuilders in the June, 1975, issue of *Sport Aviation*. The VeriEze looked different from anything else then on the market—manufactured or homebuilt. The wings were perfectly clean, with no movable surfaces. Additionally, they employed Whitcomb winglets, which further reduced drag, thus increasing their efficiency.[14] The movable control surfaces serving as elevators and ailerons were located on the canard. The VeriEze also had a unique nose-wheel setup that added to the plane's revolutionary appearance. The nose gear retracted manually, leaving the aircraft sitting with its nose on the ground when parked, making it easier for the pilot and a passenger to get into it. Once seated, the pilot started up the engine and "lowered" the nose gear, bringing the plane's nose up off the ground. After taxiing and takeoff, the pilot retracted the nose gear and left it there until lowering it again for landing. Most importantly, the VeriEze introduced a construction method that revolutionized the homebuilt industry. Early kit- and plan-built aircraft demanded a certain amount of mechanical aptitude on the part of the builder, and often required the use of specialized tools. Someone with little mechanical expertise could build the VeriEze as it required no specialized tools. Plans for the VeriEze went on sale in July, 1976.[15]

Rutan followed the VeriEze with a number of other designs for the homebuilt market that used the same construction methods, including the Quickie and the Long-EZ. By the early 1980s, he was ready to move on to even greater challenges. In 1982, while remaining with the Rutan Aircraft Factory, he founded Scaled Composites, a research firm created to focus on proof-of-concept testing and prototype construction.[16] The company has developed a number of well-known prototypes, but it is best known as the producer of Voyager, the round-the-world-flyer.

Voyager was the brainchild of Burt Rutan, his brother Dick, and Dick's friend and fellow pilot, Jeana Yeager. A number of aircraft designers had toyed with the idea of producing a craft capable of flying around the world nonstop without refueling. Such a flight would capture one of the last great aviation records left. Once they decided to accept the challenge, the Rutan brothers, Jeana Yeager, and a number of talented designers and builders at the Rutan Aircraft Factory and Scaled Composites spent nearly a decade realizing the dream. Burt led the design team and Dick and Bruce Evans led the construction team. Voyager first flew on June 22, 1984, and test flights continued over the next several years as the team worked to perfect the craft and raise the money needed to finance the flight. Finally, on December 14, 1986, with Dick Rutan as pilot and Jeana Yeager as copilot, Voyager took off on its round-the-world attempt. It returned to Edwards Air Force Base nine days later, on December 23, after achieving the record.

Scaled Composites continues to produce innovative, even ground-breaking, prototype aircraft. In addition, it also developed a show car for General Motors in 1992, the wing sail for the 1988 America's Cup boat, and the flying surfaces for the Pegasus space-launch vehicle. The Wyman-Gordon Company now owns Scaled Composites. Burt Rutan continues to serve as president and chief executive officer. The Rutan Aircraft Factory no longer sells aircraft designs, but it continues to support those who have built and continue to build those it designed. Since the mid-1970s, Rutan and his designs have earned honors from a number of organizations, including the EAA, the Aero Club of France, the Society of Experimental Test Pilots, and the National Aviation Hall of Fame.[17]

Type Clubs: Keep 'Em Flying

While plan-built and kit-built aircraft helped provide general aviation pilots with affordable new aircraft, type clubs sprang up to help keep the existing general aviation fleet airborne. In 1999, the average age of a single-engine, piston-driven aircraft with 1–3 seats was 28 years; with 4 seats, 32 years; with 5–7 seats, 25 years; and with 8 or more seats, 43 years.[18] Thus, by any definition, the types of aircraft used by general aviation pilots were aging. Moreover, many of these airplanes were "orphaned," built by companies that no longer exist. Restoring, getting parts, keeping up with airworthiness directives, and all the other tasks that go into keeping an aircraft in flying condition became increasingly difficult. Many planes, however, had devoted owners who increasingly joined together to make sure they had the parts, plans, and information needed to keep their antique and classic aircraft airworthy. Such organizations are known as type clubs.

The 2001 edition of the AOPA's annual *Airport Directory* lists sixty-five different type clubs. Some are dedicated to all aircraft produced by a particular manufacturer, including Cessna, Beech, and Piper. Many more, however, are devoted to a certain aircraft model. For example, there are different clubs for the Cessna 120/140, the Cessna 150/152, the Cessna 170, and the Cessna Airmaster. Even some of the older homebuilts, such as the Pietenpol and the Heath Parasol, have type clubs dedicated to their restoration and preservation. A number of type clubs are associated either formally or informally with the Antique Airplane Association (AAA) and/or the EAA's Vintage Aircraft Association (VAA). In addition to holding their own annual conventions, many type clubs send representatives to the annual meetings of the AAA and the VAA.[19]

At least two type clubs, the Swift Museum Foundation—the parent organization of the International Swift Association—and the Don Luscombe Aviation History Foundation (DLAHF), have tried, albeit unsuccessfully thus far, to bring vintage aircraft back into production. Both began the process of attempting to renew manufacture of their aircraft with an eye both to small-scale production and, perhaps more importantly, to increasing the parts supply. The process proved to be far more difficult and lengthy than either group anticipated, however.

In the late 1980s, the Swift Museum Foundation began negotiating with Roy LoPresti and Romeo Charlie, Incorporated, Piper Aircraft's parent company, with the aim of producing a new Swift. The foundation agreed to lease the rights to the Swift Type Certificate and to other tools and data it held to LoPresti. LoPresti and Piper, in turn, would produce a new aircraft that incorporated many of the modifications approved for Swifts over the years. This effort, however, collapsed in the face of the decline in the general aviation manufacturing sector. Although a prototype Swiftfury was flown, the money needed to begin full production never materialized. By 1992, the foundation had moved its tools, jigs, assembly fixtures, and drawings back to its headquarters in Athens, Georgia.

Four years later, the Swift Museum Foundation reached an agreement with another manufacturer, Aviat Aircraft of Afton, Wyoming. Aviat already produced three established aircraft types: the certified Pitts, the Husky, and the Christensen Eagle. Once again, the foundation leased its rights to the Swift Type Certificate, drawings, tools, jigs, and data to a second party. Both Aviat and the Swift Museum Foundation anticipated a quick return to production.

However, both parties soon realized that the process was going to be more difficult and time-consuming than either had anticipated. Because many of the Swift drawings were nearly fifty years old, Aviat needed to bring the drawings up to current standards. That alone proved challenging, however, as many of the drawings were both old and incomplete. Aviat thus had to engage in some reverse engineering in order to produce the needed documents.

By late 1998, Aviat had begun production on parts and assemblies for the new "Millennium Swift." The original goal was to have the prototype flying by the spring of 1999, but the effort suffered from distractions when the LoPresti family sued Aviat and the Swift Museum Foundation over the sale of materials from the Swiftfury project by a Florida storage company. The suit also involved the rights to produce a new Swift. The foundation and Aviat repeatedly prevailed in court, but the LoPresti family's challenges continued to slow down the project. By the beginning of the new millennium there was still no Millennium Swift, and no one could project when it would make its appearance.[20]

Efforts to bring the Lucombe back into production predated the DLAHF's recent efforts. Moody Larsen, a pilot and aircraft mechanic, bought the Luscombe factory's assets, including Aircraft Type Certificate (ATC) 694, in the early 1960s. Larsen and his partners failed to gain the necessary financing to resume production, so they sold the certificate to a group of investors in Georgia calling themselves Luscombe Aircraft for $125,000. The ATC drawings and data were subsequently moved to Georgia, but Larsen hung on to the tooling components when the Georgia group failed to pay the full $125,000. The maneuverings by both parties eventually resulted in protracted litigation.

The DLAHF entered the picture in 1992, when it agreed to buy the ATC and drawings held by the Georgia group, and the tooling, parts and spares held by Larsen. After obtaining the ATC and drawings in 1993, the Foundation entered into an agreement with Renaissance Aircraft LLC to produce new a Luscombe aircraft and parts for the existing aircraft. As with the Swift project, the process of updating the drawings to meet current standards proved challenging. In the Luscombe's case, the problem led to disagreements between the DLAHF and Renaissance Aircraft. In November, 1999, the DLAHF terminated its agreement with the aircraft manufacturer—an action that remains in litigation.[21]

The Swift Museum Foundation and the DLAHF, thanks to their efforts to bring their aircraft back into production, have been two of the more visible type clubs in the past decade. Many other type clubs are satisfied with simply providing members information and materials needed to keep their antique and classic aircraft flying. They keep their members up-to-date on the latest safety information about their aircraft by publishing magazines and newsletters, and sponsoring fly-ins and reunions at which ideas are freely exchanged. In many ways, they are at the heart of the grassroots movement in general aviation.

Ultralights and Soaring

Another way to achieve affordable flying also appeared in the 1980s: the introduction of marketable ultralights. Although ultralights existed before the 1980s, their design advanced to the point in that decade that they became attractive to a number of people looking for a quick and affordable way to simply get airborne. According to the EAA's ultralight division, the sport grew out of hang gliding in the 1970s when some enthusiasts began placing small engines on their hang gliders. The appearance of these new flying machines, not surprisingly, prompted government action. In 1982, the FAA defined an ultralight as a single-person aircraft weighing 155 pounds or less if without an engine, and 254 pounds or less with one. Powered ultralights were limited to five-gallon gasoline tanks, a top speed of fifty-five knots, and a stall speed of twenty-four knots or less. The FAA also established regulations for ultralights in Part 103 of its *Federal Aviation Regulations.*[22]

Both ultralights and the hang gliders that preceded them benefited from the development of the Rogallo wing. Francis M. Rogallo, an engineer at what was then the NACA's Langley facility, patented his flexible wing design in 1951. While he was developing the wing for use on a small, affordable aircraft, his involvement with the NACA and the National Aeronautics and Space Administration (NASA) led him to see an application of his wing in the space program. He believed that instead of using a parachute, space capsules could instead use a deployable Rogallo wing that would allow the astronauts to guide the capsule to a soft landing on the ground. After conducting some preliminary tests, NASA eventually decided to stick with parachutes and water landings.

In the mid-1960s, however, people looking for affordable ways to fly used the Rogallo wing on that era's first hang gliders. The wing made it possible for hang gliders to soar for hours and even perform some aerobatic maneuvers.[23] As hang gliders evolved into some of the earliest ultralights, the wing was adapted to this new form of affordable flying machine. Nearly thirty years after its development, the Rogallo wing was at last being used for its original purpose: making flying inexpensive.

The AOPA created a new division for ultralight pilots in 1982. The organization's Aviation Safety Foundation (ASF) established a number of programs aimed at ultralight owners and pilots, including pilot competency, training standards, and accident reporting. The ASF also worked to allow for a two-place ultralight that could be used for training. Despite these efforts, ultralight flying went into a period of steep decline in the mid-1980s. A number of factors, including a history of accidents, led to the downturn. The AOPA disbanded its ultralight division in 1984 and the ASF transferred its programs to the U.S. Ultralight Foundation and the related U.S. Ultralight Association (USUA). Thanks to improved safety and training programs, ultralights made a comeback in the 1990s. By 2001, the USUA had approximately fourteen thousand members. The EAA also created a special Ultralight Division. Ultralight pilots and their aircraft have their own meeting and flying area at the EAA's annual conventions in Oshkosh.[24]

There is a point of intersection between ultralights and soaring: hang gliders. The same devices that gave birth to the ultralight phenomenon created a certain amount of tension and controversy in the soaring community. When hang gliding first emerged as a popular sport in the early 1970s, many turned to the established Soaring Society of America (SSA) for support. At first the organization's magazine, *Soaring,* published articles about hang gliding and carried advertisements for hang gliders. In 1971, the SSA's board of directors met to consider the kind and amount of support the organization would give to the new nonpowered flying sport. They published a position paper later that year stating that the SSA would support the development of hang gliding as long as it came under FAA safety regulations. The board also decided to continue to accept advertisements for hang gliders and to help develop rules for their safe construction and operation. There were many, however, who believed that hang gliding and soaring were separate and should each have their own organization. The same year that the SSA board of directors debated its position on hang gliders, California enthusiasts formed the Southern California Hang Gliding Association. The group changed its name to the U.S. Hang Glider Association three years later, then moved its operations to Colorado in 1989. Hang gliders are now classified as ultralights and must comply with the same regulations as those craft.[25]

Similar to other sectors of general aviation, soaring experienced a number of challenges in the 1980s and 1990s. The SSA experienced a sharp drop in membership after 1980 and membership, which had been growing at a rate of more than 650 new members per year since the late 1950s, has remained flat. Since the mid-1980s, the number of individuals holding glider pilot certificates (this includes both private and commercial certificates and individuals holding multiple certificates) has also remained flat. There were 19,530 glider pilots in the United States in 1987, and 19,298 in 1999, more than a decade later. The number increased to as many as 21,721 in 1995 (a one-year increase of about 2,000 pilots), but the 1999 total represented the smallest number of glider pilots since 1987.[26]

The handful of U.S. companies involved in the glider manufacturing business began bailing out in the mid-1980s, including the Schweizer Aircraft Corporation. A second generation of Schweizers took over the family business in the 1980s and continued to follow the policy of diversification that had kept the company alive in the post–World War II period. This time, however, the diversification included the phasing out of glider production. Costs were rising, including the price of liability insurance, and U.S. manufacturers found it increasingly difficult to compete with the lower-cost fiberglass and composite gliders coming out of Europe. The company saw the market as too small to justify the expense of adopting European production methods and in 1987 built the last of a total of 2,170 gliders the company had manufactured since 1930. Schweizer Aircraft was still in business at the dawn of the twenty-first century, featuring a product line that includes helicopters—both manned and unmanned—and powered reconnaissance aircraft based on their sailplane designs.[27]

AOPA: General Aviation Goes to Washington

At the national level, the AOPA has served as general aviation's voice in Washington since its founding in 1939. It battled with federal authorities throughout the post–World War II era over what it saw as unfair restrictions and burdens being placed on general aviation pilots. In the last two decades of the twentieth century, the AOPA continued to voice the concerns of the general aviation community. The AOPA strengthened its ability to be heard in the halls of power in 1980 by forming a Political Action Committee (PAC). Many special interest groups formed PACs in the wake of the Federal Election Campaign Act of 1971, which authorized such organizations. By the end of the decade, AOPA's PAC ranked among the top one hundred in Washington, using its resources to contribute to the campaigns of key legislators serving on aviation and transportation committees.

Although a number of issues presented themselves during the 1980s, among the key challenges facing the AOPA were the consequences of the Professional Air Traffic Controllers Organization (PATCO) strike, the creation of the recreational pilot certificate, and the proposed closures of flight service stations (FSS). On August 3, 1981, a large percentage of the nation's air traffic controllers refused to show up for work. Under federal law, the strike was illegal. President Ronald Reagan responded aggressively, firing all of the air traffic controllers who refused to return to work. Almost overnight, the number of air traffic controllers in the United States fell from seventeen thousand to 9,500. The latter number included three thousand supervisors and eight hundred military controllers assigned to assist during the crisis. For the next two years, general aviation pilots faced restrictions on the number of IFR general aviation flights allowed into ATC centers daily. The AOPA worked to make sure the restrictions did not unfairly hamper general aviation operations while the nation's ATC system worked to train and employ the necessary air traffic controllers.[28]

Even as the controllers' strike and its aftermath was causing problems within the nation's ATC system, the AOPA worked to gain approval of a new type of pilot certificate—one that would make flying more affordable. In September, 1981, the AOPA proposed creating a recreational pilot certificate. Pilots holding such a certificate would require only thirty hours of training (as opposed to the forty hours required for a private pilot license), have certain restrictions placed on their flying (not above ten thousand feet, nor at night, nor for hire), and be limited to airplanes with less than 180 horsepower engines and fixed landing gear. They would also be allowed to carry only one passenger. The proposal moved ahead slowly but surely, and in 1989 the FAA announced the approval of the recreational pilot certificate, which became effective on August 31. The AOPA hoped that the recreational pilot certificate would open up the world of aviation to a large number of new pilots interested primarily in recreational flying. Compared to the number of people holding private pilot licenses, the number earning recreational pilot certificates remained quite small. By 2000, only 340 had been issued. The recreational pilot certificate program, although one of the few categories of pilot ratings that increased in the 1990s, was never large enough to offset the overall decline in the number of pilots in the United States.[29]

Finally, the 1980s also witnessed continued efforts by the FAA to close FSSs around the country. The AOPA successfully lobbied to prevent the closure of seventy-five stations in 1983, and two years later convinced the FAA to keep open fifty-one conventional centers in addition to the automated stations scheduled for commissioning beginning in 1986. The

AOPA's successes helped increase its membership to more than 280,000 by 1989. At the end of that same year, the United States had 702,659 licensed pilots, giving the AOPA a membership equal to 40 percent of the total pilot population.[30]

The AOPA was preoccupied with several issues throughout the 1990s. They included gaining passage of product liability reform legislation, addressing the drop in the overall number of pilots, and preventing the closure of endangered public-access airports. As previously noted, many people involved with general aviation placed much of the blame for the rapid and sustained decline in aircraft production on the increasing costs caused by rapidly escalating insurance premiums. In turn, they placed great hope on product liability reform legislation as a means of reviving light plane manufacturing. In 1986, Rep. Dan Glickman (Republican, Kansas) and Sen. Nancy Kassebaum (Republican, Kansas) introduced separate product liability reform bills. The measures failed to pass, however, at least in part due to strong opposition from the Association of Trial Lawyers of America.

Glickman and Kassebaum, joined by Rep. James Hansen (Republican, Utah), once again introduced legislation in early 1993. Their new statute of repose bill proposed to relieve manufacturers from product liability lawsuits after a certain period of time. While not an inclusive liability reform law, it promised to increase the availability of new aircraft and the continued production of spare parts. The AOPA, along with the General Aviation Manufacturers Association and other aviation organizations, lobbied hard for the bill's passage. They succeeded in 1994 with the passage of the General Aviation Revitalization Act, which stated that manufacturers would be exempt from lawsuits eighteen years after an aircraft was produced. Any parts or components replaced or added to the aircraft were also covered by the eighteen-year rule, in that the manufacturer would be exempt from lawsuits eighteen years after the installation of the new or replacement part or component.[31]

At first, hopes ran high that the legislation would indeed bring about an immediate and significant revitalization of the general aviation manufacturing sector. Cessna, in particular, announced that it would resume production of single-engine light aircraft as soon as such legislation was in place. While Cessna did, indeed, begin limited production of brand-new Model 172s, 182s, and 206s, seven years after the passage of the General Aviation Revitalization Act, much of the promised growth still remained to be realized.[32]

Similar to the EAA, the AOPA not only addressed the issue of the declining supply of new aircraft, it also addressed the problem of the falling supply of new pilots. In 1994, the AOPA introduced Project Pilot, which was designed to complement and build on other existing programs, including the EAA's Young Eagles program. While the EAA aimed at children, the AOPA aimed at adults. The AOPA program envisioned member pilots acting as mentors, recruiting and encouraging new student pilots by helping them find flight instructors and aviation medical examiners. Mentors would also offer continual support to student pilots once they began flight training. The goal was to inspire ten thousand people to become pilots. Although the number of individuals holding student pilot certificates increased in the late 1990s, it was a far more modest increase than hoped for by the AOPA.[33]

Finally, the AOPA addressed a crucial infrastructure issue. The number of public-use, general aviation airports—both publicly and privately owned—also declined in the 1980s and 1990s. Profitability played a part. Small airports had a hard time turning a profit to begin with, and many faced new costs, such as the replacement of old gasoline tanks with new leak-proof models. Urban and suburban sprawl resulted in formerly remote small airports being placed at risk by development and unhappy new neighbors. At one point, the AOPA estimated that one airport closed every week in the United States. Between 1969 and 1997, the number of general aviation public-use airports declined from more than seven thousand to just over five thousand. The AOPA built on its already existing programs in 1997 to create the Airport Support Network, whose members worked to keep smaller airports open. The AOPA hoped to recruit a large number of volunteers from its ranks who would keep the organization informed about threats to local airports. Once threats became apparent, the AOPA could then lend aid to local members to help them fight the airport closures.[34]

In many ways, Merrill C. Meigs Field near downtown Chicago became the program's most visible symbol. At a time when urban sprawl was forcing the closure of a number of suburban airports, waterfront redevelopment, a popular downtown economic development tool, threatened the very urban Meigs Field, which served general aviation in the Chicago area. Both private and corporate aircraft found the field advantageous due to its location, which offered convenient access to Chicago's loop. In the mid-1990s, Mayor Richard Daley moved to close the airport in order to create a park on the waterfront site. Opponents claimed that closing Meigs would force general aviation to use the city's two other airports, Midway and the already congested O'Hare. The mayor succeeded in temporarily closing the airport in October, 1996, but opposition to the action was widespread and vocal—involving not just the AOPA, but many general aviation interests. As a result, Meigs reopened in 1997 under an agreement between the city of Chicago and the state of Illinois that guaranteed the airport would remain open for five years.[35] As the deadline of February 10, 2002, approached, the AOPA, the Friends of Meigs, and other organizations continued to oppose attempts to permanently close the airport. On the other hand, Mayor Daley remained an advocate for closure. Who would prevail remained to be seen in the late summer of 2001.

Women in Aviation

By the 1980s, women had gained access to jobs in all areas of aviation—military, commercial, and general. Ironically, just as their role in aviation expanded, the number of women engaged as pilots declined. Although the drop in the number of pilots crossed gender lines, the loss of women pilots made efforts to increase both their absolute number and relative percentage in aviation challenging. Nonetheless, women did see gains in certain areas. The number of women with commercial pilot ratings increased from 4,760 (3.29 percent) in 1989 to 5,807 (5 percent) in 2000. The number of women holding airline transport ratings increased from 1,898 (1.85 percent) in 1989 to 4,411 (3 percent) in 2000. Finally, the number of female flight instructors increased from 3,074 (5 percent) in 1989 to 5,193 (6 percent) in 2000.

Meanwhile, the number of women in the pilot pipeline declined. The number of women holding student pilot certificates decreased from 17,637 (12.37 percent) in 1989 to 10,809 (12 percent) in 2000. The number of women with a private pilot license fell from 16,988 (5.79 percent) in 1989 to 14,554 (6 percent) in 2000, although their percentage in the overall private pilot population increased slightly. The total number of women pilots decreased from 42,366 (6.05 percent) in 1989 to 36,757 (6 percent) in 2000. The bottom line was that the number of women pilots declined both absolutely and relatively in almost all cases. On the other hand, the number of women holding nonpilot FAA certificates increased, including an overall rise from 10,683 in 1989 to 16,552 in 2000. The number of women rated as mechanics or "repairmen," parachute riggers, ground instructors, and dispatchers all grew in comparison to 1989 figures, while the number of women working as flight engineers declined.[36]

To promote expanded participation by women throughout aviation, Dr. Peggy Baty Chabrain organized a conference in 1990 that drew together women from all areas of the industry. The group continued to meet annually until 1994, when Dr. Baty Chabrain spearheaded the founding of Women in Aviation International (WAI), a professional nonprofit organization. Membership grew quickly, numbering over forty-eight hundred by the year 2000. In addition to holding annual conferences, WAI published a magazine and forged partnerships with NASA and the FAA to encourage careers for women in aviation.[37]

Humanitarian Aviation: Public Benefit Flying

The humanitarian flights that began after World War II grew in size and scope in during the postwar years. Missionaries from a number of different organizations used airplanes to bring food, health care, and the gospel to remote parts of the world. Groups such as the Missionary Aviation Fellowship acquired small fleets of aircraft to aid them. A number of missionaries lost their lives in these endeavors. The use of small aircraft to transport missionaries and their families received front-page coverage when the Peruvian air force mistakenly shot down a plane in April, 2001, killing a woman and her small child. The woman and her husband were serving as Baptist missionaries with their two children in remote areas of Brazil.[38]

Much of missionary aviation involved flights in overseas areas. In the United States in the last quarter of the twentieth century a new kind of humanitarian aviation developed. General aviation and business pilots had been informally helping critically ill patients, especially children, fly from small towns and remote areas of the United States to large medical centers for care for a number of years. In the late 1970s and 1980s, these pilots began to organize their efforts. In 1978, Tom Goodwin founded AirLifeLine, an organization that recruited private pilots to donate their time, skills, and aircraft to fly medical missions. Initially, the group boasted a membership of twenty-five volunteer pilots who at first concentrated on transporting medical cargo such as blood, plasma products, and organs for transplanting. In the mid-1980s, AirLifeLine pilots began flying patients unable to afford commercial travel or living in areas not serviced by commercial airlines to medical centers for treatment. In 2000, AirLifeLine pilots flew 3,700 medical missions. Another organization, Angel Flight, debuted in 1983. Like AirLifeLine, Angel Flight, which has affiliate organizations all over the country, provided transportation for patients to and from medical treatment. The volunteer pilots also transported organ donors.[39]

AirLifeLine and Angel Flight grew rapidly during the 1980s and 1990s. Eventually, these two organizations and their affiliates joined together with others providing similar public flying services to form the Air Care Alliance, an umbrella organization for charitable groups whose pilots answer the call only when financial need or other special circumstances dictate the use of volunteers. Many of the groups and organizations associated with the Air Care Alliance also fly missions for disaster or emergency relief, environmental support, and special community support. Although focused on the use of private pilots and their planes, these groups also coordinated with businesses to arrange for patients to occupy otherwise empty seats on corporate and business aircraft. They also arranged for the donation of seats on commercial airliners.[40]

By the late 1990s, the FAA recognizing the size, scope, and special needs of these mercy flights, approved a new call sign, "Compassion," to identify these public-benefit flights as medical missions. The Air Care Alliance included over forty five hundred volunteer pilots who collectively made hundreds of flights each month. As these groups grew and became more visible in the 1980s and 1990s, they also began receiving aid from other aviation organizations. Some FBOs offered them discounted fuel, and certain airports waived their landing fees. The pilots, however, paid all of the operating costs of their flights. They could, however, take tax deductions equal to their charity flight related expenses.[41]

Propellers

Before the Wright brothers were able to take to the air, they needed, among other things, a way to translate engine power into propulsion. The breakthrough came when they were able to conceptualize their propellers as vertical wings. They then used the wind tunnel data they collected while designing the wings for the Kitty Hawk Flyer and applied it to the construction of the two counterrotating propellers they used to provide the thrust for their machine.[42] General aviation entered the jet age in the 1960s, but many general aviation aircraft are still propeller driven and a number of companies emerged to provide propellers for the industry.[43] Although there are a number of specialty fabricators, the main sources for general aviation propellers were three companies with deep roots in the history of general aviation: Hartzell, Sensenich, and McCauley.

Hartzell was the first of two propeller manufacturers to set up shop near the Wright brothers' Dayton home. John T. Hartzell opened a lumber business in 1875 in Greenville, Ohio. His son, George, moved the company to nearby Piqua. George Hartzell also moved his family, including son Robert, to Oakwood, the Dayton suburb that in 1914 became Orville Wright's home. As neighbors, Orville Wright and Robert Hartzell, an aviation enthusiast, spoke often about the burgeoning aviation industry. The Hartzell Company was already a major supplier of wood for propellers, and Wright encouraged the younger Hartzell to get into the propeller manufacturing business. That opportunity came with the outbreak of war.

When Europe went to war in 1914, the Hartzell Company lost many of its customers because it had been a major exporter of American hardwoods to Europe. It needed to find alternative markets for its wood. First, the company began to produce stocks for weapons. Then, in 1917, Robert Hartzell left school and started the Hartzell Walnut Propeller Company. The new company's product was soon in great demand for use on Curtiss Jennies and locally produced Dayton-Wright DH-4s. During the 1920s and 1930s, Hartzell built propellers for a number of different aircraft, including the Aeronca C-2, a number of WACO models, and the Beech Staggerwing. It also produced propellers for the navy's airships *Akron* and the *Macon*. During World War II, the company, under contract with Hamilton-Standard, began building metal propellers.

After the war, the company began to make the transition from wood to metal propellers in its own products. First, however, it introduced the first composite propeller in 1945. Using a material of its own design called Hartzite, the company produced this unique composite propeller for the Republic Seabee. It introduced its first aluminum propeller in 1948, after essentially phasing out the construction of wooden propellers in 1946—although it continued to build a few until 1964, when it sold its propeller type certificates to Sensenich.

Hartzell Propeller was able to boast of a number of firsts during the postwar period. In addition to the first composite propeller, in 1946 it introduced the first reversible propeller system, also for the Republic Seabee. In the 1950s, the company introduced the first full-feathering propellers for light twin-engine aircraft, which were used on the Aero Commander, the Piper Apache, the Cessna 310, and the Beech Twin Bonanza. In the early 1960s, the company developed the first practical turboprop propeller. Introduced in 1964, this new three-bladed propeller was used on the Beech King Air 90. The company went on to produce four- and five-bladed versions of this same propeller.

Hartzell has also been involved with a number of experimental aircraft programs. For example, it produced a very lightweight metal propeller for use on Burt Rutan's Voyager. It also provided the sixteen-foot composite propellers used with Boeing's Condor unmanned aerial vehicle (UAV) and the four-bladed composite propeller used on the Egrett, a UAV used for atmospheric radiation measurement. Both these UAV's have set altitude records. Finally, Hartzell was involved with a number of NASA programs aimed at creating the next generation of general aviation aircraft.[44]

The saga of the Sensenich Propeller Manufacturing Company began in the 1920s in Lancaster, Pennsylvania. Brothers Harry and Martin Sensenich wanted a fast road vehicle. Using a surplus World War I aircraft engine and a propeller, the boys created a wind-driven farm wagon. After being banned from the local roads, the brothers mounted the engine on an ice sled. While they were testing the new vehicle at high speeds on the frozen Susquehanna River, the rope tethering the sled broke, the vehicle crashed, and the propeller was damaged. The brothers decided to replace it with a propeller of their own design and manufacture.

In 1932, the Sensenich brothers established their own company. They continued to build fixed-pitch aircraft propellers throughout the 1930s—first in the family barn, then in a factory in Fairfield County, Pennsylvania. During World War II, the company had four hundred employees who produced wooden propellers for military trainer aircraft. In 1948, the company diversified into the manufacture of fixed-pitch metal propellers for general aviation aircraft. It eventually expanded its original plant, which grew to eighty-seven thousand square feet on eleven and a quarter acres and also established some operations in an eighty-five-hundred-square-foot hangar at the Lancaster County Airport.

In the late 1980s, Philadelphia Bourse, Incorporated (PBI), purchased the Sensenich Corporation. The company became known as the Sensenich Propeller Company, Incorporated under PBI and had about seventy employees. In the mid-1990s, Sensenich divided into three subsidiaries: the Sensenich Propeller Manufacturing Company, the Sensenich Wood Propeller Company, and the Sensenich Propeller Company. The first subsidiary manufactured metal propellers and was located in Lancaster, Pennsylvania. The second manufactured wooden propellers and was located in Plant City, Florida. The third company serviced the propellers built by the other two subsidiaries. Philadelphia Bourse spun off the Sensenich Propeller Company in late 1995, and changed its name to Sensenich Propeller Service, with operations in Pennsylvania, Georgia, and Connecticut.[45]

The third major propeller supplier for general aviation aircraft, and the second to locate near the Wright brothers' home, was McCauley Propeller Systems.[46] In 1938, a Dayton-based aerodynamicist, Earnest G. McCauley, established the McCauley Aviation Corporation. He founded his company because he believed he could make advances in the field and increase efficiency by making certain the essential compatibility between engines and propellers. The company soon introduced the first solid-steel propeller. During World War II, it focused on the manufacture of conventional ground-adjustable solid-steel propellers, building approximately twenty thousand for the U.S. military.

Despite its work for the military during the war, the company was best known for the steel propellers it provided for general aviation aircraft. The link between McCauley and general aviation strengthened in 1960 when Cessna Aircraft purchased the company. While operating as a division of Cessna Aircraft, McCauley developed a number of innovative products, including two- and three-bladed constant-speed and full-feathering propellers. In 1979, McCauley introduced its first turbo propeller, a three-bladed, full-feathering, and reversing turboprop. A four-bladed version appeared in 1983, and a five-bladed version in 1987. The company introduced an advanced version of the five-bladed propeller, designed for use on regional airliners, in 1992. Cessna renamed the division McCauley Propeller Systems in 1996.[47]

Planes and Power Plants: NASA and the Future of General Aviation

Although the winged gospel's hold on the imagination of the American public diminished in the wake of World War II, certain parts of the dream remained alive, surfacing occasionally almost in spite of the often harsh realities. One such dream was that of personal aerial transportation. Many people have attempted over the years to design and build an afford-able, safe airplane. With the invention of the helicopter, the dream of an airplane in every garage shifted to the dream of a helicopter in every garage. As long as any type of aircraft remained relatively expensive, rela-tively more difficult to fly than automobiles were to drive, and in many ways restricted by weather conditions, attainment of the dream of per-sonal aerial transportation by either fixed-wing or rotary-wing aircraft seemed unlikely. Yet the dream never died. At the dawn of the twenty-first century, NASA sponsored new programs aimed at revitalizing gen-eral aviation. The Advanced General Aviation Transport Experiments (AGATE) program was designed to develop affordable new technolo-gies, new methods of manufacturing and certifying general aviation air-craft, and improved flight-training systems. The General Aviation Pro-pulsion (GAP) program focused on developing new propulsion systems, both intermittent combustion engines and turbine engines, with the potential of revolutionizing general aviation. A third program, the Small Aircraft Transportation System (SATS), built on the previous programs and continued to focus on the development of new avionics and a tech-nology infrastructure that would make flying extremely safe under al-most all conditions.

The AGATE program, which was built around a public-private part-nership involving NASA, industry, universities, and other governmental agencies such as the FAA, began in 1994. Members of the AGATE con-sortium are at work on projects in a number of areas. These included flight systems, propulsion sensors and controls, ice-protection systems, and a flight-training curriculum. The propulsion sensors and controls as well as the ice-protection systems partners completed their work. Other work continued, including the FAA's development of an air and ground infrastructure that would make travel by small aircraft more efficient and safe. The key goal in all of this was affordability. The program as-sumed that the new technologies must be affordable in order to truly spark a revitalization of the general aviation industry in the United States.[48]

The GAP program, housed at NASA's Glenn Research Center, began in 1996 when NASA signed agreements with Williams International and Teledyne Continental Motors to develop the two envisioned new engines. Teledyne Continental tackled the program's intermittent combustion engine element and developed a four-cylinder, liquid-cooled, two-stroke diesel engine that burns Jet A fuel and produces two hundred horsepower. In early 2001, Teledyne completed the propeller integration testing. Ground testing began that fall and was successfully completed in February, 2002, proving the new engine's viability. Williams International produced the turbine engine element of the program. The Williams engine was a lightweight, high bypass ratio, turbofan engine capable of generating seven hundred pounds of thrust. The prototype FJX-2 engine proved capable of generating 700 pounds of thrust at sea level in tests conducted at Williams International in early 2001. The engine weighed only eighty-five pounds, giving it the highest thrust-to-weight ratio (8.2) of any commercial turbofan engine. It was hoped that the availability of these new revolutionary and affordable engines would lead to the design and production of a new generation of general aviation aircraft.[49]

The most recent NASA program, SATS, was built on the GAP and the AGATE programs. It was a response not only to the long-held dream of personal aerial transportation, but also to the heavy congestion at the nation's major airports. Forty-five airports handled the vast majority of the nation's commercial air traffic. These airports, particularly the twenty or so key hub airports, were overtaxed. Their limitations contributed to the growing problems of flight delays. Those backing the SATS program pointed out that the United States has approximately fifty-four hundred public-use airports, of which only six hundred offer scheduled air carrier service. The SATS program would open up air transportation at the thousands of remaining airports not served directly by commercial carriers.

The goal of the SATS program was to develop and produce a safe, affordable small aircraft capable of carrying four to eight people. Engineers at NASA envisioned it as a pressurized vehicle powered by twin turbofan engines, perhaps like those developed by the GAP program. The key characteristic was safety. The aircraft would have highly sophisticated avionics that would allow it to fly easily and safely in nearly all weather conditions. Also essential was affordability. Proponents believed that mass production techniques and the development of a mass market would result in an affordable product.

There was some debate as to whether these aircraft, at least at first, would be privately owned and operated. Most involved with the project believed that the first of these aircraft would be operated by air taxi services. Others, however, believed that if the aircraft could be made safe enough and affordable enough, a significant percentage of the American public would purchase them for business and leisure travel.

The advent of the new sky car was heavily dependent upon the development of a technology infrastructure to support the sophisticated avionics. Program advocates described the creation of an electronic highway in the sky. Both ground-based and aircraft-based equipment would allow the pilot to easily guide the aircraft through the sky in nearly all weather and traffic conditions. Proponents pointed out that NASA spent nearly a decade on the AGATE program and some of the equipment necessary for the SATS program's success was developed as part of AGATE. Experts at NASA anticipated beginning the deployment phase in 2015 and having a fully mature system in place by 2020.

National Aviation and Space Administration officials proposed SATS as a five-year (2000–2005) proof-of-concept program. The goal was to reduce public transportation time significantly in the first generation following the introduction of the SATS vehicle. The SATS program was also connected to NASA and FAA efforts to fully modernize the nation's air traffic control system. In 2002, however, NASA commissioned a study of the SATS program by the National Academy of Science's Transportation Research Board (TRB). The report was highly critical of the program. Although it supported the development of new technologies for aircraft and airports, the TRB did not believe the program would be implemented as envisioned by NASA. In particular, it did not see the SATS program as addressing the problems associated with the projected increased demand for air transportation. Strong proponents still existed, but criticism of the program was mounting.[50]

Epilogue: September 11, 2001

Within the space of about an hour on the morning of September 11, 2001, the world as Americans knew it changed. By noon that day, only military aircraft remained airborne within the borders of the continental United States. The terrorists who flew commercial airliners into the twin towers of the World Trade Center and the Pentagon, as well as those who failed to accomplish their mission thanks to the heroic acts of passengers aboard an airliner over Pennsylvania, had brought America's aerial transportation system to a grinding halt. The events of that day have had and will continue to have profound effects on all Americans. The military air forces of the United States—air force, navy, army, and marine—found themselves taking part in a military, political, diplomatic, economic, and humanitarian effort to fight terrorism. Commercial airlines were striving to regain passengers and survive financially. General aviation is also struggling to adjust to the new conditions affecting all Americans.

In the first hours after the attacks, most of the nation's attention focused on commercial and military aviation. However, it soon became clear that *all* civilian aircraft in the United States were grounded, from Boeing 747s to Piper Cubs. In the days following the attacks, attention focused on getting commercial airliners back in the sky—and that happened, relatively quickly, albeit on reduced schedules and under heightened security. In the meantime, the general aviation fleet remained on the ground. Of particular concern were crop-dusting aircraft, which some feared terrorists might use to spread chemical or biological weapons. Once it became clear that such actions would be technologically difficult, if not impossible, America's agricultural aviation was released to fly. Others focused on flight training operations. Many sought some level of assurance that the nation's flight schools, at which a number of the alleged terrorists had received training, harbored no more would-be suicide pilots.

Restrictions on general aviation were gradually and incompletely lifted in the weeks following September 11. By mid-October, although the FAA had begun to lift the restrictions involving some major metropolitan airports, many private pilots and general aviation businesses operating out of general aviation airports falling under the "enhanced Class B airspace" surrounding thirty major metropolitan airports in the United States remained grounded.[51] Only instrument-qualified pilots flying on IFR flight plans were allowed to operate out of such airports. Flight training operations continued, but with restrictions imposed. Furthermore, no general aviation flight activity was allowed in the temporary flight restriction (TFR) areas established in the New York, Boston, and Washington metropolitan areas. The FAA finally allowed pilots to move their aircraft out of those airports over the Columbus Day holiday weekend. These were, however, essentially one-way flights: airplanes could leave, but there was no indication when they might be allowed back.[52]

A variety of general aviation operations faced difficulties under the new restrictions. Companies that towed aerial banners, for example, were barred from flying over the venues of major sporting events and other outdoor gatherings. Similarly, the nation's small blimp fleet remained pretty much grounded, as were news helicopters. General aviation airports that continued to operate under the enhanced Class B airspace restrictions, and even more so under the TFRs, faced severe hardships. Many of these airports depended on revenue from flight training operations, fuel sales, and other such day-to-day activities to make a profit. With the restrictions, their incomes fell drastically and they faced uncertain futures.

Spokespeople for general aviation were often harsh in their criticism of the continued restrictions on flying. They were especially critical of flight rules that allowed student pilots to make VFR flights in enhanced Class B airspace but kept their flight instructors and other certified pilots on the ground. The spokespeople frequently evoked long-held arguments associating flying with basic American freedoms.[53]

In December, 2001, Transportation Secretary Norman Y. Mineta, announced the lifting of enhanced Class B flight restrictions around twenty-seven major metropolitan airports, clearing the way for VFR flight operations and normal flight training to resume. This action also largely lifted the restrictions placed on news and traffic helicopters, sightseeing aircraft, blimps, and banner towers. However, the TFRs regarding sporting events and large outdoor gatherings, as well as those issued for the Washington, Boston, and New York areas, remained in place. The FAA also issued TFRs for areas surrounding the nation's nuclear power plants. Before September 11, the FAA issued very few TFRs—and then only under very special circumstances. After September 11, TFRs became a way of life for pilots in the United States. Despite strong protests from many in aviation, particularly the AOPA, they were issued frequently—often with little advance notice.[54]

As noted above, general aviation airports continued to face severe challenges in the wake of September 11. Four small airports, three in the Washington area and one in Chicago, faced particular hardships. Meigs in Chicago already faced opposition to its continued operation. The mayor seemed determined to close it in order to realize his vision of lakefront development. Meigs closed on September 11 and remained closed for a month. However, in the last months of 2001, the situation at Meigs proved that with airports all politics is local. In addition to the lakefront development he had planned for the Meigs site, the mayor also wanted to gain state support for a program to expand O'Hare International Airport. The governor of Illinois, in turn, wanted a new airport built in Peotone—a project not favored by Mayor Daley. Intense negotiations ensued. General aviation interests lobbied Illinois governor George Ryan relentlessly and a deal was announced on December 5, 2001. Meigs would stay open until 2026, barring action by the state legislature, which could not take any action in any case until after 2006. The state, meanwhile, would support the expansion of O'Hare, and Chicago's mayor would back the plan to build the new airport at Peotone. Fees paid by United Airlines and American Airlines would cover the operating deficit at Meigs.[55]

Although the situation at Meigs ultimately had a happy ending, the prospects were less promising for the College Park, Washington Executive/Hyde Field, and Potomac airports near Washington, D.C. These three airports, like others throughout the country, closed on September 11. Unlike the majority of airports in the United States, however, they remained closed for nearly six months. All three fell under the TFR imposed in the Washington, D.C., area. Two, Executive/Hyde Field and Potomac Field, were within five miles of Andrews Air Force Base, home of Air Force One. Flight schools, maintenance shops, businesses conducting aerial surveying, and crop dusting all suffered losses in the wake of September 11. Many, if not most, of these businesses, however, were back in operation within weeks. The various businesses based at the three Washington airports, in contrast, could not resume operations as quickly. Many were forced to move to other local airports. As a result, they suffered not only from the general decline in business after September 11, but also from the loss of home-based clientele and the expenses associated with moving. A number lost valuable employees. The airports themselves suffered as the rents from these businesses and the fuel revenues they generated dried up.[56]

In late February, 2002, the FAA finally allowed College Park Airport and Potomac Field to reopen. Strict security measures were imposed, however, and only pilots based at those airports were allowed to use the facilities. On the first day of operations, only about ten pilots returned to College Park, and even fewer to Potomac. Executive/Hyde Field opened shortly thereafter, but the FAA shut it down in May because of violations of the new security measures.[57] As of late June, 2002, it was still closed.

All of aviation suffered as a result of the events on September 11, 2001. General aviation and the organizations that represent it have long experience dealing with the federal government. For the most part they responded quickly, professionally, and forcefully to the challenges posed by the terrorist attacks. It was not clear when, if ever, general aviation would return to "normal." Temporary Flight Restrictions and other new security measures have changed the world in which general aviation pilots and businesses operate. Following nearly two decades of a difficult business environment and a declining number of pilots, forecasting the future of general aviation is difficult at best. It is, however, a very important part of America's aerial transportation system, providing necessary, even vital services. Moreover, it still manages to capture the imagination of at least a few dreamers hoping for a future in which many, if not most, will fly.

A Vans RV-6 homebuilt aircraft (completed in 1995) powered by a
Lycoming O-360 engine. Photo courtesy Michael G. Williams Aviation.

Notes

Preface

1. For a definition of the "winged gospel" see Joseph J. Corn, *The Winged Gospel: America's Romance with Aviation, 1900–1950* (New York: Oxford University Press, 1983), 3–27.
2. Ibid., 91–111.
3. Ibid., 71–90.
4. Ibid., 135–37.
5. Those works on balloons, dirigibles, and blimps include Tom D. Crouch, *The Eagle Aloft: Two Centuries of the Balloon in America* (Washington, D.C.: Smithsonian Institution Press, 1983); Dale Topping, *When Giants Roamed the Sky: Karl Arnstein and the Rise of Airships from Zeppelin to Goodyear*, ed. Eric Brothers (Akron, Ohio: University of Akron Press, 2000); Guillaume De Syon, *Zeppelin: Germany and the Airship, 1900–1939* (Baltimore: Johns Hopkins University Press, 2001).

Chapter 1: From First Seeds to Early Blossoms

1. For information on the Wright Exhibition Company see Tom D. Crouch, *The Bishop's Boys: A Life of Wilbur and Orville Wright* (New York: W. W. Norton, 1989), 424–39. For information on the Curtiss Exhibition Company see Cecil R. Roseberry, *Glenn Curtiss: Pioneer of Flight* (New York: Syracuse University Press, 1991), 281–307.
2. Roseberry, *Glenn Curtiss*, 302–307. Beachy is also enshrined in the National Aviation Hall of Fame (NAHF). A biography is available through the NAHF Internet site: http://nationalaviation.org.
3. For information on one of the Curtiss Flying Schools, one that offered training to civilian as well as military students, see Roseberry, *Glenn Curtiss*, 326–27. For an account of activities at the Wright Flying School near Dayton, Ohio—where both civilians and military personnel received training—see Lois E. Walker and Shelby E. Wickham, *From Huffmann Prairie to the Moon: The History of Wright-Patterson Air Force Base* (Washington, D.C.: GPO, 1986), 10–12. For information on early flight schools in Illinois see Howard L. Scamehorn, *Balloons to Jets: A Century of Aeronautics in Illinois, 1855–1955* (reprint, Carbondale: Southern Illinois University Press, 2000), 66–67, 70–72.

4. Claudia M. Oakes, *United States Women in Aviation Through World War I* (Washington, D.C.: Smithsonian Institution Press, 1978), 25–29.

5. John Underwood, *The Stinsons: A Pictorial History* (Glendale, Calif.: Heritage Press, 1976), 5–10. See also Henry Holden with Capt. Lori Griffith, *Ladybirds: The Untold Story of Women Pilots in America* (Mount Freedom, N.J.: Black Hawk, 1991), 30–32.

6. Underwood, *Stinsons,* 22–23.

7. David Young and Neal Callahan, *Fill the Heavens With Commerce: Chicago Aviation, 1855–1926* (Chicago: Chicago Review Press, 1981), 25–26, 52, 77.

8. Ibid., 45–56, 64–65. See also Scamehorn, *Balloons to Jets,* 55, 70.

9. The Baysdorfers modeled their first airplane after the Curtiss craft because of the patent fight between Curtiss and the Wright brothers. As part of their strategy in the fight, the Wrights took anyone copying their machine to court, whereas Curtiss freely allowed people to copy his design. For information on the Baysdorfers, see Robert E. Adwers, *Rudder, Stick and Throttle: Research and Reminiscences on Flying in Nebraska* (Omaha, Neb.: Making History, 1994), 67–157. See also Janet R. Daly Bednarek, "From the Baysdorfers to the Strategic Air Command: Aviation Dreams in Omaha, Nebraska, 1908–1948," *Journal of the West* 36 (July 1997): 39–41.

10. For the stories of other amateur "homebuilders" see Scamehorn, *Balloons to Jets,* 40–56; Frank Joseph Rowe and Craig Miner, *Borne on the South Wind: A Century of Kansas Aviation* (Wichita, Kans.: Wichita Eagle and Beacon, 1994), 30–35; Noel E. Allard and Gerald N. Sandvick, *Minnesota Aviation History, 1857–1945* (Chaska, Minn.: MAHB, 1993), 10–24; Michael J. Goc, *Forward in Flight: The History of Aviation in Wisconsin* (Friendship, Wisc.: New Past Press, 1998), 11–21; William F. Trimble, *High Frontier: A History of Aeronautics in Pennsylvania* (Pittsburgh: University of Pittsburgh Press, 1982), 79–84.

11. Bruce Bissonette, *The Wichita 4: Cessna, Moellendick, Beech and Stearman* (Destin, Fla.: Aviation Heritage, 1999), 9–18; Edward H. Phillips, *Cessna: A Master's Expression* (Eagan, Minn.: Flying Books, 1985), 5–33.

12. The best work on the early airmail pilots is William M. Leary, *Aerial Pioneers: The U.S. Air Mail Service, 1918–1927* (Washington, D.C.: Smithsonian Institution Press, 1985). See 253–56 for a list of fatalities among pioneer airmail pilots.

13. For a history of the early air races and air racers, see Terry Gwynn-Jones, *Farther and Faster: Aviation's Adventuring Years, 1909–1939* (Washington, D.C.: Smithsonian Institution Press, 1991), 3–99.

14. A number of biographies are available on Charles Lindbergh, as well as his own autobiographical works. One of the most recent biographies is A. Scott Berg, *Lindbergh* (New York: G. Putnam's Sons, 1998). For information on Lindbergh's life as a barnstormer, see 59–74.

15. Oakes, *United States Women in Aviation Through World War I,* 39–41; Kathleen Brooks-Pazmany, *United States Women in Aviation, 1919–1929* (Washington, D.C.: Smithsonian Institution Press, 1991), 9–10.

16. For a general biography of Bessie Coleman see Doris L. Rich, *Queen Bess: Daredevil Aviator* (Washington, D.C.: Smithsonian Institution Press, 1993). See also Brooks-Pazmany, *United States Women, 1919–1929,* 9.

17. See Bissonette, *Wichita 4;* Rowe and Miner, *Borne on the South Wind,* 52–69.

18. Mabry I. Anderson, *Low and Slow: An Insider's History of Agricultural Aviation* (San Francisco: California Farmer, 1986), 5–17.

19. Ruth Reinhold briefly explores the value of some of these early experiments in the use of aircraft, including how aerial photographs were used to help map the Grand Canyon. See Ruth Reinhold, *Sky Pioneering: Arizona in Aviation History* (Tucson: University of Arizona Press, 1982), 105. The person most identified with aerial photography is Sherman M. Fairchild. For an examination of Fairchild, his cameras, and his airplanes, as well as a look at the work of Fairchild Aerial Surveys, see Thomas J. Campanella, *Cities from the Sky: An Aerial Portrait of America* (New York: Princeton Architectural Press, 2001).

20. Crouch, *Bishop's Boys,* 338, 412, 426, 457, 458, 465–66. For information on the first Wright engine, see Howard R. DuFour, *Charles E. Taylor: The Wright Brother's Mechanician* (Dayton, Ohio: Howard R. DuFour, 1997).

21. See Louis S. Casey, *Curtiss: The Hammondsport Era, 1907–1915* (New York: Crown, 1981).

22. See Tom D. Crouch, *Blériot XI: The Story of a Classic Aircraft* (Washington, D.C.: Smithsonian Institution Press, 1982).

23. See Herschel Smith, *Aircraft Piston Engines: From the Manly Baltzer to the Continental Tiara* (New York: McGraw-Hill, 1981); Bill Gunston, *The Development of Piston Aero Engines* (Somerset, England: Patrick Stevens, 1991), 97–128.

24. For information on the Loughhead S-1 see Richard Sanders Allen, *The Northrup Story, 1929–1939* (New York: Orion Books, 1990), 4–5; idem., *Revolution in the Sky: The Lockheeds of Aviation's Golden Age* (New York: Orion Books, 1990), 9–10. The Curtiss Oriole is best know for its connection to Harold Pitcairn and especially for the fact that he used Oriole wings purchased from Curtiss on his PA-3 Orowing. See Frank Kingston Smith, *Legacy of Wings: The Harold F. Pitcairn Story* (New York: Jason Aronson, 1981), 51–53, 54, 57, 59, 62, 81–82. For information on the Bellanca CF see Jay Spenser, *Bellanca CF: The Emergence of the Cabin Monoplane in the U.S.* (Washington, D.C.: Smithsonian Institution Press, 1982).

25. See Eric Schatzberg, *Wings of Wood, Wings of Metal: Culture and Technical Choice in American Airplane Materials, 1914–1945* (Princeton, N.J.: Princeton University Press, 1999), 3–21.

26. See Fred O. Kobernuss, *WACO: Symbol of Courage and Excellence,* vol. 2 (Destin, Fla.: Aviation Heritage Books, 1999), 1–37.

Chapter 2: The "Golden Age," 1926–39

1. For a discussion of early city and state regulation of aviation, see Janet R. Daly Bednarek, *America's Airports: Airfield Development, 1918–1947* (College Station: Texas A&M University Press, 2001), 38–40.

2. For background on the development and passage of the Air Commerce Act, see Nick A Komons, *Bonfires to Beacons: Federal Civil Aviation Policy Under the Air Commerce Act, 1926–1938* (reprint, Washington, D.C.: Smithsonian Institution Press, 1989), 65–88.

3. Most works dealing with the Air Commerce Act focus on the relationship between that landmark piece of legislation and the development of commercial aviation in the United States. Indeed, the act was designed in large part to help stimulate commercial aviation. The act did, however, have ramifications for what was then known as private flying. While the Air Commerce Act itself was important, more valuable in terms of understanding its impact is a look at the regulations created as a result of the act. *United States Aviation Reports,* published annually since 1928, is an invaluable source for information on aviation regulations. For information on regulations governing pilot licensing, see Arnold W. Knauth et al., *1928 United States Aviation Reports* (Baltimore, Md.: United States Aviation Reports, 1928), 390–99.

4. Ibid., 366, 368–83.

5. The story of the development of the C-2 and C-3 is drawn from Jay Spenser, *Aeronca C-2: The Story of the Flying Bathtub* (Washington, D.C.: Smithsonian Institution Press, 1978).

6. See Bednarek, *America's Airports,* 100–102.

7. Corn, *Winged Gospel,* 98–99; Tom Crouch, "An Airplane for Everyman: The Department of Commerce and the Light Airplane Industry, 1933–1937," in *Innovation and the Development of Flight,* ed. Roger Launius (College Station: Texas A&M University Press, 1999), 166–75.

8. For information on the safe airplane program, especially the W–1, see Corn, *Winged Gospel,* 96–100; Crouch, "An Airplane for Everyman," 176–78; Fred E. Weick and James R. Hansen, *From the Ground Up: The Autobiography of an Aeronautical Engineer* (Washington, D.C.: Smithsonian Institution Press, 1988), 126–58.

9. See Corn, *Winged Gospel,* 100–104; Crouch, "An Airplane for Everyman," 178–80.

10. For an evaluation of why the program failed, see Crouch, "An Airplane for Everyman," 180–84.

11. George Hardie Jr., "The Long Road Back, Part II: The North American Light Plane Club," *Sport Aviation,* Mar., 1986, 28–30.

12. Ibid., 29–30; idem., "The Long Road Back, Part III: The Light Airplane Association of America," *Sport Aviation,* April, 1986, 30.

13. Hardie, "Long Road, Part II," 30; idem., "Long Road, Part III," 36–37.

14. Ibid.

15. See Bednarek, *America's Airports,* 102–106.

16. Claudia M. Oakes, *United States Women in Aviation, 1929–1939* (Washington, D.C.: Smithsonian Institution Press, 1991), 9; Works Progress Administration, *America Spreads Her Wings* (Washington, D.C.: GPO, 1937), 10–11; Dean Jaros, *Heroes With Legacy: American Airwomen, 1912–1944* (Niwot: University Press of Colorado, 1993), 35–37.

17. Dominick A. Pisano, *To Fill the Sky with Pilots: The Civilian Pilot Training Program, 1939–46* (Urbana and Chicago: University of Illinois Press, 1993), 1–8.

18. Ibid., 9–14, 131.

19. Ibid., 72–77.

20. Ibid., 68–72.

21. Ibid., 83–110, 111–23.

22. See Bednarek, *America's Airports*, 67–85.

23. See Janet R. Daly Bednarek, "False Beacon: Regional Planning and the Location of Dayton's Municipal Airport," *Ohio History* 106 (summer–autumn, 1997).

24. See Bednarek, *America's Airports*, 48–50, 79–88.

25. Anderson, *Low and Slow*, 23–39, 43–53, 81–139.

26. To trace the development of the Cessna Airmaster, see Joseph Juptner, *U.S. Civil Aircraft*, vol. 6, 260–63; ibid., vol. 7, 84–86; ibid., vol. 8 (Fallbrook, Calif.: Aero Publishers, 1974, 1978, 1980), 9–12.

27. See Edward H. Phillips, *Beechcraft, Pursuit of Perfection: A History of Beechcraft Airplanes* (Eagan, Minn.: Flying Books, 1992), 4–21, 25–27, 91.

28. Gwynn-Jones, *Farther and Faster*, 154–57, 161, 174.

29. Ibid., 158–61, 163, 175–76.

30. Ibid., 159–60, 172–74.

31. Ibid., 164–67, 170.

32. Ibid., 164, 165, 167, 169–72, 175, 176–78.

33. In October, 1989, *AOPA Pilot* published a multisection, fifty-year history of the organization written by Thomas H. Horne. See idem., "The Beginning: 1939," *AOPA Pilot*, Oct., 1989, 44–48.

34. Ibid., 48–50; idem., "The War Years: 40's" *AOPA Pilot*, Oct., 1989, 55.

35. Jaros, *Heroes*, 41–42.

36. See Oakes, *United States Women, 1929–1939*, 29–47.

37. See Corn, *Winged Gospel*, 71–90.

38. Jaros, *Heroes*, 29, 40, 42–44; Oakes, *United States Women, 1929–1939*, 9–11.

39. Jaros, *Heroes*, 37–38; Oakes, *United States Women, 1929–1939*, 11–14.

40. See Raymond Eugene Peters and Clinton M. Arnold, *Black Americans in Aviation* (San Diego: Neyenesch Printers, n.d.), 3–7.

41. In 1994, the Smithsonian Institution Press reprinted William Powell's work *Black Wings*, first published in 1934. This brief account of Powell's career is drawn from the introduction to the Smithsonian publication. See Von Hardesty, "Introduction," in William J. Powell, *Black Aviator: The Story of William J. Powell* (Washington, D.C.: Smithsonian Institution Press, 1994), xi–xxiv.

42. See Peters and Arnold, *Black Americans in Aviation*, 4–5; Von Hardesty and Dominick A. Pisano, *Black Wings: The American Black in Aviation* (Washington, D.C.: Smithsonian Institution Press, 1983), 12, 16–17.

43. Peters and Arnold, *Black Americans in Aviation*, 6–7; Pisano, *To Fill the Sky*, 74.

44. Pisano, *To Fill the Sky*, 74–77.

45. Smith, *Aircraft Piston Engines*, 103–108.

46. Kobernuss, *WACO*, 2:71–78, 89–112.

47. Smith, *Aircraft Piston Engines*, 118–19, 153–55, 156, 177, 180–81.

48. Ibid., 155–56, 157–59, 194–97.

49. For information on the history and development of the Taylor Cub and Piper Cub, see Chet Peek, *The Taylorcraft Story* (Terre Haute, Ind.: SunShine House, 1992), 1–11; Edward H. Phillips, *Piper: A Legend Aloft* (Eagan Minn.: Flying Books International, 1993), 1–23.

50. See John C. Swick, *The Luscombe Story* (Terre Haute, Ind.: SunShine House, 1987) 15–75; James B. Zazas, *Visions of Luscombe: The Early Years* (Terre Haute, Ind.: SunShine House, 1993).

51. Weick and Hansen, *From the Ground Up*, 126–91.

Chapter 3: For the Duration, 1939—45

1. William T. Piper with D. J. Duffin, *Private Flying: Today and Tomorrow* (New York: Pitman, 1949), 54–67.

2. Edgar F. Raines Jr., *Eyes of the Artillery: The Origins of Modern U.S. Army Aviation in World War II* (Washington, D.C.: Center of Military History, 2000), 14–29, 31–56.

3. Ibid., 325–33.

4. For information on WACO's participation in the World War II glider program and the consequences for the company, see Janet R. Daly Bednarek, "'Damned Fool Idea': The American Combat Glider Program, 1941–1947," *Air Power History* 43 (winter, 1996): 38–49.

5. Peter Jakab, *Visions of a Flying Machine: The Wright Brothers and the Process of Invention* (Washington, D.C.: Smithsonian Institution Press, 1990), 184.

6. See Terence Horsley, *Soaring Flight* (New York: Current Books, 1946), 1–5; Richard W. Wolters, *The Art and Technique of Soaring* (New York: McGraw–Hill, 1971), 23.

7. Holden with Griffith, *Ladybirds*, 58.

8. Horsley, *Soaring Flight*, 303; Paul A. Schweizer, *Wings Like Eagles: The Story of Soaring in the United States* (Washington, D.C.: Smithsonian Institution Press, 1988), 13–30.

9. Wolters, *Art and Technique*, 23; Horsley, *Soaring Flight*, 304; Paul Schweizer, *Wings Like Eagles*, 31–49.

9. William Schweizer, *Soaring with the Schweizers: The Fifty–Year History of Their Aviation Adventures* (Falls Church, Va.: Rivilo Books, 1991), 5–6, 11, 44.

10. Ibid., 1–15, 25–27, 40–42.

11. Information on the history of the Civil Air Patrol is drawn from Robert E. Neprud, *Flying Minute Men: The Story of the Civil Air Patrol* (Revised, Reprinted Washington, D.C.: Office of Air Force History, 1988), especially 21–46, 77–109. For more on CAP activity during World War II, see Howard Mingos, ed., *The Aircraft Year Book for 1945* (New York: Lanciar, 1945), 181–88.

12. The Internet site for the National Smokejumpers Association features a multipart history of the program, including background information on aerial fire fighting, at http://www.smokejumpers.com. For information on conscientious objectors involved in the smoke-jumping program during World War II, see Sarah Baker, "For Them, Enemy Was Fire" *Des Moines Register* July 16, 2000. See also, Mark Matthews, "Fighting fires, and indignities" *High Country News,* August 7, 1995, http://www.hcn.org/servlets/hcn.Article?article_id=1190.

13. See Anderson, *Low and Slow*, 116.

14. Carl Benjamin Eielson is among those enshrined in the National Aviation Hall of Fame. The biographical information on him is drawn from that organization's Internet site: http://nationalaviation.org.

15. This material is drawn from a biography of one of Alaska's famed bush pilots, Bob Reeve. See Beth Day, *Glacier Pilot: The Story of Bob Reeve and the Flyers Who Pushed Back Alaska's Air Frontiers* (New York: Henry Holt, 1957), 15–187, 188–236.

16. Ibid., 237–83. For more information on the work of the U.S. Army Corps of Engineers, see Lisa Mighetto and Carla Homstad, *Engineering in the Far North: A History of the U.S. Army Engineer District in Alaska, 1867–1992* (Missoula, Mont.: Historical Research Associates, 1997), 47–54.

17. Day, *Glacier Pilot*, 284–85.

18. Apparently about fifty women found employment as instructors with the CPTP. One historian who briefly looked at this concluded that their participation was small and the CPTP did not aggressively seek women instructors. The CAA did, however, create a program to train women instructor pilots under the direction of Phoebe Omlie. Although a proposal to train five hundred women instructor pilots was rejected, the CAA continued to support the training of women as instructors during the war. See Deborah Douglas, *United States Women in Aviation, 1940–1985* (Washington, D.C.: Smithsonian Institution Press, 1991), 7–9.

19. See Diane Ruth Armour Bartels, *Sharpie: The Life Story of Evelyn Sharp, Nebraska's Aviatrix* (Lincoln, Neb.: Dageforde, 1996).

20. For background information on Jackie Cochran, see Jaros, *Heroes*, 49–51, and Oakes, *United States Women, 1929–1939*, 32–39. For background information on Nancy Harkness Love, see Marianne Verges, *On Silver Wings: The Women Airforce Service Pilots of World War II, 1942–1944* (New York: Ballantine Books, 1991), 8–11.

21. The history of the WASPs was somewhat "lost" in the decades immediately after World War II. In the mid-1970s, the military first allowed women into the service academies and into the seats of noncombat aircraft. These women were initially celebrated as the first of their gender to fly for the military. However, the success of these young women promoted a number of other women, by then in their senior years, to come forward to remind the armed forces and the nation of their service as military pilots during World War II. Congress recognized their service by granting them veteran status in 1976. Since their rediscovery, a fairly substantial body of literature has appeared. It includes general popular histories of the program, memoirs, and some more scholarly work. Most of these books contain the essential background information on the program. For examples of the literature and information on the basic contours of the WASP program see Verges, *On Silver Wings;* Sally Van Wagenen Keil, *Those Wonderful Women In Their Flying Machines: The Unknown Heroines of World War II* (New York: Four Directions Press, 1979); Jaros, *Heroes*, 52–68; and Douglas, *United States Women, 1940–1985*, 27–56.

22. Verges, *Silver Wings*, 3–8, 22–23, 45–46.

23. For a sense of what former WASP pilots did after World War II, see Jaros, *Heroes*, 115–58.

24. For a critical evaluation of these predictions, see Pisano, *To Fill the Sky*, 131–34.

25. For a sense of how general aviation aircraft manufacturers prepared for the predicted postwar boom, see Piper, *Private Flying*, 67–69.

26. See "Airport Planning for the Future," *Western Flying,* May, 1943, 73.

27. See Don Forbes, "Airparks for Tomorrow," *Western Flying,* February, 1944, 52–53.

Chapter 4: Up from the Ashes, 1945–80

1. Roger E. Bilstein, *The American Aerospace Industry* (New York: Twayne, 1996), 146. See also Corn, *Winged Gospel,* 91–111.

2. Statistics on "General Aviation Airplanes Shipped by Unit" from 1948 through 2000 are found in General Aviation Manufacturers Association, *2001 GA Statistical Data Book,* http://www.generalaviation.org/databook/2001/index.html. The statistics on airplanes shipped by unit are on page 4.

3. Bilstein, *American Aerospace Industry,* 148–50.

4. For information on WACO aircraft, see Bednarek, "'Damned Fool Idea,'" 48. For information on Aeronca, see that company's Internet site: http://www.aeroncainc.com. For information on Luscombe, see Swick, *Luscombe Story,* 91–163.

5. Suart I. Rochester, *Takeoff at Mid-Century: Federal Civil Aviation Policy in the Eisenhower Years, 1953–1961* (Washington, D.C.: U.S. Department of Transportation, Federal Aviation Administration, 1976), 174–79.

6. See ibid., 34, 51, 60, 57–78.

7. Ibid., 169–77.

8. Rochester, *Takeoff at Mid-Century,* 176–77, 266; Thomas A. Horne, "Transitions: Fiftes," *AOPA Pilot,* Oct., 1989, 67–71.

9. Rochester, *Takeoff at Mid-Century,* 196–97, 215–16.

10. Ibid., 265–72; Horne, "Transitions," 70–71.

11. Richard J. Kent Jr., *Safe, Separated, and Soaring: A History of Federal Civil Aviation Policy, 1961–1972* (Washington, D.C.: Department of Transportation, Federal Aviation Administration, 1980), 31, 35–38; Thomas A. Horne, "Growth and Challenge: Sixties," *AOPA Pilot,* Oct., 1989, 76–77.

12. Kent, *Safe, Separated, and Soaring,* 113–15, 116–22, 190, 322–25; Horne, "Growth and Challenge," 76–82.

13. See Thomas A. Horne, "Dealing with the Feds: 70s," *AOPA Pilot,* Oct., 1989, 87–92; see also Edmund Preston, *Troubled Passage: The Federal Aviation Administration During the Nixon-Ford Term, 1973–1977* (Washington, D.C.: Department of Transportation, Federal Aviation Administration, 1987), 19–20, 57–59, 61–69, 72–77.

14. Bilstein, *American Aerospace Industry,* 146.

15. Ibid., 154.

16. Phillips, *Beechcraft,* 53–54, 56–61, 64–67.

17. See "General Aviation Airplanes Shipped by Unit," *2001 GA Statistical Data Book,* 4.

18. William Lear is enshrined in the National Aviation Hall of Fame. For biographical information, see http://nationalaviation.org/enshrinee/lear.html.

19. Bilstein, *American Aerospace Industry,* 155–57.

20. For more information on Learjets following the sale to Gates Rubber, see the

National Aviation Hall of Fame biographical entry for Harry B. Combs at http://nationalaviation.org/enshrinee/combs.html.

21. Jay Spenser, *Whirlybirds: A History of the U.S. Helicopter Pioneers* (Seattle: University of Washington Press and Museum of Flight, 1998), 3–13. The American Institute of Aeronautics and Astronautics (AIAA) has set up an Internet site to commemorate the hundredth anniversary of powered flight. That site includes a special section on the history of the helicopter. For more information, see http://www.flight100.org/history/helicopter.html.

22. Spenser, *Whirlybirds*, 428.

23. Ibid., 428–29, 431–38, 440–46.

24. Bilstein, *American Aerospace Industry*, 157–59.

25. William Schweizer, *Soaring*, 44–46.

26. Ibid., 73–79, 83–84, 89, 94, 96, 105, 109, 111, 117–19, 121, 124–25, 127–28, 130, 137–38, 142–43, 148, 153–54, 155, 158–59, 162, 168–69, 172, 179–80, 185, 189, 195–96, 199.

27. George Hardie Jr., "The Long Road Back, Part V: The American Airmen's Association," *Sport Aviation*, June, 1986, 35.

28. Ibid. For more information on the history of federal regulation of homebuilt aircraft, see Bob Burbick, "Experimental Aircraft Certificates," *Sport Aviation*, July, 1986, 60–62.

29. Hardie, "Long Road Back, Part V," 35–37.

30. George Hardie Jr., "The Long Road Back, Part VI: Founding the Experimental Aircraft Association," *Sport Aviation*, July, 1986, 57–59.

31. For more information on the history and development of the EAA see the organization's Internet site at http://www.eaa.org.

32. Peters and Arnold, *Black Americans in Aviation*, 15–17.

33. For information on the life of Neal Loving, see Neal V. Loving, *Loving's Love: A Black American's Experience in Aviation* (Washington, D.C.: Smithsonian Institution Press, 1994).

34. Peters and Arnold, *Black Americans in Aviation*, 19–21. For more information on Edward Gibbs and Negro Airmen International, see the organization's Internet site at http://www.blackwings.org.

35. See Douglas, *United States Women, 1940–1985*, 59–60, 94. Olive Ann Beach is an enshrined in the National Aviation Hall of Fame. For more on her life, see http://nationalaviation.org/enshrinee/beecholive.html.

36. Douglas, *United States Women, 1940–1985*, 76–77, 88–89. For more information on the Whirly Girls see that organization's Internet site at http://www.whirlygirls.org.

37. Douglas, *United States Women, 1940–1985*, 62–64, 74–76, 105–106.

38. Ibid., 89–90.

39. For a sense of the wide variety of activities in which women participate, see Carolyn Russo, *Women and Flight: Portraits of Contemporary Women Pilots* (Washington, D.C.: Smithsonian Institution Press, 1997). This work contains photographs and short biographies of women aviators from all parts of the United States.

40. Information on Betty Green came from her obituary, posted April 10, 1997, on

the Internet site maintained by the Mission Aviation Fellowship at http://www.maf.org. William Piper is also mentioned in the humanitarian uses of light aircraft. See Piper, *Private Flying*, 118–21.

41. Information on the history of aerial tankers can be found at the Aerial Firefighting Industry Association's Internet site at www.afia.org. In addition to the civilian tankers, since the early 1970s, some Air National Guard and Air Force Reserve units have been called on to fly aerial tankers in emergencies as backups to the civilian aerial tankers. These are C-130s equipped with the Modular Airborne Fire Fighting System (MAFFS). For more information on MAFFS, see http://www.fs.fed.us/fire/fire_new/aviation/fixed_wing/maffs.

42. For information on the Bureau of Land Management's National Interagency Fire Center, see http://www.nifc.gov. For information on the Department of the Interior's Office of Aircraft Services, see http://www.oas.gov. For a sense of aerial fire fighting at the end of the twentieth century, see Michael Maya Charles, "Long, Hot Summer," *AOPA Pilot*, Oct., 2000, 93–98.

43. See Rinker Buck, *Flight of Passage* (New York: Hyperion, 1997).

44. Anderson, *Low and Slow*, 43.

45. Ibid., 47–48.

46. Ibid., 46, 76–79, 130–31. For more information on the National Agricultural Aviation Association, see http://www.agaviation.org.

47. For information on the development of the AG-1, see Weick and Hansen, *From the Ground Up*, 241–327.

48. Anderson, *Low and Slow*, 62–67.

49. See William Schweizer, *Soaring*, 97–99, 104–105, 107–108, 113, 118, 129–30, 142, 144, 153, 173, 187–88, 193–95, 200.

50. For more information on the agricultural use of helicopters, see Spenser, *Whirlybirds*, 217, 218, 318, 320, 322, 428–31.

51. Phillips, *Piper*, 41–58.

52. Ibid., 46, 52–55, 57–58, 74, 82–88, 100–102.

53. Phillips, *Cessna*, 125–30; Donald M. Pattillo, *History in the Making: Eighty Turbulent Years in the American General Aviation Industry* (New York: McGraw–Hill, 1998), 85–6.

54. Phillips, *Beechcraft*, 18, 36–37, 44, 62–63.

55. Michael J. H. Taylor, ed., *Jane's Encyclopedia of Aviation* (New York: Portland House, 1989), 26–27.

56. Spenser, *Whirlybirds*, 214, 218–21, 385–90, 428, 429.

57. Taylor, *Jane's*, 146, 522.

58. For more information on the R-22, see http://www.robinsonheli.com/BetaII.htm.

59. Smith, *Aircraft Piston Engines*, 204–206.

60. Rick A. Leyes II and William A Fleming, *The History of North American Small Gas Turbine Engines* (Washington, D.C., and Reston, Va.: Smithsonian Institution Press and American Institute of Aeronautics and Astronautics, 1999), 441–53, 539–56.

61. Smith, *Aircraft Piston Engines*, 206–207.

62. Little has been published on the history of avionics. For more information on various products designed for the general aviation market, see the Internet sites of the two companies most involved in that market: NARCO at http://www.narco-avionics.com, and Bendix/King at http://www.bendixking.com.

Chapter 5: Dreams Once Again Deferred, Post-1980

1. See "General Aviation Airplanes by Units Shipped," *2001 GA Statistical Data Book,* 4.

2. For information on Executive Jets, Incorporated, and NetJets, including a history of the company and the concept of fractional ownership, see http://www.netjets.com/index.asp. For a look at the fractional aircraft-ownership market, see Anthony L. Velocci Jr., "Avolar Failure Belies Strength of Fractionals," *Aviation Week and Space Technology,* Apr. 1, 2002, 36–37.

3. For a discussion of the issue of liability and the cost of aircraft, see John S. Yodice, "Product Liability," *AOPA Pilot,* Feb., 1988, 31–33.

4. For information on Quicksilver aircraft, see http://www.quicksilveraircraft.com.

5. For a sense of the growth of general aviation manufacturing in the late 1990s, see "Raytheon Aircraft Leads 1995 Sales," *AOPA Pilot,* Mar., 1996, 28; "GAMA: Most deliveries since 1990," *AOPA Pilot,* Apr., 1997, 43; "GAMA proclaims 1997 'a banner year,'" *AOPA Pilot,* Apr., 1998, 32–33; "Aircraft billings and shipments highest since 1984," *AOPA Pilot,* Apr., 1999, 42–43. The last article listed notes that general aviation manufacturers shipped more than two thousand aircraft in 1999, the first time they had done that since 1984. However, the article also pointed out that the industry shipped more than seventeen thousand aircraft in 1978.

6. See "Pilots by Certificate and Rating," *1997 GA Statistical Data Book,* 16, available at http://www.generalaviation.org/pages/statistics.shtml. See also the information available at the FAA's Internet site at http://www.faa.gov. The FAA's Aviation Policy and Plans Division publishes *U.S. Civil Airman Statistics* annually. Information on pilots and student pilots can be found in Table 1, "Estimated Active Airman Certificates Held, December 31, 1991–2000," in the 2000 edition of that publication, available at http://www.api.faa.gov/civilair/DocList.asp?ID=33.

7. For information on the background of the Young Eagles program and the most current information on the number of young people flown, see http://www.eaa.org.

8. Information on amateur-built aircraft can be found at the FAA's Internet site: http://www.faa.gov. The FAA's Aviation Policy and Plans Division published a *Statistical Handbook of Aviation, 1996.* This publication is available on-line at http://www.api.faa.gov/pubs.asp?Lev2=2. Statistics on amateur-built experimental aircraft are found in Table 8.2, "Active General Aviation Aircraft by Aircraft Type."

9. See James Fallows, *Free Flight: From Airline Hell to a New Age of Travel* (New

York: Public Affairs, 2001), 39–42, 85–98, 106–31. This work essentially focuses, rather uncritically, on Cirrus as it relates to NASA's Small Aircraft Transportation System and related programs. In many ways, this work acts as something of an advertisement for the company and the NASA program. One can certainly see the lasting influence of the winged gospel on aviation enthusiasts such as James Fallows in this work. Fallows is a private pilot who flies a Cirrus.

10. Vera Foster Rollo, *Burt Rutan: Reinventing the Airplane* (Lanham, Md.: Maryland Historical Press, 1991), 21, 28, 32

11. It is uncertain why the Wright brothers chose to place their horizontal stabilizer (which they called a forward rudder and is now known as an elevator) ahead of the wings, but they quickly discovered the benefits of this configuration, especially in a stall. A stall occurs when an aircraft's wings exceed a critical angle of attack. Lift is disrupted and the aircraft basically stops flying. In conventional aircraft, the nose can pitch downward suddenly, causing the plane to rapidly lose altitude. If the aircraft is low enough when this happens, it can crash before the pilot is able to take action to arrest the stall. Although the Wrights were not certain exactly what a stall was or how it occurred, they found that their gliders with the canard configuration prevented the sharp nose-down reaction of a conventionally configured aircraft. This was because the canard stalled before the wings, which continued to provide lift. As the canard regained lift, it would automatically level the aircraft. For a discussion of the Wrights' use of the canard configuration, see Jakab, *Visions of a Flying Machine*, 70–73.

12. Jack Cox, "VeriViggen Vignette," *Sport Aviation*, Mar., 1975, 58.

13. Rollo, *Burt Rutan*, 39–40, 44.

14. For information on Whitcomb winglets, see "How Things Work: Winglets," *Air and Space*, Aug.-Sept., 2001, 38–39.

15. Jack Cox, "Burt Rutan's VeriEze ... A Sneak Previews," *Sport Aviation*, June, 1975, 21–23; Burt Rutan, "Rutan VeriEze to be Available to Homebuilders," *Sport Aviation*, July, 1975, 50, 69; Jack Cox, "VeriEze Update," *Sport Aviation*, Apr., 1977, 13.

16. Rollo, *Burt Rutan*, 88–93, 106–109, 121–32, 138.

17. Ibid., 96–97, 133–37, 162–63, 184–201. For information on the current activities of Scaled Composites and a biographical sketch of Burt Rutan, see http://www.scaled.com. Additional biographical material about Rutan, who is enshrined in the National Aviation Hall of Fame, is available at http://www.nationalaviation.org/enshrinee/rutan.html.

18. For information on the age of the general aviation fleet, see "Fleet by Age," *2001 GA Statistical Book*, 11.

19. Information on the type clubs is drawn from the 2001–2002 edition of the *AOPA Airport Directory*. The information is also available on-line to AOPA members only at http://www.aopa.org.

20. Information on the Swift projects is drawn from the newsletters of the Swift Museum Foundation (previously The International Swift Association). The newsletter is published monthly. See especially the following editions: vol. 18, no. 12 (Nov. 7, 1986); vol. 20, no. 9 (Aug. 7, 1988); vol. 21, no. 4 (Mar. 7, 1989);

vol. 22, no. 1 (Dec. 7, 1990); vol. 22, no. 11 (Oct. 7, 1991); vol. 23, no. 12 (Nov. 7, 1992); vol. 25, no. 1 (Dec. 7, 1993); vol. 27, no. 1 (Dec. 7, 1994); vol. 28, no. 12 (Nov. 7, 1996); vol. 30, no. 12 (Nov. 7, 1998); vol. 31, no. 5 (Apr. 7, 1999); vol. 31, no. 8 (July 7, 1999); vol. 31, no. 12 (Nov. 7, 1999); and vol. 33, no. 6 (May 7, 2001).

21. Information on the Luscombe projects is drawn from the Luscombe Association's newsletter. The newsletter is published every two months and includes an update from the Don Luscombe Aviation History Foundation. See especially the following editions: no. 105, July-Aug., 1993; no. 107, Nov.-Dec., 1992; no. 108, Jan.-Feb., 1994; no. 109, Mar.-Apr., 1994; no. 144, Jan.-Feb., 2000; no., 147, July-Aug., 2000; and no. 149, Nov.-Dec., 2000.

22. The definition of ultralights is found in Part 103 of the *Federal Aviation Regulations (FAR)*. The FAA publishes its *Aeronautical Information Manual/Federal Aviation Regulations (AIM/FAR)* on an annual basis. The *FARs* are available on-line at http://www.faa.gov. Background on the sport can be found at http://www.eaa.org/ultralights/index.html and at http://www.usua.org.

23. For information on the background of the Rogallo wing, see Timothy R. Gaffney, "Hanging on to a Dream," *Dayton Daily News,* Mar. 18, 2002, 1B.

24. Thomas A. Horne, "The Foremost Advocate: Eighties," *AOPA Pilot,* Oct., 1989, 98–99. See the EAA's Ultralight Division Internet site at http://www.eaa.org/ultralights/index.html and the United States Ultralight Association's Internet site at http://www.usua.org.

25. See Paul Schweizer, *Wings Like Eagles,* 251–52, 255–56, 257–58. See also the U.S. Hang Glider Association's Internet site at http://www.ushga.org.

26. Schweizer, *Wings Like Eagles,* 343–44. For statistics on glider pilot's certificates, see the FAA's *Statistical Handbook of Aviation, 1996,* Table 7-8, "Estimated Active Glider Pilots By Class of Certificate, December 31, 1987–1996," 7–13; and *U.S. Civil Airman Statistics 1999,* Table 8, "Estimated Active Glider Pilots By Class of Certificate," 1 1, both available at http://www.api.faa.gov/civilair/DocList.asp?ID=34.

27. William Schweizer, *Soaring,* 203–11, app. 11; Paul Schweizer, *Wings Like Eagles,* 345–46; for information on current products, see the corporation's Internet site at http://www.sacusa.com.

28. Horne, "Foremost Advocate," 97–98.

29. Ibid., 99, 106–107. For statistics on recreational pilot's licenses, see *U.S. Civil Airman Statistics 2000,* Table 1, 1–2.

30. Horne, "Foremost Advocate," 100, 101, 107.

31. For background on the fight to gain passage of product liability reform, see Thomas B. Chapman, "Working the Hill," *AOPA Pilot,* Sept., 94, 2–5.

32. When the liability reform act passed in 1995, Cesnna Aircraft anticipated that it alone would soon be producing between 1,900 and 2,000 piston-engine aircraft a year. Six years later, in 2001, the entire sector produced only 2,816 aircraft, including just over 1,900 piston-engine aircraft. Cessna had the largest share of the market, selling 912 piston aircraft. General aviation aircraft sales overall fell 6.6 percent in 2001, with piston-engine sales falling 12.8 percent to 1,581 units. Projections for 2002 were cautious. Mooney Aircraft declared bankruptcy on

July 27, 2001, and Advanced Aerodynamics and Structures purchased it in early 2002. Cirrus, meanwhile, was forced to look overseas for the investment capital it needed to expand production. See Thomas A. Horne, "Manufacturers Face the Future," *AOPA Pilot*, Sept., 1994, 5; "GA airplane makers set record," *AOPA Pilot*, Apr., 2001, 56; "Mooney declares bankruptcy," *AOPA Pilot*, Sept., 2001, 58; "Cirrus turns the corner," *AOPA Pilot*, Oct., 2001, 54; "GA billings up in 2001, but deliveries drop," *AOPA Pilot*, Apr., 2002, 55; "Mooney chief aims to create GA conglomerate," *AOPA Pilot*, May, 2002, 56.

33. See "AOPA Project Pilot," *AOPA Pilot*, Apr., 1994, 2. Between 1994 and 1999, the number of individuals holding student pilot's licenses increased only slightly— from 96,254 to 97,359. In 2000, the number of student pilots dropped to 93,064. The statistics on student pilots come from *U.S. Civil Airman Statistics 2000*, Table 1, 1–2.

34. See "Fighting for Airports," *AOPA Pilot*, Nov., 1997, 4; "Airport Support Network" *AOPA Pilot*, Feb., 1998, 4.

35. For a sense of the battle over Meigs, see "Mayors versus Aiports," *AOPA Pilot*, Mar., 1996, 4; "AOPA Appeal to Illinois Members Pays Off in State Legislation on Meigs Field," *AOPA Pilot*, Jan. 1997, 8–9; "Chicago mayor hopes to speed demise of Meigs," *AOPA Pilot*, Feb., 1998, 35; Michael Collins, "What fate Meigs?" *AOPA Pilot*, June, 2000, 71–75.

36. The statistics on women pilots are drawn from on-line editions of the *U.S. Civil Airmen Statistics* for 1998 and 2000, Table 2, "Estimated Women Airmen Certificates Held," 1–3, in each of those publications.

37. For more information on Women in Aviation International, see the organization's Internet site at http://www.wiai.org.

38. The plane shot down in Peru belonged to the Association of Baptists for World Evangelism in Harrisburg, Pennsylvania. For more information on the incident, see http://www.abwe.org/family/peru_incident/peru_tragedy.htm.

39. For more about the history of AirLifeLine, see Michael Collins, "Compassion in Action," *AOPA Pilot*, Mar., 2001, 65–69. See also the organization's Internet site at http://www.airlifeline.org/a1/servlet/visit. For more information on Angel Flight, see that organization's Internet site at http://www.angelflight.com.

40. For information on the Air Care Alliance, see that organization's Internet site at http://www.aircareall.org.

41. For more information on the FAA and public-benefit flying, see Tom LeCompte, "Center, This is Compassion Seven–One–Golf," *Air and Space*, Mar., 2000, 72–77. For more information on the humanitarian use of general aviation since 1990, see Thomas B. Haines, "Aviation's Ambassadors," *AOPA Pilot*, Jan., 1992, 62–67; David A. Rozansky, "On Volunteer Wings," *AOPA Pilot*, Feb., 1998, 63–70; Peter A. Bedell, "Aid in Appalachia," *AOPA Pilot*, Mar., 2000, 83–87.

42. For more on the Wrights and their development of the first airplane propeller, see Peter Jacob, *Visions of a Flying Machine: The Wright Brothers and the Process of Invention* (Washington, D.C.: Smithsonian Institution Press, 1990),

43. One of the most famous of the early propeller manufacturers was the Hamilton-Standard Propeller Corporation. This company was formed through

the merger of Hamilton Aero Manufacturing and Standard Steel Propeller under the corporate umbrella of the United Aircraft and Transport Corporation (later United Aircraft Corporation). Standard provided the adjustable metal propeller Charles Lindbergh used on the "Spirit of St. Louis" in 1927, and in 1933 received the Collier Trophy for its development of the controllable pitch propeller. During World War II, the company and its subcontractors produced over five hundred thousand propellers. After the war, however, Hamilton-Standard made a corporate decision to diversify and removed the word *propeller* from its corporate name. For more on the corporate history of Hamilton-Standard (now known as Hamilton Sundstrand), see http://www.hamilton-standard.com/cda/details/0,3401,CLI1_DIV1_ETI177,00.html.

44. Information on Hartzell's history can be found at http://www.hartzellprop.com/history/index_history.htm.

45. Information on the history of Sensenich propellers can be found at http://www.sensenich.com. Additional information is available at the Internet sites of its major subsidiary, the Sensenich Wood Propeller Company, at http://www.sensenichprop.com, and at the Internet site of the company spun off by PBI: Sensenich Propeller Service, Incorporated, http://www.sensenichpropeller.com.

46. In March, 2002, McCauley's parent company, Cessna Aircraft, announced that it planned to close the McCauley Accessory Division near Dayton and move its operations to Columbus, Georgia (Jason Roberson, "McCauley May Move to Georgia," *Dayton Daily News,* Mar., 1, 2002, 1E).

47. Information on McCauley's history can be found at http://www.mccauley.textron.com.

48. For more on AGATE, see http://oea.larc.nasa.gov/PAIS/AGATE.html. See also Fallows, *Free Flight,* 68–70, 173.

49. For information on the GAP program, see http://www.grc.nasa.gov/WWW/AST/GAP. See also Fallows, *Free Flight,* 173–76, 181.

50. For more on the SATS program, see http://www.sats.nasa.gov. See also Fallows, *Free Flight,* 173, 224. In addition to his book, Fallows also wrote a magazine article that spells out his enthusiastic assessment of NASA programs for the public. See James Fallows, "Freedom of the Skies," *Atlantic Monthly,* June, 2001, 37–49. *Aviation Week* examined the program in a more critical light, especially in terms of its dependence on the continued operation of a number of smaller regional airports. See John Croft, "Small Airports: To Be or Not To Be?" *Aviation Week and Space Technology,* Apr. 15, 2002, 58–61. See also "No SATS-isfaction," *Aviation Week and Space Technology,* June 17, 2002, 25.

51. Class B airspace is the FAA's designation for the airspace surrounding the nation's thirty major metropolitan airports. It basically resembles an upside-down, three-tiered wedding cake. The inner ring is the airspace in the airport's immediate vicinity. Restrictions apply from ground level up to a certain altitude. In the second ring, restrictions begin at a certain altitude above the ground and continue up to the same altitude covered by the inner ring. In the outer or third ring, restrictions begin at an even higher altitude above the

ground and, again, continue up to the same altitude covered by the inner and second rings. Aircraft flying within Class B airspace must be in two-way contact with flight controllers and have an altitude-encoding transponder. Aircraft, however, are allowed to fly under or over Class B airspace without meeting those requirements. Enhanced Class B airspace involves changing from an up-side-down wedding cake to a solid cylinder. In enhanced Class B airspace, restrictions begin at ground level and continue up to infinity. The single ring includes all airspace within a twenty nautical mile radius of the airport. As already noted, additional restrictions are placed on aircraft flying within enhanced Class B airspace.

52. One can follow the course of the FAA response to the September 11 attacks through the agency's Internet site at http://www.faa.gov. It contains electronic copies of notices to airmen (notams), press releases, and other publications. Of particular interest are press releases from October 12 and 21, and December 19, 2001.

53. The AOPA detailed its organizational response to the restrictions imposed after September 11 in a series of articles published in November, 2001. See "America Under Siege: An Aviation Prespective," *AOPA Pilot*, Nov., 2001, 73–81.

54. See "TFRs," *AOPA Pilot*, Mar., 2002, 4. For an announcement concerning TFRs around the nation's nuclear plants, see the FAA press release dated October 30, 2001, available at http://www.faa.gov/apa/pr/pr.cfm?id=1451.

55. "CGX," *AOPA Pilot*, Feb., 2002, 4, 16.

56. Mark Huber, "A Price Too High," *Air and Space*, June-July, 2002, 58–65.

57. Michele Berk, "College Park Airport, Potomac Field resume some flights," *Baltimore Business Journal*, Feb. 25, 2002, available at http://www.bizjournals.com/baltimore/stories/2002/02/25/daily3.html.

Sources for the History of General Aviation

The literature on the history of general aviation is perhaps best described as scattered. There are so-called buff books on just about every type of light aircraft ever built in the United States, and many of the more popular models have inspired several books. Beyond these ready sources on the planes and the people who built them, the story of general aviation is a little more challenging in terms of finding the various pieces. A few works have attempted at least to give an overview of the general aviation industry—again, primarily focusing on the planes and the people who built them. But literature that reaches beyond the planes and their manufacturers is relatively rare. A few articles have been written, and there are a number of works dealing with other aspects of aviation history that occasionally touch on the world of general aviation. For the rest, the story must be pieced together using back issues of aviation-related magazines and Internet sites devoted to certain general aviation corporations, organizations, and activities. In fact, for certain types of general aviation activity and certain aviation organizations, the only readily available source of information is their Internet sites. The various sources used specifically for this work are found in the notes. This essay will reference most all of those sources, plus a number of others of value to those exploring the history of general aviation.

If one wants to begin with an overview of general aviation, perhaps the best place to start is Roger Bilstein's *Flight in America* (Baltimore: Johns Hopkins University Press, 2001). Now in its third edition, this is an excellent textbook on the history of aviation in the United States. Many of the chapters have sections devoted to developments in general aviation. Reading the text also provides a larger context within which to view the history of general aviation. The most thorough book dealing with the history of the light aircraft manufacturing sector is Donald M. Pattillo's *A History in the Making: 80 Turbulent Years in the American General Aviation Industry* (New York: McGraw-Hill, 1998). Although the book sometimes tends to become a descriptive list of manufacturers, planes, and performance specifications, it does provide an overview of many of the forces that have shaped the general aviation manufacturing industry. Bilstein also provides an overview of the aviation/aerospace industry in *The American Aerospace Industry: From Workshop to Global Enterprise* (New York: Twayne, 1996). This work, although focused on the manufacturers of commercial and military aircraft, rockets, and missiles, contains sections in various chapters dealing with general aviation manufacturing concerns. One of the latest works to offer an overview, albeit a somewhat uncritical one, of some of the latest developments in general aviation, as well as many of the hopes for its future, is James Fallows's *Free Flight: From Airline Hell to a New Age of Travel* (New York: Public Affairs, 2001).

There was an attempt in this work to place the history of general aviation within broader contexts and frameworks not only within the history of aviation, but also within U.S. history. The slowly evolving relationships between both women and aviation and African Americans and aviation unfolded within the broader context of the twentieth century women's and civil rights movements. The rising fuel costs of the 1970s and the globalization of American industry in general helped shape developments within the general aviation manufacturing sector. In terms of placing general aviation within the broader context of the American response to technology, the most valuable source is Joseph Corn's *The Winged Gospel: America's Romance with Aviation, 1900–1950* (New York and Oxford: Oxford University Press, 1983). While dealing with America's response to all types of aviation, Corn gives particular attention to the general aviation sector, particularly in his chapter dealing with the "airplane for everyman." He makes clear the variety of hopes and dreams Americans held concerning the airplane through World War II. A helpful companion piece that offers something of a corrective to some of Corn's interpretation is Tom D. Crouch's "An Aircraft for Everyman: The Department of Commerce and the Light Airplane Industry, 1933–1937" in Roger D. Launius's *Innovation and the Development of Flight* (College Station: Texas A&M University Press, 1999). Crouch clearly outlines the extent to which aircraft manufacturers viewed the possibility of the mass production of an affordable aircraft with a greater realism than some of the more vocal evangelists of the winged gospel. Another work that offers a certain conceptual framework for viewing the history of general aviation is Eric Schatzberg, *Wings of Wood, Wings of Metal: Culture and Technological Choice in American Airplane Materials, 1914–1945* (Princeton, N.J.: Princeton University Press, 1999). This work examines some of the nontechnical rationales behind the move from wood to metal in aircraft construction. While Schatzberg focuses primarily on commercial and military aircraft, it became clear to me while conducting research for this book that general aviation aircraft designers embraced the same view on the "modernity" of metal as a construction material.

A number of other works, although not focused on the subject, provide important background information and offer frameworks with which to view the history of general aviation. One of the best is Tom D. Crouch's *The Bishop's Boys: A Life of Wilbur and Orville Wright* (New York: W. W. Norton, 1989). An outstanding biography, it also provides a number of insights into aviation's earliest years. C. R. Roseberry's *Glenn Curtiss: Pioneer of Flight* (Syracuse, N.Y.: Syracuse University Press, 1992) is in many ways a somewhat defensive portrait of another aviation pioneer. It, too, provides a window into the world of aviation during the first decades of the twentieth century. Air racing is detailed extensively in Terry Gwynn-Jones's *Farther and Faster: Aviation's Adventuring Years, 1909–1939* (Washington, D.C.: Smithsonian Institution Press, 1991). Dominick A. Pisano explores the history of the depression era government-sponsored program to train pilots in *To Fill the Sky with Pilots: The Civilian Pilot Training Program, 1939–1945* (Urbana and Chicago: University of Illinois Press, 1993). His work examines the nature of the relationship between the federal government and general aviation and demonstrates that the relationship was often difficult. Fred Weick designed a number of important general aviation aircraft including the Ercoupe and the Piper Pawnee. His story is told in Fred Weick and James R. Hansen, *From the Ground Up: The Autobiography of an Aeronautical Engineer* (Washington, D.C.: Smithsonian Institution Press, 1988). Another recent memoir—Rinker Buck's *Flights of Passage: A Memoir* (New York: Hyperion, 1997)—offers insight into the world of general aviation flying and a sense of the devotion some have to it. The author and his older brother made a transcontinental flight in an Aeronca Champ in 1966. Among the many themes developed in the book, Buck explores why he, his brother, and their father all developed a love of flying. For a contemporary and insider's sense of how light aircraft manufacturers viewed the role of general aviation in the United States and the potential of the post–World War II market, see William T. Piper's (with D. J. Duffin) *Private Flying: Today and Tomorrow* (New York: Pitman, 1949). It is interesting to note that this work contains a chapter specifically devoted to women's role in aviation. There seemed to be a sense of the importance of general aviation to the ability of women to participate at all in the world of flying. My own work on the history of airports, *America's Airports: Airfield Development, 1918–1947* (College Station: Texas A&M University Press, 2001) provides some sense of the infrastructure issues facing general aviation.

In honor of the fiftieth anniversary of the Air Commerce Act of 1926, the FAA sponsored a series of books covering the history of federal aviation policy in America. While each work seems to focus primarily on the role of the federal government in the promotion of commercial aviation, they also detail the history of policies dealing with general aviation. The first of these books, reprinted by the Smithsonian Institution Press, was Nick A. Komons's *Bonfires to Beacons: Federal Civil Aviation Policy under the Air Commerce Act, 1926–1938* (Washington, D.C.: Smithsonian Institution Press, 1989). The next in the series, John R. M. Wilson's *Turbulence Aloft: The Civil Aeronautics Administration Amid Wars and Rumors of Wars, 1938–1953* (Washington, D.C.: U.S. Department of Transportation, Federal Aviation Administration, 1979), carries the story through World War II and the Truman Administration. The critical Eisenhower era is examined in Stuart I. Rochester, *Takeoff at Mid-Century: Federal Civil Aviation Policy in the Eisenhower Years, 1953–1961* (Washington, D.C.: U.S. Department of Transportation, Federal Aviation Administration, 1976). More than the other works in the series, this one focuses on the often contentious relationship between the federal government and general aviation, particularly its chief voice in Washington, the AOPA. The next book in the series, Richard J. Kent Jr., *Safe, Separated, and Soaring: A History of Federal Aviation Policy, 1961–1972* (Washington, D.C.: Department of Transportation, Federal Aviation Administration, 1980), traces the history of aviation policy through the Kennedy and Johnson administrations and Richard Nixon's first term in office. Finally, taking the story up to the fiftieth anniversary of the Air

Commerce Act, is Edmund Preston's *Troubled Passage: The Federal Aviation Administration During the Nixon-Ford Term, 1973–1977* (Washington, D.C.: Department of Transportation, Federal Aviation Administration, 1987).

There are two invaluable works on the development of piston engines for light aircraft. The first is Herschel Smith's *Aircraft Piston Engines: From the Manly Baltzer to the Continental Tiara* (New York: McGraw-Hill, 1981). Smith organized his study by engine type (i.e. rotary, radial, inline). The second work, Bill Gunston's *The Development of Piston Aero Engines,* 2d ed. (Great Britain: Patrick Stephens, 1999), chronologically traces the history of engine design. Another recent work, Richard A. Leyes II and William A. Fleming's *The History of North American Small Gas Turbine Aircraft Engines* (Washington, D.C.: AIAA and Smithsonian Institution Press, 1999) thoroughly examines the development of the types of gas turbine engines employed in general aviation.

The most comprehensive source for information on aircraft through the early post–World War II period is Joseph P. Juptner's nine-volume *U. S. Civil Aircraft* (Los Angeles: Aero, 1962–1981). The work provides considerable detail on all the aircraft that received Approved Type Certificates from the Department of Commerce between 1925 and 1957. The Smithsonian Institution's National Air and Space Museum also sponsored a series of books dealing with famous aircraft in its collection. Three of those books detail the histories of general aviation aircraft. The first, Tom D. Crouch's *Blériot XI: The Story of a Classic Aircraft* (Washington, D.C.: Smithsonian Institution Press, 1982), provides information on the third basic type of aircraft (in addition to Wright and Curtiss models) flown in the United States before World War I. Jay P. Spenser's *Aeronca C-2: The Story of the Flying Bathtub* (Washington, D.C.: Smithsonian Institution Press, 1978) details the history of the country's first affordable aircraft. Finally, Spenser's *Bellanca C. F.: The Emergence of the Cabin Monoplane in the United States* (Washington, D.C.: Smithsonian Institution Press, 1982) tells the tale of the cabin monoplane that served as the first in a long line of important designs by Giuseppe Bellanca. Spenser also wrote one of the more comprehensive books on the history of the helicopter in America, *Whirlybirds: A History of the U.S. Helicopter Pioneers* (Seattle: University of Washington Press and Museum of Flight, 1998).

Another good source for basic information is the *Aircraft Yearbook* and its successor publications, *The Aerospace Yearbook* and *Aerospace*

Facts & Figures. The *Aircraft Yearbook* began publication in 1919, sponsored by the Manufacturers Aircraft Association. In 1921, that group reorganized as the Aeronautical Chamber of Commerce. It reorganized and renamed itself again after World War II, adopting the name Aircraft Industries Association of America. Finally, in 1959 it adopted its current name: Aerospace Industries Association of America. Throughout its long history, this organization of aviation and aerospace companies has published an annual volume under the various titles listed above outlining basic facts, figures, and trends in the industry. These works also contain extensive essays on some of the important themes, trends, and developments. For example, the 1945 edition contains an essay on the activities of the Civil Air Patrol during World War II.

As noted, there is considerable buff literature on individual airplane manufacturers and even on individual airplane models. Written by dedicated enthusiasts, these works are short on a broader theoretical or thematic context, but often rich in detail. The list of available works could be almost limitless. However, the following are a representative sample of the literature available. The origins of some of the most prominent early light aircraft manufacturers are detailed in John Underwood's *The Stinsons: A Pictorial History* (Glendale, Calif.: Heritage Press, 1983) and Bruce Bissonette's *The Wichita 4: Cessna, Moellendick, Beech, and Stearman* (Destin, Fla.: Aviation Heritage, 1999). For more details on the companies founded by the Wichita "gang," see Edward H. Phillips's *Cessna: A Master's Expression* and *Beechcraft: Pursuit of Perfection, A History of Beechcraft Airplanes* (Eagen, Minn.: Flying Books, 1985 and 1992), Bruce Bissonette's *Travel Air: A Photo History* (Destin, Fla.: Aviation Heritage, 1996), and Edward H. Phillips's *Travel Air: Wings Over the Prairie* (Eagan, Minn.: Flying Books, 1982).

The history of the Taylor-Piper aircraft line is detailed in Chet Peek's *Taylorcraft: The Taylorcraft Story* (Terre Haute, Ind.: SunShine House, 1992) and Edward H. Phillips's *Piper: A Legend Aloft* (Eagan, Minn.: Flying Books, 1993). The Don Luscombe's work has attracted a remarkable amount of attention. Books on aircraft manufactured by companies headed by Luscombe include John Underwood's *Of Monocoupes and Men: A Pictorial History* (Glendale, Calif.: Heritage Press, 1973), James B. Zazas's *Visions of Lucombe: The Early Years* (Terre Haute, Ind.: SunShine House, 1993), Frank R. Saletri's *The Luscombe: No Wood, No Nails, No Glue* (Hollywood, Calif.: Agony House, 1982), and John C. Swick's *The Luscombe Story: Every Cloud Has a Silvaire Lining* (Terre Haute, Ind.:

SunShine House, 1987). Another aircraft manufacturer that has inspired a good deal of buff literature is WACO. Books on WACO detail not only the general history of the company, but also the histories of particular models produced. WACO books include Fred O. Kobernuss's *WACO: Symbol of Courage and Excellence,* vol. 1 (Terre Haute, Ind.: SunShine Books, 1992) and *WACO: Symbol of Courage and Excellence,* vol. 2 (Destin, Fla.: Mystic Bay and Aviation Heritage Books, 1999), as well as Raymond H. Brandly and Bonnie Jean Borisch's *Taperwing WACOs* (n.p.: Raymond H. Brandly, 1984).

Other examples of buff literature include Bill Wright's *Rearwin: A Story of Men, Planes, and Aircraft Manufacturing During the Great Depression* (Manhattan, Kans.: Sunflower University Press, 1997), G. Dale Beach's *It's A Funk: A Story of the Funk Twins* (Destin, Fla.: Aviation Heritage and Aviation Publishing, 1985, 1997), Stanley G. Thomas's *The Globe/Temco Swift Story* (Destin, Fla.: Aviation Heritage and Aviation Publishing, 1996), and Chet Peek's *The Spartan Story* (Destin, Fla.: Aviation Heritage, 1994). For a general look at the planes of the golden age, see Geza Szurovy's *Wings of Yesteryear: The Golden Age of Private Aircraft* (Osceola, Wisc.: MBI, 1998). These represent just a sampling of the works available.

There is also something of a buff history of the agricultural aviation industry. Written by Mabry I. Anderson, *Low and Slow: An Insider's History of Agricultural Aviation* (San Francisco: California Farmer, 1986) provides a brief history of the industry. While much of it focuses on the South, it includes chapters on agricultural aviation in the various regions of the United States. Another source for information on the history of agricultural aviation is the National Agricultural Aviation Association's Internet site.

Not only did the Schweizer brothers provide the majority of the nation's gliders, they also produced much of the available literature on the history of soaring. Older brother Paul Schweizer wrote a history of soaring in America. His book, *Wings Like Eagles: The Story of Soaring in the United States* (Washington, D.C.: Smithsonian Institution Press, 1998), sometimes reads a little bit like the minutes from the meetings of the Soaring Society of America. It does, however, provide a good sense of the sport's history in the United States. Younger brother William Schweizer focused on the history of the company his older brothers founded. In *Soaring with the Schweizers: The Fifty-Year History of Their Adventure Aviation Adventures* (Falls Church, Va.: Rivilo Books, 1991), he details the family's personal history as well as the business history of their company, taking the story up to the point at which control of the company moved from the original generation to the sons of the founders. Other books on the history of soaring include Terence Horsley's *Soaring Flight* (New York: Current Books, 1946) and Richard W. Wolters's *The Art and Technique of Soaring* (New York: McGraw-Hill, 1971).

The Internet is replete with Web pages paying homage to aircraft of all kinds. A search on just about any make or model of aircraft will produce a number of possible sources. These sources vary greatly in quality. Perhaps a better way to search for information on individual makes or models of aircraft would be to start with type clubs. Like buff literature and Web pages, almost every make and/or model of light aircraft has a type club dedicated to its preservation. The basic motto behind these clubs is "keep 'em flying." A source for information on these type clubs is the *AOPA Airport Directory,* published annually by the Aircraft Owners and Pilots Association (AOPA). It is available in both print and on-line versions, although one must be a member of the AOPA to access the on-line version. The directory contains an extensive list of associations and type clubs, including contact information for each.

Another source for information on general aviation, particularly in the years before World War II, are the various state aviation histories. Although it has been pointed out that technology in America has not developed in a way that respected state boundaries, these histories do focus on a wide variety of aviation activities, including general aviation. Some of the best examples of these state histories include Roger Bilstein and Jay Miller's *Aviation in Texas* (Austin: Texas Monthly Press, 1985), Howard L. Scamehorn's *Balloons to Jets: A Century of Aeronautics in Illinois, 1855–1955* (reprint, Carbondale: Southern Illinois University Press, 2000), William F. Trimble's *High Frontier: A History of Aeronautics in Pennsylvania* (Pittsburgh: University of Pittsburgh Press, 1982) and Ruth M. Reinhold's *Sky Pioneering: Arizona in Aviation History* (Tucson: University of Arizona Press, 1982). Others include Frank Kingston Smith and James P. Harrington's *Aviation and Pennsylvania* (Philadelphia: Franklin Institute Press, 1981), Frank Joseph Rowe and Craig Miner's *Borne on the South Wind: A Century of Kansas Aviation* (Wichita, Kans.: Wichita Eagle and Beacon, 1994), Robert E. Adwers's *Rudder, Stick, and Throttle: Research and Reminiscences on Flying in Nebraska* (Omaha, Neb.: Making History, 1994), Michael J. Goc's *Forward in Flight: The History of Aviation in Wisconsin* (Friendship, Wisc.: New Past Press, 1998), and Noel E.

Allard and Gerald N. Sandvick's *Minnesota Aviation History, 1857–1945* (Chaska, Minn.: MAHB, 1993). Aviation has played an important role in the history and development of Alaska. To get a sense of the evolution of aviation in the Far North, see Beth Day Romulo's *Glacier Pilot: The Story of Bob Reeve and the Flyers Who Pushed Back Alaska's Air Frontiers* (New York: Holt, 1957).

Much of the literature on women in aviation has focused on those women who during World War II flew for the Army Air Forces as WASPs. In many ways, the WASPs were "lost to history" following their disbandment in late 1944. They "reappeared" in the 1970s as women began to expand their roles, particularly in military aviation. Since their rediscovery, a fairly substantial literature has appeared. This literature includes general popular histories of the program, memoirs, and more scholarly work. Most of these works contain the program's essential background information. For examples of the literature and information on the basic contours of the WASP program, see Marianne Verges's *On Silver Wings: The Women Airforce Service Pilots of World War II, 1942–1944* (New York: Ballantine Books, 1991) and Sally Van Wagenen Keil's *Those Wonderful Women in Their Flying Machines: The Unknown Heroines of World War II* (New York: Four Directions Press, 1979). Other works focus on women's efforts to gain entry into military and/or commercial aviation. This is a bit curious, however, because until the 1970s, women were limited to participation in general aviation. Nevertheless, the literature on women pilots offers important glimpses into the many other aviation activities in which women engaged.

The Smithsonian Institution Press published a series of short books on women in aviation. Each provides a helpful overview of the major individuals, events, and themes from a number of time periods. The series begins with Claudia M. Oakes's *United States Women in Aviation through World War I* (1978). It continues with Kathleen Brooks-Pazmany's *United States Women in Aviation, 1919–1929* (1991). Oakes wrote a second volume for the series, this one covering the depression years, entitled *United States Women in Aviation, 1930–1939* (1991). The series concludes with perhaps the best book in the series, Deborah G. Douglas's *United States Women in Aviation, 1940–1985* (1991). Another good book examining the history of women in American aviation that offers insight into the various roles women were able to play (and those from which they were excluded) is Dean Jaros's *Heroes Without Legacy: American Airwomen, 1912–1944* (Niwot: University Press of Colorado, 1993). A recent book by Carolyn Russo, *Women in Flight: Portraits of Contemporary Women Pilots* (Washington, D.C.: Smithsonian Institution Press, 1997), offers both photographic and descriptive portraits of women working in aviation in the 1990s. Leslie Haynsworth and David Toomey's *Amelia Earhart's Daughters: The Wild and Glorious Story of American Women Aviators from World War II to the Dawn of the Jet Age* (New York: William Morrow, 1998), like much of the literature on women aviators after World War II, examines women's attempts to break into military and/or commercial flying. It especially focuses on the group of women who worked to become the nation's first female astronauts in the early 1960s. Nonetheless, by providing details of the lives of these women, the book offers insights into the various aviation careers open to women in aviation in the 1950s and 1960s.

The topic of women in aviation also includes its share of buff literature, much of it focused on the World War II WASPs. Other works, however, examine women performing different roles in aviation. An example of such literature, this one focused especially on early-twentieth-century women pilots, is Henry M. Holden with Captain Lori Griffith, *Ladybirds: The Untold Story of Women Pilots in America* (Mount Freedom, N.J.: Black Hawk, 1991). Although it deals with the biography of a WASP, Diane Ruth Armour Bartels's *Sharpie: The Life Story of Evelyn Sharp, Nebraska's Aviatrix* (Lincoln, Neb.: Dageforde, 1996), clearly outlines the job opportunities available to women aviators in the 1930s. There are also numerous biographies of some of the more prominent women of aviation's golden age, including Amelia Earhart and Jackie Cochran.

Just as much of the literature on women aviators focuses on the story of the WASPs of World War II, much of the literature on African-American aviators focuses on the story of the Tuskegee Airmen of the same era. While works on the Tuskegee Airmen sometimes touch on how these young men came to aviation, they focus almost exclusively on their military flying experiences. Other works are available that focus more on the activities of African Americans in general aviation. Raymond Eugene Peters and Clinton M. Arnold researched and published a short work on African Americans in aviation through the 1970s and early 1980s. Entitled *Black Americans in Aviation* (San Diego, Calif.: Neyenesch Printers, n.d.), it provides information on a number of pioneer African Americans as well as traces the involvement of blacks in aviation through such statistics as the number holding pilot licenses at various points in time. Based on a National Air and Space Museum exhibit, Von Hardesty and

Dominick Pisano's *Black Wings: The American Black in Aviation* (Washington, D.C.: National Air and Space Museum, 1983), offers an overview of African American involvement in aviation primarily through World War II. Although most the biographies and autobiographies focus on African-American military pilots, Neal V. Loving's autobiography, *Loving's Love: A Black American's Experience in Aviation* (Washington, D.C.: Smithsonian Institution Press, 1994), tells the story of an African American who devoted his life to general aviation. For an examination of African-American pilots during the golden age of general aviation there is the Smithsonian Press's reprint of *Black Wings*. With an introduction by Von Hardesty, *Black Aviator: The Story of William J. Powell* (Washington and London: Smithsonian Institution Press, 1994) faithfully presents the most important published work of this pioneer aviator. There is also Doris L. Rich's biography of Bessie Coleman, *Queen Bess: Daredevil Aviator* (Washington and London: Smithsonian Institution Press, 1993). Another source of information on African Americans and aviation is the Internet site maintained by Negro Airmen, International (NAI). It offers not only a history of the organization itself, but it details the wide variety of careers held by African Americans in aviation and explains the organization's current activities aimed at promoting greater African American involvement in aviation.

The practice of "smokejumping" and the dangers associated with it and aerial fire fighting achieved a certain level of visibility with the appearance of Norman Maclean's *Young Men and Fire* (Chicago and London: University of Chicago Press, 1992). Another recent work, Murry A. Taylor's *Jumping Fire: A Smokejumper's Memoir of Fighting Wildfire* (New York: Harcourt, 2000), vividly portrays the life of a smokejumper in Alaska. Neither work delves much into the history of smokejumping, but both touch on it at least briefly. The use of aviation in fire fighting is one of the topics for which Internet sites are invaluable sources of information. The National Smokejumper Association's site includes a history of smokejumping in the United States, and the Aerial Firefighting Industry Association provides background information on the development of air tankers. Other information can be found at Web sites maintained by the U.S. Forest Service, Bureau of Land Management, and National Interagency Fire Center.

Many of the organizations involved in general aviation publish their own magazines and newsletters. These also are good sources of information on various topics. The AOPA's *AOPA Pilot* is one of the most valuable. This monthly magazine reports on the issues, challenges, and promises of general aviation. While often boosterish in nature, it also occasionally offers a critical examination of the various problems faced by general aviation. The EAA's *Sport Aviation* contains a wealth of information on both the organization and topics and trends in the homebuilt aircraft world. *Vintage Airplane* does the same for those involved in restoring aircraft. The EAA's "warbird," ultralight, and acrobatic divisions also publish their own magazines, and the American Institute of Aeronautics and Astronautics publishes a journal entitled *Aerospace America*. While the focus of the latter tends to be on developments in military and commercial aircraft and space vehicles, the journal also periodically covers developments in general aviation. *Air and Space,* a publication of the Smithsonian Institution, has printed a number of articles dealing with a variety of general aviation themes and topics ranging from technology to public-benefit flying to the plight of small airports. *Aviation Week and Space Technology* is another important source on developments in general aviation, particularly in terms of federal actions and industry trends. Other publications that are of value include *AG Pilot, Western Flying,* and *Flying Magazine.* As with the literature on light aircraft, the publications listed here are also something of a representative sample of those available.

Finally, as noted, the Internet offers access to a great deal of information on a wide variety of general aviation organizations, associations, and businesses. It also hosts sites that make biographical information available. Although social and political historian Sam Hays has argued that such sources may likely prove temporary, for the present they are available and accessible (Samuel P. Hays, *A History of Environmental Politics Since 1945* [Pittsburgh: University of Pittsburgh Press, 2000], ix). In addition to the sites already mentioned in this essay and others created by a variety of aviation business concerns, Web pages offering information on general aviation include those of the Air Care Alliance, the Aircraft Owners and Pilots Association, Angel Flight, the Civil Air Patrol, the Experimental Aircraft Association, the Federal Aviation Administration, the General Aviation Manufacturers Association, the International Black Aerospace Council, the National Business Aviation Association (formerly the National Business Aircraft Association), the National Aeronautics and Space Administration, the National Air and Space Museum (with special pages on both women and African Americans in aviation), the National Aviation Hall of Fame (an excellent source of biographical information), the Ninety-Nines, the U.S. Ultralight Association, and Women in Aviation International. Many of these sites provide links to others offering additional information.

As a synthetic work aimed at providing a general overview, this book in many ways only scratches the surface of the history of general aviation and the sources available. There is still a tremendous opportunity for greater, more in-depth research into many of the themes, topics, and developments outlined here. One of the most interesting involves the persistence of the idea that large numbers of Americans will one day take to the sky in personal flying machines—at least among a sometimes influential core of "true believers." What is it about this vision of the future that allows it to persist in the face of an often hostile reality? Many company and organizational archives remain untapped. Many individuals still await examination by perceptive and knowledgeable biographers. Military aviation has probably witnessed the most extensive and critical examination, followed by commercial aviation. The history of general aviation is still a rich field waiting to be fully explored.

Index

Photos are indicated with an italicized *f*.

A-4 Pirate engines (Menasco), 57
A-series engines (Continental), 57, 64*f*
Abbott, Robert S., 14
Advance Aircraft, 22
Advanced Aerodynamics and Structures, 165–66*n*32
Advanced General Aviation Transport Experiments (AGATE), 145
Aerial Experiment Association, 19
Aerial Fire Control Experimental Project, 76
Aerial Observation Post Program, 66–68
aerial photography, 17, 98, 155*n*9
aerial tankers, 108, 162*n*41. *See also* fire fighting
Aero Club of America, 8–9, 12, 27, 44
Aero Commander aircraft, 115
Aero Design and Engineering Corporation, 115
Aero Mist-Master, 109
Aeronautical Corporation of America (Aeronca). *See* Aeronca (company)
Aeronautics Branch, U.S. Commerce Department, 31
Aeronca (company): golden age period, 29–30, 57; post-World War II years, 90; World War II era, 67, 69
African American aviators: birdmen era, 6, 14–15; golden age period, 38–39, 51–54; post-World War II years, 103–105; winged gospel mythology, xii; World War II era, 79–80
AG-1 prototype (Weick's), 111
AG-2 aircraft (Transland), 112

AG-3 Pawnee aircraft, 111
AGATE program, 145
Ag-Cat aircraft, 112
agricultural aviation: birdmen era, 16–17; golden age period, 26, 42–43; post-1980s, 148; post-World War II years, 88, 98, 109–12; World War II era, 77
aileron system, 18–19
Air Care Alliance, 141
Air Commerce Act, 27–28, 35, 40, 156*n*3
aircraft design. *See* design innovations
aircraft manufacturing. *See* manufacturing sector
Aircraft Owners and Pilots Association (AOPA). *See* AOPA (Aircraft Owners and Pilots Association)
Air Force Academy, U.S., 100
Air Force One, 115
AirLifeLine, 140–41
Air Mail Act, 25
airmail services, 8, 25, 32, 50, 78
air-marking program, 36, 37–38, 50
Airmaster aircraft, 44
airport construction/improvements: golden age period, 26, 31, 36–37; World War II era, 74, 79
airport operators/operations: birdmen era, 7, 9; golden age period, 26, 40–42; post-1980s, 138–39; post-World War II years, 103; Sept. 11 impact, 148–50; World War I, 7. *See also* flight schools
Airport Supply Network, 138
air racing, 13, 26, 44–47, 48–49, 104
Air Tractor, Incorporated, 112
air traffic controllers, 135–36. *See also* navigation aids

Air Transport Command, 81
Alaska, 77–79
Alexander Eaglerock (aircraft), 43
Allen, Edmund T., 34
Allen, Thomas C., 52
Allison, 117
ambulance services, 99, 140–41
American Airmen's Association, 101
Anderson, C. Alfred "Chief," 52–53
Angel Flight, 141
Antiques/Classic Division of EAA, 103
AOPA (Aircraft Owners and Pilots
    Association): golden age period, 47–
    48; post-1980s, 125, 133–34, 135–39;
    post-World War II years, 92, 93–94;
    World War II era, 73
Apache aircraft, 114
"Apprentice Program," 60
Aristocraft aircraft, 70
Army, U.S., 97
Army Air Corps, 32, 66–67, 75
Army Air Forces (AAF), 39–40, 68–70, 72,
    73
Army Air Service, 16–17, 29
Arnold, Henry H. "Hap," 68
A-series engines (Continental), 57, 64f
ASO aircraft (WACO), 43
Association of Baptists for World
    Evangelism, 166n38
Aviat Aircraft, 131–32
Aviation Safety Foundation (AFS), 133–34
avionics, 117–18

B-series engines (Menasco), 57
Baldwin, Thomas Scott, 19
balloons, 5, 9
Banning, James Herman, 52
barnstormers, 12–15
Baty Chabrain, Peggy, 140
Baysdorfer, Charles, 9–10, 154n9
Baysdorfer, Gus, 9–10, 154n9
Baysdorfer, Otto, 9–10, 154n9
Beachy, Lincoln, 5–6
Beech, Olive Ann, 106, 161n35
Beech, Walter Herschel, 15–16, 45, 50
Beechcraft/Beech Aircraft: golden age
    period, 44, 45–46, 50; post-1980s, 124;
    post-World War II years, 90, 95, 106
Bell, Alexander Graham, 19

Bellanca, Giuseppe, 21
Bellanca CF aircraft, 21
Bell Helicopters, 98, 115–16
Bendix, Vincent, 45
Bendix Trophy, 45, 46, 47, 49
Bessie Coleman Aero Club, 51
Bilstein, Roger, xv
birdmen era: overview, 3–4; African
    American aviators, 6, 14–15; barn-
    storming/exhibition flying, 5–7, 10, 11–
    15; development of aviation, 2f, 4–12;
    manufacturing/design sector, 8, 9–12,
    15–22, 141–42, 164n1; women aviators,
    6–7, 14–15
black aviators. See African American
    aviators
Black Wings (Powell), 51–52
Blériot Type XI aircraft, 11, 19
Bogardus, George, 101–102
Boise Interagency Fire Center, 108
Bonanza series aircraft, 115, 124
British Air Transport Auxiliary (ATA), 81
Brown, Walter, 32
Brucker, Clayton, 22
Bruckner, Clayton, 70
B-series engines (Menasco), 57
Buck, Rinker, 109
Buffett, Warren, 123
Bureau of Air Commerce, 27–28, 33–34,
    36, 50
bush pilots, 77–79
business aviation, 26, 43–44, 94–96, 115,
    122–23

CAA. See Civil Aeronautics Administra-
    tion (CAA)
C-series aircraft (Aeronca), 29–30, 57
C-series engines (Continental), 116
canard configuration, 18, 127–28, 164n1
Carson, Rachel, 110
Central Airlines, 50
Central States Aero Company, 59–60
certification of aircraft: golden age
    period, 28, 35–36; post-World War II
    years, 101–102, 124, 126–27
Cessna, Clyde, 10–12, 16, 44
Cessna, Roy, 11
Cessna Aeroplane Exhibition Company,
    12

Cessna Aircraft: golden age period, 44; post-1980s, 86*f*, 120*f*, 124, 137, 144, 165–66*n*32, 167*n*46; post-World War II years, 90, 114–15
Cessna clubs, 130
CF aircraft (Bellancan), 21
CG-4A gliders, 70
Challenger Air Pilots' Association, 52
Chamberlain, Clarence, 21
Cherokee aircraft, 114
Chicago, Meigs Field dispute, 138–39, 149–50
Chicago Aero Club, 8–9
Chicago Defender, 53
"Chummy" (aircraft), 58
Cicero Field, 8–9
Cirrus Aircraft, 127, 163–64*n*9, 165–66*n*32
Civil Aeronautics Act, 35–36, 40
Civil Aeronautics Administration (CAA): golden age period, 36, 38; post-World War II years, 90–94, 101–102; World War II era, 79, 159*n*8. *See also* Federal Aviation Administration (FAA)
Civil Air Patrol, 73–75, 107–108
Civilian Pilot Training Program (CPTP): golden age period, 36, 38–40, 53; World War II era, 80–81, 83, 153*n*8
Civilian Public Service (CPS), 76–77
Civil Works Administration (CWA), 31, 37
Class B airspace, 148, 149, 167–68*n*51
Cleveland National Air Races, 45
Cochran, Jackie, 49, 81, 82
Coffee Scholl of Aeronautics, 52
Coleman, Bessie, 14–15
College Park Airport, 150
Collier Trophy, 96, 166–67*n*43
"The Comet" (aircraft), 9
Commerce Department, 31
commercial aviation: golden age period, 27, 40, 47, 50, 156*n*3; post-1980s, 125–26, 139; post-World War II years, 103, 105–106
Condor aircraft, 143
Continental, Green v., 103
Continental engines: golden age period, 57, 58, 61; post-World War II years, 86*f*, 116–17, 120*f*; World War II era, 64*f*
Convair, 114

Cord, E. L., 56
Corn, Joseph, xi, xiii
crop dusting. *See* agricultural aviation
C-series aircraft (Aeronca), 29–30, 57
C-series engines (Continental), 116
Curtiss, Glenn: design sharing philosophy, 9, 10, 154*n*9; design/structure of aircraft, 18–19, 20, 21; promotion of flying, 5
Curtiss Flying School, 6

Daley, Richard, 138–39, 149–50
Davis, Doug, 45, 47
DDT (dichlorodiphenyl trichloroethane), 110
DeHavilland Moth aircraft, 43
Delta Air Service, 42, 43
Delta Laboratory, 42
Department of Agriculture, 16–17
design innovations: birdmen era, 17–22, 141–42, 164*n*11; golden age period, 54, 55, 59–62; post-1980s, 127–29, 142–44; post-World War II years, 113–16. *See also* manufacturing sector
DGA-3 aircraft (Howard's), 46
Dietz, Conrad, 30
dirigibles, 5–6, 9
Dohse, John, 29–30
Don Luscombe Aviation History Foundation (DLAHF), 131, 132
Doolittle, Jimmy, 46
Drew, Andrew, 9

E-2 Taylor Cub aircraft, 58–59
E-series engines (Aeronca), 30, 57
E-series engines (Curtiss), 19
EAA. *See* Experimental Aircraft Association (EAA)
EAA Aviation Foundation, 103. *See also* Experimental Aircraft Association (EAA)
Eagle Parachute Company, 76
Egrett aircraft, 143
Eielson, Carl Benjamin, 77–78, 158*n*4
Eisenhower, Dwight D., 92, 115
Elmira, New York, 71–72
emergency services, 99, 140–41
Engineering and Research Corporation (ERCO), 61–62

engines: birdmen era, 17–21; golden age
    period, 24f, 28–29, 54–59; post-1980s,
    146; post-World War II, 86f, 112–13,
    116–17; World War II era, 64f
Ercoupe aircraft, 33, 61–62
E-series engines (Aeronca), 30, 57
E-series engines (Curtiss), 19
European aircraft/engines, xiii, 20, 70,
    100–101
Evans, Bruce, 129
Executive/Hyde Field, 150
Executive Jets, 123
exhibition flying, 5–7, 10, 11–15
Experimental Aircraft Association
    (EAA), 102–103, 104–105, 125, 134
experimental aircraft category, 126–27.
    See also homebuilt aircraft

FAA. See Federal Aviation Administra-
    tion (FAA)
Fairchild, Sherman M., 155n9
Fairchild 6-370 engines, 57
Fairchild KR-21A aircraft, 24f
Fallows, James, 163–64n9
Farthest North Aviation Company, 78
Federal Aviation Administration (FAA):
    post-1980s, 124, 126–27, 133, 141; post-
    World War II years, 71, 92–94, 107, 110;
    Sept. 11 response, 148–51. See also Civil
    Aeronautics Administration (CAA)
Federal Emergency Relief Administration
    (FERA), 37
federal legislation: overview, xiii–xiv;
    golden age period, 25, 26–28, 35–36,
    40, 156n3; post-1980s, 137; post-World
    War II years, 90, 92–93. See also Civil
    Aeronautics Administration (CAA);
    Federal Aviation Administration
    (FAA)
Federation Aeronautique Internationale,
    14, 27, 48–49
Filene's, 98
fire fighting, 75–77, 99, 108–109, 162n41
Fisk, George, 107
fixed-base operators/operations. See
    airport operators/operations; flight
    schools
FJX-2 engines (Williams), 146
Flight of Passage (Buck), 109

flight schools: birdmen era, 2f, 6, 7, 9, 11–
    12, 76; golden age period, 51, 52; post-
    1980s, 125; post-World War II years,
    103–104; World War I era, 7
Flokerts, Clayton, 59–60
Flying Circus (Ruth Law's), 14
"Flying Silos" (aircraft), 46
Fokker, Anthony, 21
Ford, Henry, xv–xvi
Ford Motor Company, xv–xvi, 69–70
Forest Service, U.S., 75–77, 108–109
Forsythe, Albert E., 52–53
Fort, Cornelia, 81–82
Franklin engines, 67–68, 116

G-164 aircraft (Transland), 112
Galloway, Robert, 30
GAP program, 145, 146
Gates Rubber Company, 96
Gee Bee aircraft, 46
general aviation, defined, xi
General Aviation Propulsion (GAP), 145,
    146
General Aviation Revitalization Act, 137
George, Harold, 81
Gettysburg, Pennsylvania, 110
G. Fox and Company, 98
Gibbs, Edward A., 105
Gillies, Betty Huyler, 82
GL-2 gliders (Roche's), 29
glass composite materials, 128
Glickman, Dan, 137
gliders, 29, 68–72, 99–101, 133–35
G model aircraft (grasshoppers), 67
golden age period: overview, 25–27, 62;
    African American aviators, 51–54;
    agricultural aviation, 26, 42–43, 42–
    44; airport operations, 40–42; air
    racing, 44–47; AOPA emergence, 47–
    48; federal legislation/programs,
    36–40; homebuilt aircraft, 34–36;
    licensing/certification, 27–28;
    manufacturing/design sector,
    28–34, 54–62; women aviators,
    48–50
Gooch, Ulysses "Rip," 103
Goodwin, David P., 76
Goodwin, Ted, 140
Grand Central Terminal Airport, 41

Granville, Zantford D. "Granny," 46
"grasshoppers" (aircraft), 67–68
Graves, Henry S., 75
Greene, Betty, 107
Green v. *Continental Airlines,* 103
Grumman Aircraft, 95, 112
Gulfstream (company), 112
Gulfstream I, 95

Haizlip, Jimmy, 46
Halaby, Najeeb, 93
Hall, John Waldorf, 9
Hall-Scott engines, 20
Hamilton-Standard Propeller Corpora-
    tion, 166–67*n*43
hang gliders, 133–35
Hansen, James, 137
Harlem Airport, 52
Harmon Trophy, 78
Hartranft, Joseph B, Jr., 47–48
Hartzell, George, 142
Hartzell, John T., 142
Hartzell, Robert, 142
Hartzell Company, 142–43
Hartzell Walnut Propeller Company, 142
Hartzite, 142
Heath, Edward, 35
Heath Parasol aircraft, 35, 130
helicopters, 96–97, 106, 115–16
Henderson, Clifford, 45
Heron, Samuel D., 55
Hinckely, Robert H., 38
Hisso engines, 20
Holman, Charles "Speed," 45–46
homebuilt aircraft: golden age era, 34–36;
    post-1980s, 126–27, 128–29, 152*f;* post-
    World War II years, 99, 101–103
Howard, Benny, 46
Huff-Daland Airplane Company, 17, 42,
    43
humanitarian aviation, 107–108, 140–41,
    166*n*38

Ingalls, Laura, 45, 49
Innes, Walter, Jr., 16
insurance, 123, 137, 165–66*n*32
Inter-city Airlines, 81
Interior, U.S. Department of, 108–109
Interstate aircraft, 68

J-1 engines (Lawrance's), 55
J-5 engines (Wright Aeronautical), 55
J-series aircraft (Piper), 43, 58, 59
Jacobs engines, 56
Jamouneau, Walter, 58
Jenny aircraft, 19, 20
JN-4D Jenny aircraft, 19, 20
Johnson, E. A., 41
Johnson Flying Service, 41
J-series aircraft (Piper), 43, 58, 59
"June Bug" (aircraft), 10
Junkin, Elwood "Sam," 22

Kassebaum, Nancy, 137
Kelly Act, 25, 27
King Air aircraft, 95
Kinner K-5 engines, 24*f*
kit aircraft. *See* homebuilt aircraft
Kronfeld, Robert, 71

L-4 aircraft (Piper), 64*f*
L-series aircraft (grasshoppers), 67–68
Laird, Emil Matthew "Matty," 15, 45–46
Laird Super Solution aircraft, 46
Larsen, Moody, 132
Law, Ruth, 14
Lawrance, Charles, 55
Lear, William, 95–96, 160*n*18
Lear Jet, 95–96
Levine, Charles, 21
liability insurance, 123, 137, 165–66*n*32
licensing/licenses: birdmen era, 6, 9;
    golden age period, 27–28, 35; post-
    1980s, 124–26, 136, 137, 166*n*33
Lillie, Max, 9
Lindbergh, Anne Morrow, 71
Lindbergh, Charles, 13–14, 166–67*n*43
Lippisch, Alexander, 71
Lockheed (company), 95–96
Lockheed Orion aircraft, 45
Lockheed Vega aircraft, 45, 55
Long, Leslie, 35, 36
LoPresti, Roy, 131
Loughhead S-1 aircraft, 20–21
Love, Nancy Harkness, 37, 81
Love, Robert, 81
Loving, Neal V., 104–105
"Loving's Love" (aircraft), 104
L-series aircraft (grasshoppers), 67–68

Ludington, C. Townsend, 47–48
Luscombe, Don, 59–61
Luscombe Aircraft, 132
Luscombe-series aircraft, 60–61
Lycoming engines, 56, 67–68, 116

manufacturing sector: birdmen era, 8, 9–
    12, 15–16; golden age period, 25–26,
    28–34, 43–44, 49–50, 54–62; post-
    1980s, 122, 137, 142–44, 163*n*5, 165–
    66*n*32; post-World War II, 88–90,
    94–96, 106, 111–18; World War II era,
    66. *See also* design innovations;
    homebuilt aircraft
Martin, Glenn, 9
Maule, 124
Max Lillie Flying School, 7
McCauley Accessory Division, 167*n*46
McCauley Aviation Corporation, 144
McCauley Propeller Systems, 144
McCloskey, Helen, 37
McCormick, Harold, 8–9
McCreery's, 98
medical services, 99, 140–41
Meigs Field, 138–39, 149–50
Menasco engines, 57
Merrill C. Meigs Field, 138–39, 149–50
"Mike" (aircraft), 46
military-related aviation, World War I, 7.
    See also World War II era
"Millennium Swift" (aircraft), 131–32
Mineta, Norman Y., 149
missionary aviation, 107, 140, 166*n*38
Mission Aviation Fellowship, 107
Mississippi Valley Aircraft Service, 109
"Mister Mulligan" (aircraft), 46, 47
Model 4 aircraft (Luscombe), 60–61
Model 8 aircraft (Luscombe), 61
Model 9 aircraft (WACO), 22
Model 10 aircraft (WACO), 55
Model 17 aircraft (Beechcraft), 44
Model 18 aircraft (Beechcraft), 44
Model 47 Ranger helicopter, 115
Modern Mechanics and Inventions, 35
Moellendick, Jacob Melvin "Jake," 15–16
Moisant Exhibition Company, 10
Mono-Aircraft Company, 60
Monocoupe aircraft, 59–60
Mooney Aircraft, 124, 165–66*n*32

Moorehouse, Harold, 29–30
Mosely, Zack, 74
mosquito spraying, 110
Mystery Ship (aircraft), 45–46

NASA programs, 133, 145–47, 163–64*n*9
National Advisory Committee on
    Aeronautics (NACA), 32–33
National Aerial Applicators Association,
    111
National Agricultural Aviation Associa-
    tion, 111
National Air Marking Program, 37, 50
National Airmen's Association, 53
National Air Races, 44–47, 49
National Business Aircraft Association,
    92
National Gliding Association, 71
National Interagency Fire Center
    (NIFC), 108
National Pilots Association, 92
navigation aids: golden age period, 36,
    37–38, 50; post-World War II years,
    90–92, 93–94, 117–18
Negro Airmen International, 105
NetJets, 123
New Deal programs/policies, xiii–xiv, 31,
    36–40
Ninety-Nines, 82, 106
North American Aviation, 89, 95–96
Northrup, Jack, 20–21
Noyes, Blanche, 37, 49

O-series engines (Continental), 86*f*, 116–
    17, 120*f*
O-series engines (Lycoming), 116
Office of Aircraft Services, 109
Oldfield, Barney, 6
Omlie, Phoebe, 37, 159*m*8
172 series aircraft (Cessna), 115, 120*f*
Oregon, homebuilt aircraft, 36
Oriole aircraft, 21, 155*n*24
O-series engines (Continental), 86*f*, 116–
    17, 120*f*
O-series engines (Lycoming), 116
OX-5 engines (Curtiss), 19, 20, 22, 56

PA-3 Orowing aircraft, 114
PA-23 Apache aircraft, 114

PA-28 Cherokee aircraft, 114
Pan-American Goodwill Flight, 52–53
parcel delivery services, 98
PATCO strike, 135–36
Peru, missionary aviation, 140
"Pete" (aircraft), 46
"Phantom" (aircraft), 60
Philadelphia Aviation Country Club, 47
Philadelphia Bourse, Incorporated (PBI), 144
Pietenpol Air Camper aircraft, 34–35
Pietenpol aircraft, 130
Piper, William, 58–59
Piper Aircraft: golden age period, 43, 58, 59; post-1980s, 124; post-World War II years, 90, 95, 111, 113–14; World War II era, 64f, 66, 67–68, 69
Pitcairn, Harold, 21, 155n24
Poberezny, Paul, 102
Poole-Galloway engines, 30
Popular Aviation, 35, 48
Popular Flying, 101
post-1980s: overview, 121–22; airport operators/operations, 138–39; homebuilts/gliders, 126–30, 133–35; licensing/licenses, 124–26, 136, 137, 166n33; manufacturing/design sector, 122–24, 126–29, 137, 142–44, 146, 163n5, 165–66n32; September 11 impact, 147–51; women aviators, 139–40
Post Office, U.S., 8, 25, 32, 50, 78
post-World War II years: overview, 87–88; African American aviators, 103–105; agricultural aviation, 88, 98, 109–12, 148; federal regulation, 90–94; fire fighting, 108–109; humanitarian aviation, 107–108; manufacturing/design sector, 86f, 88–90, 94–103, 111–18; women aviators, 105–107
Potomac Field, 150
Powell, William J., 51–52
Pratt and Whitney, 55, 56, 117
Prince, Norman, 9
Professional Air Traffic Controllers Organization (PATCO) strike, 135–36
Project Beacon, 93
Project Horizon, 93
Project Pilot, 125, 138
Project Tightrope, 93

propellers, 141–44, 166–67n43
PT-6 Turboprop engines, 117
Public Works Administration (PWA), 31–32
Pulitzer, Joseph, 44–45
"pusher" design, 18, 127–28
PZL (company), 116

Queen Aeroplane Company, 11
Queen Air aircraft, 95
Quesada, Elwood "Pete," 92–93
Quick Aeroplane Dusters, 17
Quicksilver aircraft, 124
Quimby, Harriet, 7

R-680 engines (Lycoming), 56
R-series helicopters, 116
Ranger engines, 57
Ranger helicopters, 115
Rathbun, John B., 35
Reagan, Ronald, 136
recreational pilot certificates, 136
Renaissance Aircraft LLC, 132
Rentschler, Frederic, 55
Republic Aviation, 89
Richardson Highway, 77
Richey, Helen, 37, 50, 105–106
Roadable Aircraft Competition, 104–105
Robbins Airport, 52
Robinson R-22 helicopters, 116
Roche, Jean, 29
Rockwell-Standard, 111
Rogollo, Francis M., 133
Romco Charlie, Incorporated, 131
R-series helicopters, 116
Rutan, Burt, 127–30
Rutan, Dick, 129
Rutan Aircraft Factory, 127, 128, 130
Ryan, George, 150

S-2 Thrush aircraft, 111
sailplanes, 71. *See also* gliders
sales statistics: post-1980s, 122, 163n5, 165–66n32; post-World War II, 88–89, 95, 100. *See also* manufacturing sector
Santos-Dumont, Alberto, 97–98
SATS program, 146–47
Scaled Composites, 129–30
Scarab engines, 56

Schlemmer, Roger E., 30
Schweizer, Ernie, 72
Schweizer, Paul, 72
Schweizer, William, 72
Schweizer Aircraft Company, 72, 99–101,
    112, 135
Sensenich, Harry, 143
Sensenich, Martin, 143
Sensenich Propeller Manufacturing
    Company, 142–44
Sentinel aircraft, 67–68
September 11 impact, 147–51
SGU-1-1 gliders (Schweizer), 72
Sharp, Evelyn, 80–81, 82
Sharples, Laurence, 47–48
Sharples, Philip, 47–48
Siddeley, Hawker, 106
Sikorsky, Igor, 97–98
Silent Spring (Carson), 110
"Smilin' Jack" (comic strip), 74
Smith, John Story, 47–48
smokejumpers, 75, 76–77
Snow, Leland, 111–12
Soaring Society of America, 71, 134
Solution aircraft, 45–46
Southern California Hang Gliding
    Association, 134
Southern Dusting Company, 17
Spencer, Chauncey E., 53
"Spirit of Booker T. Washington"
    (aircraft), 52–53
SR-20/22 aircraft (Cirrus), 127
Staggerwing aircraft, 44, 45
Standard Steel Propeller, 166–67n43
Stearman, Lloyd Carlton, 15–16
Stearman aircraft, 43, 109
steel-tube construction, beginnings, 16,
    17, 21
Stick and Rudder Club (New York), 105
"stick" control systems, 19
Stinson, Katherine, 7–8, 9, 10
Stinson, Marjorie, 7
Stinson Municipal Airport, 7
Stinson School of Flying, 7
student pilots. See licensing/licenses
submarine searches/patrols, 73–74
Super Parasol kit, 35
Super Scarab engines, 56, 60
Swallow aircraft, 15

Swallow Airplane Manufacturing
    Company, 15–16
Swift aircraft, 131–32
Swift Museum Foundation, 131–32

Taperwing gliders, 69
Taylor, C. G., 58
Taylor, Charles E., 18
Taylor, Gordon, 58
Taylor Aircraft, 58–59
Taylor Brothers Aircraft Corporation, 58
Taylorcraft, 58, 67, 69
Taylor Cub aircraft, 58–59
Teledyne Continental, 146
temporary flight restrictions (TFRs),
    148–51
Texas A&M University, 111
TG-series gliders, 69, 72
Thaden, Louise, 37, 45, 49, 50
"The Comet" (aircraft), 9
Thompson, Charles, 45
Thompson Trophy, 45–46, 47
310 series aircraft (Cessna), 86f, 115
Tiara engines, 117
timeshare ownership, 122–23
tractor configuration, 19, 128
training programs, federal, 36, 38–40. See
    also flight schools
Transland Company, 112
Travel Air 4000 aircraft, 43
Travel Air Company, 50
Travel Air Manufacturing Company, 16
Tri-Pacer aircraft, 114
Tunner, William, 81
Turboshaft 250-series engines, 117
Turner, Roscoe, 45, 46, 47
Turner-Laird Super Solution aircraft, 46
Tuskegee Institute, 53
Twin Beech aircraft, 44
"Twin Stinson" prototype, 114
type clubs, 130–32

ultralights, 133–35
UPF-7 gliders (WACO), 69
U.S. Hang Glider Association, 134
U.S. Ultralight Foundation, 134

Vagabond aircraft, 114
Vandalia field, 41

Vans RV-6 aircraft, 152*f*
variometers, 71
Velie, Willard L., 60
VeriEze aircraft, 128–29
VeriViggen aircraft, 127–28
Vidal, Eugene, 31–32, 33–34
Vigilant aircraft, 67–68
VK-30 aircraft (Cirrus), 127
Vought, Chauncy "Chance," 9
Voyager, 129, 143
VS-300 helicopters (Sikorsky's), 97
Vultee-Stinson aircraft, 67–68

W-1 series aircraft (Weick's), 32–33
WACO Aircraft Company, 21–22, 55, 68, 69–70, 89–90
WAFS (Women's Auxiliary Ferrying Squadron), 81–82
Wallace, Dwayne, 44
Wallace, Dwight, 44
Warbirds of America, 103
Warner engines, 56, 60
Warren School of Aeronautics, 51
War Training Service (WTS), 39
Wasp engines, 55
Wasp Junior engines, 56
WASPs (Women's Airforce Service Pilots), 82, 159*n*21
Wayne School of Aeronautics, 104
Weaver, George "Buck," 15, 21–22
Weaver Aircraft Company, 15, 21–22. *See also* WACO Aircraft Company
Wedell, Jimmy, 46–47
Wedell-Williams aircraft, 47
Wedell-Williams Air Service, 46
Weeks Act, 75–77
Weick, Fred, 32–33, 59, 61, 111
Whirlwind engines, 54–55
Whirly Girls, 106
White, Dale L., 53
Wichita Aero Club, 12
Wichita Airplane Company, 15
Wilkins, Sir Hubert, 78
Williams, Harry, 46–47
Williams International, 146
Wilson, Gill Robb, 48, 73
winged gospel mythology, xi–xii
wing-warp system, 18–19
Wolf, Alfred L., 47–48

women aviators: birdmen era, 6–7, 14–15; golden age period, 37–39, 45, 48–50, 53–54; post-1980s, 139–40; post-World War II years, 105–107; winged gospel mythology, xii; World War I, 7–8; World War II era, 80–82, 159*n*8, 159*n*21
Women in Aviation International (WAI), 140
Women's Advisory Committee on Aviation, 107
Women's Air Derby, 45, 49
Women's Airforce Service Pilots (WASPs), 82, 159*n*21
Women's Auxiliary Ferrying Squadron (WAFS), 81–82
Women's Flying Training Detachment (WFTD), 82
Woolman, C. E., 42
Works Progress Administration (WPA), 36–37
World War I, 7–8, 12, 14
World War II era: overview, 65–66; aerial observation programs, 64*f*, 66–68, 73–74; agricultural aviation, 77; Alaska aviation development, 78–79; fire fighting, 76–77; glider programs, 68–70, 72; women aviators, 80–82
Wright Aeronautical, 20, 55
Wright-Bellanca 2 aircraft, 21
Wright brothers: design/structure of aircraft, 18–19, 164*n*1; flight schools, 2*f*, 6, 7; patent dispute, 154*n*9; promotion of flying, 4–5
Wright Field, 41
Wright-Hispano Suiza engines, 20
Wright Whirlwind engines, 54–55
WR series aircraft (Loving's), 104–105
Wycliffe Bible Translators, 107
Wyman-Gordon Company, 130

XCG-series gliders (WACO), 69
XR-4 helicopters (Sikorsky's), 97

Yeager, Jeana, 129
Young Eagles, 125

Ziff-Davis Publishing Company, 47–48

ISBN 1-58544-257-7

90000